Misadventures in Archaeology

The Life and Career of Charles Conrad Abbott

Carolyn D. Dillian and Charles A. Bello

University of Pennsylvania Museum of Archaeology and Anthropology | Philadelphia

Library of Congress Cataloging-in-Publication Data

Names: Dillian, Carolyn D., author. | Bello, Charles A., author.
Title: Misadventures in archaeology : the life and career of Charles Conrad
    Abbott / Carolyn D. Dillian, and Charles A. Bello.
Other titles: Life and career of Charles Conrad Abbott
Description: Philadelphia : University of Pennsylvania Museum of
    Archaeology and Anthropology, [2020] | Includes bibliographical
    references.
Identifiers: LCCN 2019044533 | ISBN 9781949057058 (hardcover) | ISBN
    9781949057065 (ebook)
Subjects: LCSH: Abbott, Charles C. (Charles Conrad), 1843-1919. |
    Archaeologists--United States--Biography. | Archaeology--United
    States--History. | Naturalists--United States--Biography. | Delaware
    River Valley (N.Y.-Del. and N.J.)--History.
Classification: LCC CC115.A23 D55 2020 | DDC 930.1092 [B]--dc23
LC record available at https://lccn.loc.gov/2019044533

Distributed for the University of Pennsylvania Museum of Archaeology and
Anthropology by the University of Pennsylvania Press.

Printed in the United States of America on acid-free paper.

Contents

Contents

Figures

Abbreviations

CCA/PU: Charles Conrad Abbott Papers (C0290), Manuscripts and Special Collections, Firestone Library, Princeton University.

CCA-FWP/HPM: Charles Conrad Abbott and Frederic Ward Putnam Correspondence (UAV 677.38), Peabody Museum, Harvard University.

CCA-JSR/PANS: Charles Conrad Abbott and Julia Stockton Robins Correspondence (Collection 162), Philadelphia Academy of Natural Sciences.

CCA-LC/HPM: Charles Conrad Abbott and Lucien Carr Correspondence (Accession 79-42), Peabody Museum, Harvard University.

CCA/PANS: Charles Conrad Abbott notes copied by H. W. Fowler (Collection 162), Philadelphia Academy of Natural Sciences.

CCA-NHW/HPM: Charles Conrad Abbott and Newton H. Winchell correspondence, Peabody Museum, Harvard University.

Charles Conrad Abbott and the Birth of Professional Archaeology

In 1893, in critique of the American Paleolithic, William Henry Holmes published a short article in which he remarked "The fact is that the field has, up to this time, been occupied mainly by amateurs who have not mastered the necessary fundamental branches of science. The work done is mainly their work, the literature produced is mainly their literature, and the world has received its impressions from this source. This no doubt is an unavoidable condition of the evolution of archaeologic science....But the time has now come for a change—for the opening of an era when scientific acquirements of the highest possible order shall be brought to bear upon these questions" (Holmes 1893a:29). As a leading figure in the search for an American Paleolithic, amateur archaeologist Charles Conrad Abbott (Fig. 1.1) was the implicit target of Holmes's rebuke.

Abbott trained as a medical doctor, not an archaeologist, but in the mid-19th century, when he first embarked on archaeological research and publishing, his pedigree as a well-educated member of the gentlemanly class was enough to gain entry into the discipline (Hinsley 1976, 1981; Parezo and Fowler 2007; Taylor 1995). Merely a few decades later, Abbott's lack of an academic degree or specialized training in archaeology proved a barrier to access. Abbott's life spanned a shift towards professionalization of the field that occurred at the end of the 19th century and beginning of the 20th. His ascent, and subsequent decline, paralleled the evolution of the field from one in which amateurs contributed to archaeological debate to one that

1.1 Portrait of Charles C. Abbott, undated; Charles Conrad Abbott Papers (C0290), Box 15 Folder 2; Manuscripts Division, Department of Rare Books and Special Collections, Princeton University Library.

was the exclusive domain of university-trained and government scholars. By the turn of the century, Abbott's lack of formal education in archaeology resulted in his exclusion from professional circles, and his intransigence in insisting on an American Paleolithic in the face of scientific data falsifying his hypotheses further contributed to his reputation as an unqualified dilettante in a rapidly professionalizing field.

In this book, we examine the life and career of Charles Conrad Abbott across this transition in archaeology from amateur hobby to professional science. Abbott was a prolific writer, leaving behind personal diaries covering much of his adult life that are now housed in the Manuscripts and Special Collections Division of Firestone Library, Princeton University, as well as extensive correspondence and published works that document the rise and fall of his career. As the principal advocate of an American Paleolithic, in which he argued for a human presence in the Delaware Valley in great antiquity, Abbott gained notoriety, if not scholarly fame, despite his avocational rank. His public engagement with Holmes and others on both sides of the Paleolithic debate provides us with a rich record of published academic and popular articles and editorials. By the 1890s, when geological and archaeological data casting doubt on his hypotheses emerged in publications authored by those with advanced academic degrees, government jobs, or professional training in the field, a truculent Abbott refused to accept defeat by what he termed a Washington "clique" (CCA/PU Box 2, Folder 5; August 21, 1887), and the written record turned acrimonious. But what Abbott viewed as an attack by an insider faction was also in part the manifestation of changes in the field. As an amateur, and an irascible one at that, Abbott soon found himself left behind.

ARCHAEOLOGY AND THE PROFESSIONALIZATION OF SCIENCE

The trajectory of archaeology as a scientific field is often traced from antiquarianism to scholarly discipline (Trigger 1989). Frequently members of an aristocratic class, 18th and 19th century antiquaries were concerned with collecting the relics of the past but often neglectful of archaeological provenience, explanation, or cultural context. As interest in interpretation of the past—rather than mere collecting—grew through the 19th century, members of the educated middle and upper class, such as clergymen, civil servants, merchants, doctors, lawyers, and country squires, embraced archaeology (Hudson, 1981:12; Taylor 1995; Trigger 1989:14). These were professions that allowed the "spare time" (Hudson 1981:12) for archaeological pursuits, which permitted amateur practitioners to labor uncompensated, or in the case of Charles Conrad Abbott, minimally compensated for work in the field.

Archaeology was not unique in experiencing a rise of amateur scholarship in the 19th century. For example, Victorian gentlemen scholars popularized the study of natural history, and the title of 'naturalist' was embraced by anyone with interest and leisure time to muse in writing on the world around them (Barber 1980). Naturalists often focused on collecting unusual specimens—of plants, animals, and minerals—for museums where they could be preserved, cataloged, and displayed (Rudwick 2005), but travel to foreign places was dangerous and expensive, so for many, maps, pictures, and illustrations democratized the field by bringing nature to the armchair amateur scholar (Rudwick 2005), leading also to the professional field of scientific illustration. Abbott dabbled as an amateur naturalist as well as in archaeology, though this body of work received less attention—and less criticism—than his archaeological oeuvre.

Studies of the sociology of occupations identify characteristics of professionalism as including "formal education and entry requirements; a monopoly over an esoteric body of knowledge and associated skills; autonomy over the terms and conditions of practice; collegial authority" and others (Anleu 1992:24). The first Ph.D. granted in archaeology in the United States was in 1894 to George Dorsey, a student of Frederic Ward Putnam, and soon after that, academic institutions and museums required their faculty and staff to be legitimized through their academic credentials (Kehoe 1999:5), rather than self-taught like Charles Conrad Abbott. This created an expanding divide between amateur and professional; and an elite class of scholars, government employees, and professors inaugurated a scholarly community that fostered isolation of, and disdain for, those who were not members (Levine 1986).

Joseph Henry, the first secretary of the Smithsonian Institution, founded in 1846, engineered institutional efforts to bring scientific methods to American archaeological practice. He reprinted reports on European archaeology in the annual report of the Smithsonian Institution, which included methodological advances such as controlled excavations, recording, and stratigraphy (Trigger 1989:107–108). For example, Adolphe Morlot's *General Views on Archaeology* was translated and published by the Smithsonian Institution in 1861. It outlined European excavations of stratified middens (Morlot 1861; Randall 2015), which influenced methods used in American excavations of shell mounds and middens along the Atlantic coast in the 1860s (Randall 2015; Trigger 1989:108). Notably, Jeffries Wyman, of Harvard University, used stratigraphic methods similar to those described in Morlot's publication in his own mid-19th century excavations of shell middens in Florida (Wyman 1875), and within the context of a burgeoning scientific archaeology, this work represents an early effort to use standardized, professional field recording techniques (Bourque 2002; Kirakosian 2015; Randall 2015; Trigger 1986).

The Bureau of Ethnology (later renamed the Bureau of American Ethnology [BAE]), created in 1879 under the supervision of the Smithsonian Institution, initially had a mission to conduct ethnographic research, but soon became the driving force for a greater empirical approach to archaeological research. With the benefit of federal funding, BAE archaeologists were able to complete far-reaching projects with the assistance of staff who held advanced degrees in geology, natural history, biology, and other fields (Hinsley 1976). Amateur archaeologists, such as Abbott, chafed under greater scrutiny of their methods brought about by a wider awareness of proper practice (McKusick 1970, 1988; Trigger 1989:128), and which in some cases exposed outright fraud (McKusick 1970, 1988), but American archaeology as a whole was experiencing a movement towards greater professionalization of the discipline and federal agencies were an important driver of this transition (Trigger 1989:127).

It has been argued that the linear evolution of the archaeologist from amateur to professional is not as straightforward as it may appear (Levine 1986; Taylor 1995). In demoting the amateur, the professional legitimized their own place within the scholarly hierarchy, and in the case of late 19th and early 20th century American archaeology, created a robust cadre of professionals that eschewed research conducted by amateurs (Taylor 1995). As admission to the field of archaeology gained increasingly rigorous requirements, amateurs such as Abbott were downgraded to less prestigious roles (Hudson 1981; Stebbins 1979), such as that of unpaid field assistant, which was Abbott's job title at Harvard's Peabody Museum. This boundary between amateur and professional was important for those who wished to maintain control over expert knowledge in the field (Shaeffer 2016:19).

History and sociology of science research demonstrates that professionalization progressed through a series of discrete stages: (1) preemption of esoteric knowledge by a select group, making it incomprehensible to the amateur scholar; (2) institutionalization and formal associations among colleagues who share this esoteric knowledge; (3) legitimation of full-time roles in esoteric scholarship; finally leading to (4) professional autonomy and control of the discipline (Daniels 1967). Abbott was witness to and victim of this process, while vehemently resisting the progressive stages that relegated him further into the amateur realm. His contributions fell within the early phases of democratic science, in which scientific knowledge is part of a "fact-gathering" stage, when all participants, whether formally trained or not, have the opportunity to contribute (Daniels 1967:155; Kuhn 1962:15). By the 1890s, the preemption of esoteric knowledge of archaeological materials by professional scholars positioned Abbott as an amateur not to be taken seriously. He retrenched amongst his "facts" and resorted to bitter name-calling in response. In published memoirs later in life, he quipped "but if people would stick to facts and not their relation thereto, I still maintain, the world would be happier" (Abbott 1906a:169).

CHARLES CONRAD ABBOTT'S FAMILY AND EDUCATION

Like many amateur archaeologists in the 19th century (Hudson 1981; Taylor 1995; Trigger 1989), Charles Conrad Abbott was a member of an elite social class. Born in Trenton on June 4, 1843 into a prominent, though not necessarily wealthy, Quaker family, his father, Timothy Abbott, was a successful hardware merchant in Philadelphia and then later worked as a banker, becoming President of the Mechanics National Bank in Trenton. Timothy Abbott later gave up that position to become the Vice-President and Treasurer of the Trenton Iron Company (Hunter and Tvaryanas 2009:4–45). His mother was Susan Conrad, daughter of Solomon White Conrad (1779–1831), a Professor of Botany and Lecturer in Mineralogy at the University of Pennsylvania. His maternal uncle, Timothy Conrad (1803–1877) was one of America's early paleontologists. Charles was the youngest child of the family and had one sister, Mary, and two brothers, Joseph and Francis.

Charles attended the Trenton Academy, located on Academy Street (formerly Fourth Street) in Trenton, from 1852–1858. The 1850s were arguably the most successful period of the Trenton Academy's history. David Cole, an educational leader in New Jersey, was the school's principal at the time, and grew enrollments to 143 students, the largest student body in its 100 year history (Murray 1899:127). Abbott's classmates included members of the Trenton elite: attorneys, playboys, industrialists, and businessmen such as S. Meredith Dickinson, Ion H. Perdicaris, and Washington and Ferdinand Roebling (Hughes 1929). Of these classmates, Abbott remained in contact with Washington Roebling during adulthood, and visited him from time to time. In his diaries for example, Abbott recorded one such visit on June 7, 1875, "called on Washington Roebling, who is a sort of semi-invalid at present. Went to same school and have known him many years" (CCA/PU Box 2, Folder 2). Roebling served as chief engineer in the construction of the Brooklyn Bridge and suffered from complications of decompression sickness acquired while fighting a fire in the pressurized atmosphere of one of the two pneumatic caissons that supported the bridge foundation (McCullough 1992).

Following graduation from the Trenton Academy, Abbott matriculated at the University of Pennsylvania, earning both a B.A. in 1861 and an M.D. in 1865, writing his thesis on diphtheria, though his education was briefly interrupted by the Civil War. Abbott enlisted as a Private in Company A, New Jersey 1st Infantry Regiment on June 17, 1863. His military service was in response to a plea for volunteers from the Governors of Pennsylvania, New Jersey, and New York, for troops to halt the aggressive northward movements of General Robert E. Lee's Confederate soldiers during the summer of 1863. This Civil War event became known as the "Pennsylvania Emergency" and culminated in the Union victory at the Battle of Gettysburg, although it does not appear that Abbott's Company fought in that battle. Company A soldiers were returned to Trenton a mere thirty days later and discharged, with a formal note of appreciation from Pennsylvania Governor Curtin for their service (Stryker 1876:1429).

Though he held a medical degree from a prestigious Ivy League university, Abbott was a terrible doctor. His abrasive personality and an overall indifference towards medicine contributed to a poor bedside manner. Despite his shortcomings, he continued to be listed in the Trenton, New Jersey, city directory as a practicing physician through 1873. According to one of his biographers, "the Doctor was a reluctant physician. His overriding preference for natural science needed little inducement—from the whistle of a bird or the splash of a turtle in a creek. When he should have been holding office hours, he was more often to be found making studious observations on the natural life of the Delaware Valley. His little black bag was more likely to contain bird's nests than bandages" (Aiello 1968:32).

In 1867, Charles married Julia Boggs Olden, of Princeton, New Jersey, who was the oldest daughter of the wealthy and influential Job Olden, a merchant and brother of New Jersey Governor, Charles S. Olden (Hageman 1879:250). They had three children who lived to adulthood, Maria Olden Abbott (1867–1956), Richard Mauleverer Abbott (1871–1943), and Julia Boggs Abbott (1874–1957). A fourth child, Arthur Brenton Abbott (1883–1888) died in childhood, an event that sent Charles into a deep depression. He wrote in his diary that he was in Cambridge, Massachusetts, at Harvard "until the morning of 17th, when I was called home arriving at 10:45pm, to find Arthur dead and Maria, Dick, and Julie Jr. sick, the latter nearly recovered. Scarlet fever the scourge. Crushed beyond all resurrection, I fear." (CCA/PU Box 2, Folder 5; February 6–17, 1888). Despite professional successes, Charles referred to the year 1888 as "the unhappiest year I can remember" (CCA/PU Box 2, Folder 5; Dec. 31, 1888).

When Charles and his family moved to the family farm, which he named "Three Beeches" near Bordentown, New Jersey (Fig. 1.2), in 1874, he finally embarked upon what would be his life's work. Three Beeches contained extensive archaeological deposits covering almost 10,000 years of prehistory, and many of Abbott's Native American artifacts were surface collected during walks on this property. It was also at this time that Abbott began the daily diaries that chronicled his scholarly and personal activities, which form a valuable primary source for this volume.

During these early years at Three Beeches, Abbott published several articles on nature studies in the area around his home, but his first foray into his American Paleolithic in print occurred in 1872, with the publication of "The Stone Age in New Jersey" in the journal *The American Naturalist*. In this text, Abbott carefully described a series of prehistoric artifacts and offered readers a brief insight into his theories about ancient humans in the Americas, for which he would ultimately be known.

> We judge of our 'Indians' by those relics that are now the only trace of their former existence, and finding stone implements as rude as those

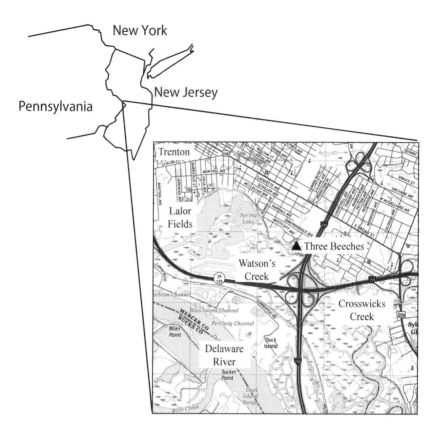

1.2 Topographic map of Three Beeches and surrounding area showing modern development and features discussed in the text. USGS Topographic Quadrangle: Trenton East, N.J., 2016.

of Abbeville...we naturally conclude that the fashioners of such 'flints' were so primitive as to be incapable of a migration from Asia....We cannot but think that there was an autochthonic people here in North America (Abbott 1872:146–147).

Throughout his life, Abbott continued to promote the idea of a deep antiquity of humans in the Americas, while collecting artifacts from New Jersey and Pennsylvania for leading archaeological museums. Abbott supplemented his meager farm income with articles, books, and essays on archaeology and nature. He first articulated his nascent theories about an American Paleolithic in several publications including his early expanded tome *The Stone Age in New Jersey* (Abbott 1877a), articles printed by the journal *The American Naturalist* (Abbott 1872, 1876a), and in the *Reports of the Peabody Museum* (Abbott 1877b, 1878). But in 1881, Abbott published *Primitive Industry*, his most influential book, which included a definitive essay on the "paleoliths" of the Trenton gravels, alleged by Abbott to be evidence of human occupation of great antiquity. This volume, which reached a wide audience of amateur and professional scholars, forced Abbott to defend his theories in print and at scholarly meetings against a growing community of professional archaeologists, and earned him the reputation for which he is most well-known: failed seeker of the Paleolithic in the New World.

FAMILY INFLUENCES

Charles Conrad Abbott's scholarly family and the introductions they provided, helped him gain initial acceptance in academic circles. His grandfather, Solomon White Conrad, was a Professor at the University of Pennsylvania and his uncle, Timothy Abbott Conrad, was a malacologist, who published numerous books and articles on extant and fossil mollusks. Timothy Conrad was employed as a geologist for the State of New York, and then later as a paleontologist for the New York Geological Survey but was known to produce work that was riddled with errors and omissions. For example, in an introduction to *Republication of Conrad's Fossils of the Medial Tertiary of the United States*, editor William Healey Dall stated "Mr. Conrad had several peculiarities: he wrote his letters and labels frequently on all sorts of scraps of paper, generally without date or location. He was naturally careless or unmethodical, and his citations of other authors' works cannot safely be trusted without verification, and are usually incomplete" (Dall 1893:vii–viii). Conrad had little patience for accurate record-keeping, and appeared to be suffering from memory loss at least by age sixty, and possibly much earlier (Abbott 1895a). In fact, it was noted he even "on several occasions has re-described his own species" (Dall 1893:viii).

Timothy Abbott Conrad inadvertently served as a rancorous familial model for Charles Abbott's professional behavior. For example, during the 1830s, Conrad became embroiled in a controversy with Isaac Lea over the publication and description of a series of mollusk fossils from Claiborne, Alabama. Both Conrad and Lea separately published differing descriptions of the collections in 1833. Then in 1853, twenty years later, Conrad published an article in which the first sentence outlined an objective to give synonymies to the descriptions published by Lea. He then followed that with twenty-five pages of corrections on Lea's work (Academy of Natural Sciences, Finding Aid to Collection 270, Lea and Conrad Controversy papers 1855). Further illustrating his spiteful inclinations, in 1848, Conrad published a lengthy poem entitled "The New Diogenes, a Cynical Poem" that Charles described in a biography of Conrad as "some twenty-five hundred lines of fault-finding" (Abbott 1895a). But despite Conrad's culpabilities, Charles revered his uncle's career in science and nature, and in many ways, sought to emulate the career trajectory of both his uncle and his grandfather, with scholarly recognition gained through collecting and describing specimens (Aiello 1968). Abbott wrote admiringly in a biography of Conrad that he and colleagues were naturalists who "collected eagerly and studied carefully their 'finds' and spicily defended their positions" (Abbott 1895a:257). It is further likely that Timothy Conrad provided an introduction for the young Charles to the Philadelphia Academy of Natural Sciences, of which Charles's grandfather, Solomon, was also an early member.

In addition to opening doors towards membership in scholarly societies, Timothy Conrad's influence also exposed Charles Conrad Abbott to debates on the antiquity of the earth, which played a major role in his arguments on the American Paleolithic. Abbott identified artifacts in what he interpreted as glacial deposits in the Trenton gravels, and this formed the foundational evidence for his hypotheses about the antiquity of human occupation in the Delaware Valley. Conrad's work included mapping and recording ice age geologic strata in New York, but Conrad was not interested in archaeology. In his diary, Abbott wrote "It is always pleasant to discuss relics, which have occupied much of my attention since 1870. I see in them more than seems to be apparent to others and few are interested at all. Uncle Tim Conrad only sniffs when I speak of them" (CCA/PU Box 2, Folder 1; March 15, 1875).

EVOLVING ARCHAEOLOGICAL PARADIGMS

Charles Conrad Abbott's life and career straddled a period of changing attitudes towards science and the natural world, as archaeologists and naturalists of the latter half of the 19th century were beginning to classify, describe, and explain the world around them in increasingly scientific terms and using increasingly modern methods of observation and documentation (Anleu 1992; Barber 1980; Grayson 1983; Hinsley 1981; Hudson 1981; Kehoe 1999; Levine 1986; Rudwick 2005; Shaeffer 2016; Stebbins 1979; Taylor 1995; van Riper 1993). As early as the 17th century, amateur archaeologists, geologists, and naturalists identified fossilized remains of extinct animals, which raised questions among the learned class about the antiquity of the earth. Most scholarship during this time focused on biblical texts as a primary source of data, and the academic elite were typically theologians (Grayson 1983; Morrell and Thackray 1981; van Riper 1993). For example, using genealogical data gleaned from the Bible, Archbishop James Ussher calculated that the world was created in 4004 BC (1650[1658]), to which Dr. John Lightfoot of Cambridge University specified that the event happened on October 23 at nine o'clock in the morning (1642). But, fossils of extinct animals hinted that the earth must be older than 6,000 years, and the association between these fossils and stone artifacts clearly indicated a human presence in deep antiquity (Grayson 1983).

As early as the 16th century, Georgius Agricola, Ulisse Aldrovandi, and superintendent of the Vatican Gardens, Michele Mercati, who studied ethnographic specimens from the New World, posited that stone tools represented prehistoric technology (Heizer 1962:62; Trigger 1989:53). By the 18th century, it was generally accepted that the earth's history far surpassed a brief 6,000 year span of time (Grayson 1983; Hinsley 1981; Rudwick 2008:5; van Riper 1993). When Acheulean handaxes were found in England in 1797 by John Frere in association with animal bones at a depth of four meters, the report published by the Society of Antiquaries included the comment that they were from a remote but undated past (Grayson 1983; Heizer 1962:71; van Riper 1993), building on emerging data in geology. James Hutton in *Theory of the Earth* (1788) argued that geologic strata result from natural processes that could still be observed, and later continuing that theme, Lyell's *Principles of Geology* (published between 1830–1833) synthesized much of the geologic knowledge of preceding scholars and argued that modern phenomena could be observed to explain an ancient geological record that accrued over a very long period of time. By expanding the depth of the earth's history, Lyell's publication created an opportunity for a greater antiquity of humanity to be considered.

Paleolithic archaeology and the question of humanity's antiquity relied on evolutionary perspectives emerging in the field of geology (Grayson

1983; Meltzer 2015; van Riper 1993). Georges Cuvier (1769–1832), a French scholar and paleontologist who documented extinct animals in the geologic record, was convinced that the earth had experienced a series of catastrophic events, such as the Great Flood described in the book of Genesis (1813; Fagan 2005:21; Rudwick 2008). Others, such as William Daniel Conybeare (1830; Rudwick and Conybeare 1967; Rudwick 1970) and William Buckland (1823, 1836) tended to agree, though the details of sequential catastrophes varied. However, Buckland later changed his mind and published works arguing that glaciation could explain the geologic phenomena documented in the stratigraphic record (1836; Rudwick 2008:427).

During the first half of the 19th century, the intersections and divisions between religion and science rose to the forefront of conversations within the British Association for the Advancement of Science, one of the earliest professional associations, as burgeoning scientific fields demonstrated explanations of natural phenomena that did not require divine intervention (Morrell and Thackray 1981). The first to publicly theorize the processes that lead to biological change through time was Jean-Baptiste Lamarck in an 1809 publication entitled *Philosophie Zoologique*. Lamarck believed that evolution occurred through the inheritance of acquired characteristics that were the result of adaptation to a wide range of environments. Lamarck's explanations of evolutionary processes gained widespread acceptance during the latter half of the 19th century, as the Neo-Lamarckism school of thought was popularized by Edward Drinker Cope and other paleontologists (Gill 1897; Grayson 1983; van Riper 1993). Charles Conrad Abbott was corresponding extensively with Cope, whom he had met through the Philadelphia Academy of Natural Sciences, during the late 1880s (CCA/PU Box 2), though Abbott's diaries do not specifically reference conversations about Lamarck's ideas.

Lamarck, Lyell, and other 18th and 19th century scholars influenced Charles Darwin's thinking (Bowler 1988; Grayson 1983; Moore 1979; Ruse 1979) and contributed to the ideas about natural selection outlined in his 1859 *On the Origin of Species*. In this volume, Darwin stated that the changes that are visible in species through time are the result of natural selection. Variation exists within a population, and differences between individuals help determine who can survive and reproduce. Some heritable traits give individuals more reproductive success than others, and these advantageous traits will be passed on to the next generation. At no point in *On the Origin of*

Species did Darwin address *human* evolution, but the applicability of natural selection to humans was certainly implied. It was not until Darwin's 1871 publication *Descent of Man and Selection in Relation to Sex* that he proposed that humans evolved from earlier species as a result of natural selection. In other words, he stated, we are no different from other animals and plants. Darwin also speculated that our ancestors may be found in Africa, since the living species most similar to humans, such as gorillas and chimpanzees, could be found there.

Darwin's publication generated debate among scholars, most famously through the event of June 30, 1860, in which more than 400 men and women gathered in Oxford for a discussion on natural selection, led primarily by Samuel Wilberforce, the Bishop of Oxford; Thomas Henry Huxley; and Joseph Dalton Hooker, Director of the Royal Botanical Gardens (James 2005:171). The meeting, though poorly documented in contemporaneous accounts, is and was even by the late 19th century, heralded as an early polarization of science and religion, but such an oversimplification obfuscates the complicated relationship that existed even as early as Darwin's first foray into evolutionary theory (James 2005). Darwin's theories about evolution, and particularly its application to human evolution, were anathema to many 19th century Christians for two reasons: first, Christians believed that humans were created by God in present form, and in God's image. And second, if humans did evolve, and Lyell and others were correct in their assessment of the earth's age, then calculations based on biblical passages indicating the world was created 6,000 years ago must also be wrong. Many people were unable to reconcile their Christian beliefs with new scientific theories about evolution and sought explanations for geologic phenomena that could be based in some aspect of biblical text (Bowler 1988; Grayson 1983; Montgomery 2012; Ruse 1979; Symondson 1970). Even Darwin initially followed William Paley's ideas of natural theology, in which the process of biological adaptation was evidence of a divine author, but later became a self-professed agnostic who attributed species' change solely to natural selection (von Sydow 2005:153).

The rate of new discoveries published by amateur archaeologists, paleontologists, and geologists accelerated through the 19th century. French, Belgian, and English scholars, such as Paul Tournal, Jules de Christol, Philippe-Charles Schmerling, and John MacEnery documented human remains and associated artifacts in situ adjacent to the fossils of extinct species in the early part of the century (Grayson 1983; Meltzer 2015; van Riper 1993). Soon after that, Jacques Boucher de Perthes of France published prehistoric stone tools from the Somme River Valley that were recovered in association with the bones of extinct animals, leading him to conclude that these stone tools must have been made and used at the time that those animals lived—during or before the last ice age (1847, 1857). In 1863, Thomas Henry Huxley published *Man's Place in Nature*, which summarized his analysis of the Neanderthal remains discovered in 1856 in the Neander Valley. Huxley documented the anatomical similarities between the fossilized remains and those of modern apes and humans, noting that the skull retained features similar to those of chimpanzees. The same year, Lyell (1863) published *The Geological Evidences of the Antiquity of Man*, which established a geologic context for Paleolithic archaeology.

ABBOTT'S AMERICAN PALEOLITHIC

It was within this scientific environment that Abbott began collecting artifacts on his farm and researching human antiquity within the Delaware Valley. Abbott drew strong parallels between his own research, which he believed demonstrated Pleistocene occupation of the New World, and the findings that were gaining traction in the Old World. His earliest publication on the American Paleolithic in *The American Naturalist* in 1872 referenced the work of John Frere, Jacques Boucher de Perthes, and Charles Lyell, and drew heavily on John Lubbock's highly popular 1865 publication, *Pre-Historic Times* (Abbott 1872). As his career as an archaeologist ascended, with some financial remuneration for his collections at Harvard's Peabody Museum and later as the first curator of the American Section at the University of Pennsylvania Museum of Archaeology and Anthropology (now the Penn Museum), his status as a well-connected, and well-educated member of the Trenton elite facilitated access to this scholarly world.

However, as professional archaeologists began to examine, and ultimately dismantle, his American Paleolithic, his theories and his place in the scholarly community declined precipitously, and Abbott did not handle it well. Though Abbott perhaps did not initially intend to become an iconoclast, his conclusions regarding the antiquity of humans in the Delaware Valley as a pre-Ice Age, autochthonic population (Abbott 1872:146), thrust him into the scientific spotlight and were ultimately rejected by the newly established academic and professional community. His refusal to concede in the face of mounting scientific evidence, and his hostile replies in print, marked him as a mere amateur who did not need to be taken seriously by a growing cadre of professional archaeologists. His later years and writings, both personal and archaeological, were colored by animosity about the lack of scholarly acceptance for human antiquity in the Delaware Valley and his marginalization from a now exclusive community of intellectuals. In his last book, written in 1912, *Ten Years' Diggings in Lenape Land*, he continued to stubbornly insist on a great antiquity of prehistoric humans in New Jersey.

Abbott's later years were filled with writing and full-time residence at Three Beeches until it was destroyed by fire on November 13, 1914 (*Daily State Gazette,* 14 November 1914), and he spent the last five years of his life in a rented apartment, away from the farm he so loved. He died on July 27, 1919, of Bright's disease, a kidney infection, at the age of 76. His grave is located in Trenton's prestigious Riverview Cemetery, not far from his Three Beeches farm, where a glacial boulder serves as his monument (see Fig. 10.5).

2

The Move to Three Beeches and the History of the Abbott Farm

"January 2, 1875: Not everything one needs, grows on the farm, and certainly I can find no dollars blooming among the bushes. Golden rod is very different from golden coins."

--Charles Conrad Abbott (CCA/PU Box 2, Folder 2)

Amateur archaeologists of the 19th century typically collected artifacts exposed on the surface of agricultural fields in areas near where they lived (Hudson, 1981; Trigger 1989), and Charles Conrad Abbott was no exception. Abbott's family farm, where he identified an alleged American Paleolithic, contained an unusual confluence of environmental conditions that favored more or less continuous occupation from prehistoric until modern times, as evidenced by a rich and well-documented archaeological record. Today, the property is considered archaeologically significant for its contributions to our understanding of the Archaic through Woodland periods in the Delaware Valley, and archaeological investigations over the past 150 years, beginning with Abbott's inexpert surface collecting, have greatly increased our knowledge of the trajectory of human occupation in the region (Cavallo 1987; Cross 1956; Dumont and McLearen 1986; Foss 1986; McLearen and Fokken 1986; Perazio 1986; Stewart 1986a, 1986b, 1987, 1998; Volk 1911; Wall and Stewart 1996; Wall et al. 1996a, 1996b, 1996c).

Despite his failed efforts towards an American Paleolithic, Abbott was the first to bring the prehistory of this portion of the Delaware Valley to a larger audience, and the history of Abbott's family's tenure at Three Beeches farm and neighboring properties is important for understanding the environmental and historical context of Charles Conrad Abbott's work. The Abbotts were a prominent family and well-established as landowners in this area of Trenton. His family's elite reputation, his access to a farm dense with archaeological artifacts, and his uncle and grandfather's scholarly status provided initial entry into intellectual circles, although as the field evolved, a family pedigree and control of a farm that held important archaeological sites were no longer enough to bestow the scholarly respect Abbott felt he deserved. However, he gained initial fame by publicizing the claim of an ice age occupation of the Delaware Valley based on the artifacts collected on his Three Beeches farm, and the farm figures prominently in the account of the rise and fall of Charles Conrad Abbott and the American Paleolithic.

ARRIVAL OF THE ABBOTTS

In 1689, Charles Conrad Abbott's ancestors settled in what would become Mercer County, New Jersey. Charles's great-great-great grandfather John Abbott arrived in the United States from England as an indentured servant to local farmer William Watson. After completing his five-year service, John Abbott purchased and combined multiple landholdings totaling over 800 acres along Crosswicks Creek and the Delaware River (Hunter and Tvaryanas 2009). The property, then known as Abbottville, was used for both agricultural and commercial enterprises, including a tannery and distillery. In the 18th century, the Abbotts constructed a landing, wharf, and storehouse on Crosswicks Creek, and John Abbott's son Timothy operated at least one boat to transport products to market. Crosswicks Creek, which ran westward from the high terrace above the Delaware River down through low-lying marshes, was wider and deeper in the 17th and 18th century than it is today, allowing goods to be sent downriver to Philadelphia. An overland transport route along the bluffs was improved with the construction of a drawbridge over Crosswicks Creek in 1763, permitting the growth of commercial farms along the high terrace connecting Trenton to Bordentown and points further south (Hunter and Tvaryanas 2009). The Abbott family property was ideally situated to take advantage of these transportation routes as well as prime

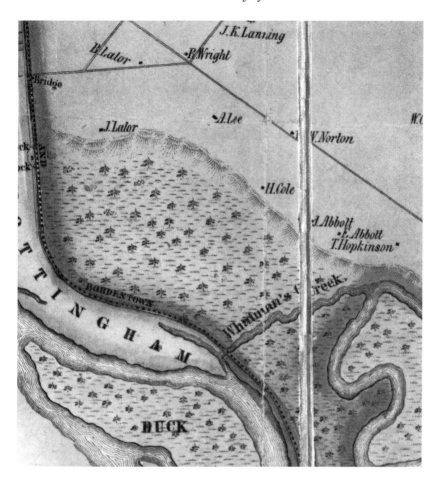

2.1 Depiction of Charles Conrad Abbott's future home on an 1849 map of Mercer County, New Jersey, labeled here in the center of the map as the home of J. Abbott, who was grandfather to Charles Conrad Abbott. Map of Mercer County, New Jersey, J. W. Otley and James Keily, published by L. van der Veer, Camden, New Jersey, 1849. Retrieved from the Library of Congress, https://www.loc.gov/item/2004629246/.

agricultural and timber land. When Charles Conrad Abbott was a boy, almost 200 years after John Abbott's initial arrival in New Jersey, much of this property remained in the Abbott family, including a large block of farmland on the high bluffs overlooking Crosswicks Creek and the Delaware River.

Historic maps depict the Abbott family holdings from the mid-19th century. The 1849 Otley and Keily map of Mercer County, New Jersey (Fig. 2.1) illustrates the farm of J. Abbott, who was Joseph Abbott, great-grandson

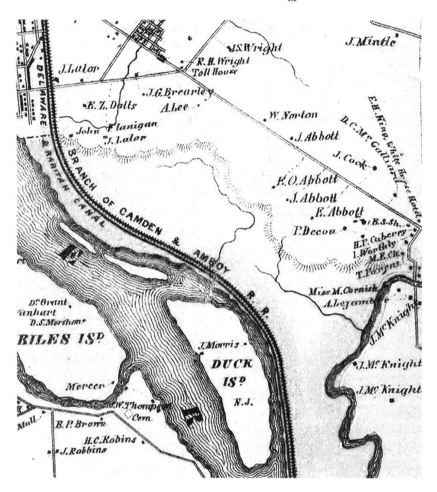

2.2 Depiction of Charles Conrad Abbott's future home on an 1860 map of Trenton and Philadelphia, labeled here as the home of J. Abbott. Map of the Vicinity of Philadelphia, From Actual Surveys, D. J. Lake and S. N. Beers, published by J. E. Gillette and Co., Philadelphia, Pennsylvania, 1860. Retrieved from David Rumsey Map Collection, http://www.davidrumsey.com/luna/servlet/detail/RUMSEY~8~1~200338~3000966:Map-Of-The-Vicinity-Of-Philadelphia.

to the original John Abbott, and grandfather to Charles Conrad Abbott. This farm, at the time known as "Prospect Hill" would eventually become Charles Conrad Abbott's farm, which he renamed "Three Beeches" in 1874. In an unpublished history, Charles described the farm as he remembered it in the late 1840s as:

much as nature fashioned it, although there was no heavy timber standing, but the trees were old enough and large enough to make it a real forest. As a place wherein to wander at any time of year, these woods were ideal for one interested in nature and not simply by an aimless spirit of adventure such as characterizes the average boy. There was enough variety of surface condition to attract every form of wood-loving wildlife and one bubbling spring surrounded by trees and hidden by huckleberry bushes, was a delight to me, it seeming so remote from civilization (CCA/PANS).

By 1860, the Lake and Beers map of the area shows more development with three Abbott family farms on the bluff overlooking Crosswicks Creek and the Delaware River (Fig. 2.2). In the center is Prospect Hill/Three Beeches, still owned in 1860 by Charles's grandfather Joseph Abbott. The Three Beeches farmhouse was built in 1807 and consisted of a two-story frame house, which along with several outbuildings, incorporated elements of structures that had been erected on the property even earlier by the Watson family (Louis Berger and Associates, Inc. 1998). At some point between 1860 and 1874, the farm passed into the hands of Charles's aunt Susan Abbott.

It was during these years of the mid-19th century, when the farms were owned by aunts, uncles, and grandparents, that Charles spent time there as a child. His visits to the family properties influenced his decision to pursue life as an archaeologist and naturalist as he got older. Early diaries detailed new discoveries and excitement about the surrounding countryside and opportunities to pursue his love of the outdoors. Abbott wrote of his childhood memories that "I early learned to love it and sat there many an hour, jejunely recording childish impressions, absolutely happy." He continued snootily "yet often stooping from such high estate to pity the toilers in the adjacent fields" (CCA/PANS). His apparent distaste for physical farm labor manifested at an early age.

Surrounding Three Beeches, Abbott family farms and neighboring properties also contained extensive prehistoric archaeological deposits. Notably, to the north were several farms owned by the Lalor family (see Figs. 2.1, 2.2), where Abbott established what he termed an "argillite culture" and collected artifacts (Abbott 1907). Later excavations by Ernest Volk on the Lalor fields were sponsored by Harvard's Peabody Museum and primarily designed to evaluate Abbott's claims of great antiquity. Volk's excavations revealed argillite assemblages from the Late Archaic through Woodland periods in the subsoil of the bluff but offered no evidence of Abbott's American Paleolithic (Volk 1911).

The neighborhood surrounding the family farms was largely agricultural in the mid-19th century, facilitating Abbott's almost-daily archaeological surface collecting, however, urban sprawl rapidly expanded during the late 19th and early 20th century. In 1885, new transportation routes, including two trolley lines, extended south from Trenton along Lalor Street to the Delaware and Raritan Canal and passed immediately east of Three Beeches, bringing picnickers to parklands along the bluff and Riverview Cemetery, and allowing commuters an easy route into Trenton proper. Though Charles took advantage of the easy transportation to Trenton, Philadelphia, and beyond, he dismayed at the new developments in his neighborhood that it "surely changed from the poetical to the prosaic. The nearby town grew rapidly and farm after farm was converted into town lots. An 'improvement' this, it considered by the common herd of humanity, but not from my point of view and finally there was little left of the old charm" (CCA/PANS).

THE LANDSCAPE OF THE ABBOTT FARM

The Abbott family farms were located approximately three miles downstream from the falls of the Delaware, which marked the northern terminus of the tidal portion of the Delaware River. This feature created an ecologically rich setting, with high bluffs overlooking low-lying marshes where Crosswicks Creek flowed into the Delaware River near Bordentown. Crosswicks Creek drained an area of approximately 140 square miles, originating ten miles from the Delaware River. This was an important watercourse for Three Beeches farm, along with Watson's Creek located directly below the bluff, and drained the marshland into the river. All three watercourses contributed to the overall agricultural fertility of the property.

Crosswicks and Watson's Creeks featured conspicuously in Abbott's naturalist writings and would have provided key resources for prehistoric Native American inhabitants of the area, a causative factor to Three Beeches' archaeological prominence. Watson's Creek was described by Abbott as "a piece of some remote wilderness dropped in the midst of long-cultivated, civilized surroundings, Watson's creek, now almost a thing of the past, was richer in aquatic life than any other stream I ever saw" (CCA/PANS).

Situated on these high bluffs overlooking these marshes and the confluence of Crosswicks and Watson's Creeks with the Delaware River, the Abbott family farms were also positioned to take advantage of a wide range of ecological settings that included rich agricultural soils and upland forests. The upland terrain was relatively flat, cut by the Crosswicks Creek drainage, and ranged from approximately 40–60 feet above sea level. Sediments on these uplands typically consisted of several feet of eolian (windblown) Holocene sands that were deposited between 2,000–6,000 years ago (Hunter and Tvaryanas 2009). To the north of the upland farms was Riverview Cemetery, which was present during Abbott's occupation of the farm, and remains a prominent feature today. To the south, the upland bluff extends towards Bordentown. To the east was Hamilton Township and central New Jersey's heartland, composed of small farms and farming communities in the mid-19th century. To the west, beyond the marshes, ran the Delaware and Raritan Canal and the Camden and Amboy Railroad, both of which paralleled the main channel of the Delaware River, separated by a low-lying sandbar island known as Duck Island.

The lowland marshes below the farms ranged from approximately 10–12 feet above sea level, and are today much wetter than they were during Abbott's childhood. Ecological changes resulting from drainage modifications due to railway and canal construction limited the natural drainage of marshy lowlands. This caused water to back up into meadows that were agriculturally productive during the 19th century. Sediments in this area consist of gradually accumulated, marshy deposits such as organics, silts, sands, and clays from recent Holocene overbank flooding of the Delaware River, Watson's Creek, and Crosswicks Creek.

The ecological setting of the Abbott farms was important for the historic settlement of the farmland by Charles's ancestors, but also very important in the selection of this location by its Native American inhabitants in prehistoric times. It was the combination of upload forests, lowland marshes, large and small waterways, and productive soils that would have made this such an attractive location. Charles's archaeological collections from the property, and subsequent, more scientifically rigorous excavations, have revealed thousands of years of prehistoric occupation and an exceptionally rich history of people in the region.

THE MOVE TO THREE BEECHES FARM

Charles and his wife Julia lived in Trenton for the first seven years of their marriage, but in 1874, Job Olden, Charles Conrad Abbott's father-in-law and a wealthy Princeton merchant, fulfilled Charles's childhood dream of living full-time on one of the Abbott family farms. He generously purchased the Prospect Hill farm from Abbott's aunt Susan for the young Abbott family, who moved in on March 16, 1874 and renamed it "Three Beeches" after a cluster of trees on the property (Fig. 2.3). Olden's will outlined the purchase and associated gifts for running the farm:

> I have bought a farm situated in the Township of Hamilton, in the County of Mercer, aforesaid known as the Abbott Farm and lately owned by Miss Susan Abbott, containing about one hundred and nine acres, and have furnished the house thereon, and have put stock and implements of husbandry on said farm, with a view of securing a home for my said daughter and of devising the said farm to my said daughter and her children in lieu of the legacy aforesaid, to the extent of ten thousand dollars, the value I place on said farm and property (New Jersey, District and Probate Courts, Mercer County. Ancestry.com; *New Jersey, Wills and Probate Records, 1785–1924*).

Abbott was thrilled with the purchase of Three Beeches for his family's use, which he never would have been able to afford on his own. Despite loving the farm, Abbott deeply resented being beholden to his father-in-law for this purchase (CCA/PU Box 2, Folder 2; December 31, 1875). In *A Naturalist's Ramblings About Home*, Abbott wrote of the trees that were his farm's namesake "I have often wondered that these sole remaining traces of the primeval forest did not die of chagrin when they saw how sadly changed everything was about them. However, they still stand as glorious monuments of a splendid long ago, guarding a little space of air if not of earth" (1884a:191). He was drawn by the ideal of the gentleman farmer and a pull towards nature and away from medicine, a career he openly despised. The farm gave him the opportunity to pursue these dreams. The family farms along the bluff had been a magical place during his childhood. He wrote: "The farm proper, or what constituted the Three Beeches when I moved there in 1874, was an unusual one in many ways....It was

2.3 Newspaper photograph of Three Beeches farm captioned: "Here's a dismal view of where I live—C.C.A." Charles Conrad Abbott Papers (C0290), Box 15, Folder 2; Manuscripts Division, Department of Rare Books and Special Collections, Princeton University Library.

because of this ideal condition, so unusual in this region that I had with a minimum of effort the opportunity to visit...A maximum of conditions" (CCA/PANS).

Interestingly, however, it appears that Job Olden did not fully trust his son-in-law to manage the farm properly and maintained legal ownership of Three Beeches. The 1875 Everts and Stewart map depicted Three Beeches as a property owned by J. I. Olden (Fig. 2.4). Olden's purchase of Three Beeches was clearly for his daughter Julia's benefit, and a statement in his will specifically instructed that the deed to the property to pass to Julia's heirs, and not to Charles, in the case that she predecease her husband. Abbott's uncle John remained on the farm to assist in its operations, and

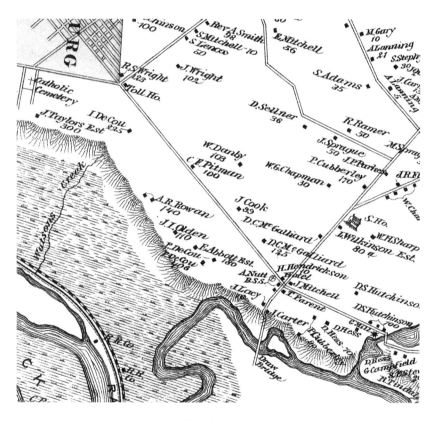

2.4 Depiction of Charles Conrad Abbott's home on an 1875 map of Mercer County, New Jersey, labeled here in the center of the map as J. I. Olden, who was Job Olden, the father-in-law of Charles Conrad Abbott. Combination Atlas Map of Mercer County, New Jersey, Published by Everts and Stewart, Philadelphia, Pennsylvania.

Charles found himself caught between two competing interests. He stated in his diary that "Uncle John was then living here, and he and Mr. Olden continually disagreed about the conduct of the farm, so that I wasn't by any means lying on a bed of roses" (CCA/PU Box 2, Folder 2).

Job Olden's will was very explicit about the farm's purpose:

> I do hereby give, devise and bequeath unto my said daughter Julia O. Abbott during her natural life, the use, possession, profits, and income of said farm with the stock, implements thereon aforesaid, all subject to her own control and not to the control of her husband, nor liable for his debts; and at her death, I give, devise, and bequeath the said farm and the other said property to the child or said children of her the said Julia; their heirs and assigns forever if she shall have any child or children her surviving, and in case she should have no lawful issuance surviving her, then I give devise and bequeath the same to her brother and sisters equally share and share alike their heirs and assigns forever (New Jersey, District and Probate Courts, Mercer County. Ancestry. com; *New Jersey, Wills and Probate Records, 1785–1924*).

Job Olden's control over Three Beeches was perhaps understandable, as he must have known Charles had little enthusiasm for farm labor—or any labor, for that matter. Much of the farm work was done by hired workers who were supervised by his uncle John Abbott. Instead, Charles preferred to spend his time in scholarly quests, such as his explorations of archaeology and nature. On January 26, 1875, he wrote "Uncle John and Johnnie attended to the farm, and I suppose I should have been interested, at least, but I fear I can never learn to be a farmer" (CCA/PU Box 2, Folder 2). He simply did not have the constitution, or the will, for farm chores. Instead, he preferred to sleep late, nap often, and follow his archaeological and naturalist pursuits. In *Clear Skies and Cloudy*, Abbott wrote "there is danger in the unsunned air of early morning, and insanity is the result of too frequent lungfuls of the day at dawn; that farmers lose their sanity because of early rising, and, if not quite so bad as this, at least their mental strength is prematurely weakened" (1898a:96). Charles appeared to be in little danger of succumbing.

The farm produced vegetables, grains, and hay for the household and for sale in nearby cities such as Philadelphia and Trenton, where canneries purchased and processed large quantities of vegetables. Abbott's diaries provide little information about farm accounts, other than payments to farm workers, but he occasionally mentioned planting and tending to crops such as rye, tomatoes, watermelons, cauliflower, onions, strawberries, and eggplants. He also briefly mentioned chickens and a cow, though these were apparently for household use, and not large scale livestock operations.

However, he quickly discovered that the farm's revenue, even with the assistance of several farmhands, would not adequately support a growing family, and at this point, Abbott began his literary and archaeological endeavors as a means to supplement a meager farm income, as well as began writing the daily personal diaries that provide insight into his thoughts and activities for much of his adult life.

> January 1, 1875: Happening to be sitting at my desk and recalling incidents of the past very disagreeable nine months and a half [since moving to the farm]. I concluded to keep a diary, yet the wisdom of it is problematical, as I have found living here not what I expected in many respects, and the farm's income, this year, so small that the sentiment which so urged me on now wears the front of mockery (CCA/PU Box 2, Folder 2).

Overall, farming appeared to be a losing proposition. On June 30, 1875, Charles lamented "Is it worthwhile to keep on? I cannot take interest in farm life as I should, or the real work is too hard for me, and the financial aspect is anything but encouraging. If Uncle John was really a businessman it would be very different" (CCA/PU Box 2, Folder 2). However, the farm's failures may not have been entirely Charles's, or his Uncle John's, fault. Reconstructions of drought cycles, linked to La Niña sea surface temperature oscillations and tree-ring data suggest that the mid-Atlantic United States experienced several years of drought between 1870–1877 (Herweijer et al. 2006), meaning that Charles and his family moved to the farm right in the middle of a severe, multiyear drought.

Historical evidence of drought conditions can be gleaned from some of Abbott's diary entries, too. He lamented the failure of his crops in 1874 "Was a remarkably dry summer and corn-crop a fizzle" (CCA/PU Box 2, Folder 2). More suggestively, on January 28, 1875, he wrote "As the rain no longer supplies us with water, had to cart a lot from the mill-pond. In all the years Grandfather had this rain, about twenty, and while Aunt Sue lived here. There seems to be no end of trouble. Is the farm hoo-dooed?" (CCA/PU Box 2, Folder 2).

Ironically, other fields suffered from too much water, not too little. Anthropogenic changes affected the natural drainage of the marshland below the bluffs, which had previously provided rich agricultural lands, primarily for hay, but presumably other crops as well, during the 18th and early 19th centuries. Construction of the Delaware and Raritan Canal occurred between 1830–1834 and ran parallel to the Delaware River along the edge of the marsh below the Abbott family farms. The canal, once completed, blocked some of the direct drainage outflow into the River. Compounding the canal's effects, construction of the Camden and Amboy Railroad just a few years later, between 1839–1840, created a large earthen berm along the River. These substantial earth-moving projects profoundly affected Three Beeches, though the effects were gradual. Tidal flow and drainage of the marsh were impeded by the railroad berm and the canal, which caused water to back up behind the canal and railroad embankments, with a single culvert providing drainage for Watson's Creek. All water now shunted into Crosswicks Creek to the east, rather than directly into the Delaware River (Hunter and Tvaryanas 2009). As a result, the meadows below the bluff were unable to drain properly and quickly flooded, forming marshy lands that could no longer be farmed.

Marsh drainage was further hampered by extensive clay deposits underlying the property. This clay may have been used by prehistoric potters, contributing to the farm's archaeological significance, but was also an important industrial resource in the 19th century. The DeCou family, who had purchased property adjacent to Three Beeches, began mining operations in the 1860s, digging from the exposed bluff into the hillside at a depth of about 20 feet. Miners constructed tunnels extending as much as 200 feet into the bluff, with timber supports for the roof. Clay mining only occurred for a few years, but continued elsewhere in the vicinity at least through the late 19th century (Hunter and Tvaryanas 2009). These mining activities, and associated dredging of Crosswicks Creek for shipping the clay to factories throughout New Jersey, accelerated erosion and channeling of the Creek and hastened the decline in productivity of neighboring farmland.

Unfortunately, Abbott was oblivious to the natural and man-made changes undermining the farm's success. He was unaware that a large-scale, multiyear drought was occurring throughout much of the eastern United States at the time that he relocated to the farm. Furthermore, he would not have understood the impacts of the canal and railway construction on the marsh's drainage, as the effects were both gradual and cumulative. Instead, he only knew that his Uncle John was unable to make the farm work, and that he, Charles, was not successful as a farmer, though he was quick to transfer blame to others. He had ultimately failed at the task handed to him by his father-in-law, which exacerbated tension between the two men. On New Year's Eve 1875, he wrote in his diary "This tells the story of the first whole year of the farm. Why it was a failure in many ways was due to my lack of knowledge and of capital. John R. Abbott, too was a dismal failure and greatly complicated my troubles instead of helping me out. As worthless a man as ever lived. I will not say more but live in hopes that things will better themselves as time runs on. I am learning some things that will be useful in the future and of most importance is to be my own master and not at the beck and nod of those here or in Princeton [his in-laws]" (CCA/PU Box 2, Folder 2).

ARCHAEOLOGICAL SIGNIFICANCE

As farming proved to be a relatively fruitless occupation, archaeological and literary endeavors became an important source of income. Charles Conrad Abbott collected thousands of prehistoric Native American artifacts from the fields surrounding Three Beeches and on neighboring farms. Most of these artifacts are today in the collections of the Peabody Museum at Harvard University, but others are scattered between the Pitt Rivers Museum at Oxford University, the Penn Museum, the New Jersey State Museum, and the Smithsonian Institution, with a few individual artifacts at other museums. Serendipitously for Abbott, the high bluff on which his house was located contains an almost continuous band of deposits of prehistoric archaeological material. There are twelve recorded archaeological sites on the bluff between Riverview Cemetery and White Horse Circle, which includes Three Beeches farm, and ten have been recorded in the lowland below the bluff. There may be additional unrecorded sites as well, particularly in the low-lying marshes (Hunter and Tvaryanas 2009).

Modern-day professional archaeological survey and excavation of the bluff confirmed Abbott's assertions of thousands of years of Native American occupation of the region, though not at the great antiquity that he alleged. Archaeological sites have been mapped and, in many cases, professionally excavated as part of cultural resources compliance activity for federally funded projects such as highway construction, specifically for the I-195 and I-295 rights-of-way (Wall et al. 1996a). Professional excavations were also conducted by Works Progress Administration projects with the Indian Sites Survey, under the direction of Dr. Dorothy Cross (1956). These excavations have revealed intact, multicomponent archaeological sites depicting thousands of years of prehistoric occupation. Many of the bluff-top sites consisted of Middle and Late Woodland period occupations that included storage pits, caches, and large quantities of lithic material and pottery sherds (Cross 1956; Hunter and Tvaryanas 2009), but there is evidence of extensive, diachronic occupation spanning 10,000 years of prehistory.

Based on his collections, Abbott concluded that there were three distinct periods of occupation represented at Three Beeches. The first was what he called the "Paleolithic" culture, represented by stone "paleoliths," which were rough, bifacially-worked argillite nodules that were recovered from what he deduced to be glacial gravels. He identified these artifacts as manufactured by either ancestors to modern Native American people, or by a separate, earlier population that was later replaced by Native Americans. He subsequently grew more convinced of the latter (Abbott 1878) and later proposed that this period represented habitation of the Delaware Valley by an earlier human, which he called *Homo delawarensis*, living during and immediately following the last glaciation (Abbott 1912:128).

In Abbott's view, the Paleolithic in New Jersey slowly died out with the retreat of glacial ice, but was replaced by a second wave of occupation, by ancestral Native American people, that continued to use argillite stone tool material, yet manufactured highly standardized spear points and other implements. Abbott referred to this intermediate occupation as the "argillite culture" or "argillite man" in his personal and professional writings (Abbott 1907). These argillite artifacts were frequently found in yellow sands of the Three Beeches farm, approximately two feet below the ground's surface. Extensive collecting by Abbott, and later excavations by Ernest Volk on the Lalor fields to the north of Three Beeches, revealed argillite assemblages in the subsoil of the bluff (Abbott 1907; Volk 1911). The "yellow sands" within which the argillite culture was found were distinct from the lower glacial gravels and the organic soils above. Given that the chronology of the argillite culture occupation was contingent on stratigraphic positioning and technology, it was important for Abbott, and later Volk, to ascertain the age and depositional nature of these sediments, which appeared to be intact water or wind deposited sands containing bands of reddish iron oxides. Abbott and Volk recognized that these sediments were younger than the glacial gravels, but older than modern topsoil, bracketing the age of the artifacts within them to an intermediate period (Abbott 1907; Volk 1911).

The technology represented by argillite spearpoints was also used to ascertain chronology. Abbott argued that prehistoric cultures improved their stone tool-making abilities through time and believed that rougher, less-refined artifacts reflected earlier cultures, while more well-made pieces indicated later occupation, particularly when viewed in the context of their stratigraphic position relative to the glacial gravels. Therefore, the argillite artifacts of the yellow sands reflected improvements in stone tool-making ability from early, Paleolithic culture, but not the skilled toolmakers of more recent Native American occupation. Abbott wrote that these artifacts were "a marked advance over the palaeolithic implements, and yet is so uniform in pattern and so inferior in finish, when compared with the average flint implement of the Indian, that it has been assigned to an earlier date than the latter" (1883a:319). He concluded that his argillite culture was perhaps related in some way to Eskimo populations, both having an ancestral line traced back to Paleolithic occupation of the Old World.

Much of the stratigraphically provenienced data from the "argillite culture" comes from Ernest Volk's excavations at Lalor fields, which he published twenty-two years after beginning the research (Volk 1911). Volk assembled his data according to Abbott's interpretations of three distinct strata representing three chronological horizons. He attempted to remain true to Abbott's interpretations, though regrettably, Abbott never actually conducted controlled excavations, so his work was problematic from the outset. Dr. Dorothy Cross, who later directed large-scale excavations of the Abbott Farm in the 1930s, noted some significant shortcomings in Volk's publication: "With little interpretation and very few conclusions, the reader must judge the validity of the presentation for himself....For example, only material which was supposed to be the product of the 'Dweller of the Yellow Soil,' such as chipped quartzite pebbles, argillite implements, and the like, are listed as being found in the 'yellow sand.' All other material, which must have been numerous, was regarded as intrusive, and omitted" (Cross 1956:8).

Stratigraphically positioned above the yellow sand of the argillite culture, Abbott identified what he interpreted to represent recent Native American occupation. This "modern" prehistoric level was located within the "black soil" or uppermost organic soil on the bluff. Artifacts from this level included stone arrow points made of quartz, chert, and jasper, as well as prehistoric pottery, ground stone artifacts, bone and antler, shell, copper, and other materials (Cross 1956). However, Abbott was only superficially interested in these more recent habitation levels, focusing more of his attention on earlier evidence of what he argued was Paleolithic occupation. Subsequent excavations by Dorothy Cross and later cultural resource management undertakings have revealed an extensive archaeological sequence from prehistory through contact with Euro-American settlers.

THE ARCHAEOLOGICAL RECORD OF THE ABBOTT FARM

Today, extensive archaeological survey and excavation have revealed multiple chronological periods of occupation that do not necessarily correspond to the three stratigraphic horizons described by Abbott. The earliest prehistoric period represented at Three Beeches is not a Paleolithic horizon, but instead is the Archaic (8000–1000 BC). This time period marked a gradual environmental transition associated with the retreat of ice age glaciers at the beginning of the Holocene. Subsistence strategies of the Archaic show a trend towards increased efficiency and diversity in exploiting resources (Caldwell 1958; Smith 1986). Archaic peoples remained largely mobile hunters and gatherers who moved frequently to exploit a variety of seasonally available resources, with a pattern towards increased sedentism and smaller territory through time. Archaeological evidence indicates that small groups of hunting and gathering people in the Eastern United States often reoccupied camps in favorable locations and may have returned to a larger base camp during specific times of the year (Chapman 1973).

The Archaic period on the Three Beeches farm is represented by several individual sites located on the bluff near Abbott's farmhouse. Cross and later archaeologists identified large side- and corner-notched projectile points, bannerstones, grooved axes, semi-lunar knives, scrapers, drills, netsinkers, hammerstones, and other lithics in situ, and Abbott's collections at the Peabody Museum at Harvard University include many identifiable Archaic period lithics. Lithic artifact manufacture was dominated by argillite raw material, but chert, jasper, quartzite, and quartz were also used. Many of the artifacts were located within the "yellow sands" of Abbott's and Volk's investigations (Cross 1956; Wall et al. 1996a), and Abbott's "argil lite culture" appears rooted firmly in the Archaic period.

The Archaic transitioned into the Woodland period (1000 BC–1600 AD). During this time, the archaeological record documents continuing changes in the way in which Native Americans interacted with each other and their surroundings (Williams and Thomas 1982). Woodland period sites at Three Beeches included sites on both the bluff and the associated lowlands, which are today dominated by wetlands, but were drier and more well drained in prehistory. Stone tools including projectile points, scrapers, axes, flakes, and other lithic artifacts were common on these sites, including raw materials such as chert, jasper, quartz, and argillite. Steatite vessels, specifically bowls, were also found in Woodland sites. The most notable change in artifact assemblages from Archaic to Woodland period sites is the introduction of ceramic pottery, which became a common prehistoric artifact type, with plain and decorated vessels present. Other Woodland artifacts included netsinkers, bannerstones, bone and antler implements, copper, mica, and caches of argillite blades (Cross 1956; Wall et al. 1996a). Abbott's artifact collections at the Peabody Museum at Harvard University also contain Woodland period artifacts, though Abbott appears to have been less interested in later prehistoric occupation. Projectile points, knives, scrapers, bannerstones, and netsinkers were commonly collected during Abbott's fieldwalking on his property.

Sites within and immediately adjacent to Abbott's farm illustrate prehistoric Native American occupation of the area spanning both the Archaic and Woodland periods. Unfortunately, unlike professional archaeological excavation conducted in the 20th century by Cross and others, Abbott neglected to document the locations where many of his artifacts were found. Many of his diaries simply recorded entries such as the one on May 26, 1875 "After supper, walked to lane gate and searched corn field for Indian relics" or the one on February 11, 1876 "After dinner at 'drawbridge,' getting a large lot of relics" (CCA/PU Box 2, Folder 2). The latter entry provides some more useful provenience information in that it likely refers to the bridge over Crosswicks Creek as indicated on the 1875 Everts and Stewart map of Hamilton Township, New Jersey (Fig. 2.3). A more typical entry can be found on October 1, 1876 "In afternoon, went on a hunt for Indian relics. This is always fun and sometimes exciting, when a new shape turns up and speculation begins as to its significance" (CCA/PU Box 2, Folder 2). Most of Abbott's artifacts from his farm are in the collections of the Peabody Museum at Harvard University, and what provenience data are available are recorded in the accession records of the Museum. Many simply state that artifacts are from "Trenton" but occasional pieces are specific to farm (i.e., Abbott's farm, DeCou's farm, or others), or if collected from a railroad cut or erosional surface, may record depth. This lack of archaeological provenience frustrates attempts to reconstruct prehistoric site characteristics, but was not unusual practice by amateur archaeologists in the latter half of the 19th century.

THREE BEECHES TODAY

Today, the Abbott Farm is recognized as a National Historic Landmark with multiple archaeological sites and historic properties listed on the National Register of Historic Places. But, modern development encroaching into the area around Three Beeches has enveloped the property into the outer reaches of the city of Trenton. Highway construction impacted the upland terraces, with interchanges of U.S. Routes 195 and 295, and New Jersey Route 29 intersecting within the immediate vicinity of the Three Beeches farm. Hamilton Township constructed a sewage treatment plant on Crosswicks Creek, and an abandoned landfill is present just beyond the Three Beeches property boundary. Below Three Beeches, an oil tank farm was constructed on Duck Island in the Delaware River in the first half of the 20th century. On the low-lying fields, poor drainage and rising water levels in the tidal portion of the Delaware River resulted in expanded wetlands and marshes that remain largely undeveloped beyond the railway and canal lines that were also present during the 19th century. Much of this low-lying area has passed into public ownership, including the John A. Roebling Memorial Park, operated by Mercer County, and the National Register of Historic Places listed Delaware and Raritan Canal State Park, operated by the state of New Jersey. Yet Abbott was the first to argue that this land contained important data on the prehistory of Native American people, and though his theories of their origins were ultimately overturned, Charles Conrad Abbott and the Abbott Farm, where many of the alleged American Paleolithic artifacts originated, remain vital to our understanding of the prehistoric past and the changing views of archaeological science during the late 19th and early 20th centuries.

3

Frederic Ward Putnam and the Peabody Museum of Archaeology and Ethnology, Harvard University

In 1866, George Peabody, a New England banker and one of the founders of what would ultimately become J.P. Morgan Chase bank, established the Peabody Museum of Archaeology and Ethnology at Harvard University with a $150,000 bequest (approximately $2.25 million today). His endowment was earmarked for the establishment of the Peabody Professor-Curator, the purchase and development of artifact collections, and the construction of a museum building to house and display archaeological and ethnographic materials. At the same time, Peabody provided similar gifts for museums at Yale University in 1866 (the Yale Peabody Museum of Natural History), and Salem, Massachusetts in 1867 (the Peabody Academy of Science, which is now the Peabody Essex Museum and formed through a merger of the Essex Institute and the East Indian Marine Society), creating a foundation of natural history museums throughout New England and setting the stage for competitive specimen collecting between these institutions. To illustrate how explicit this rivalry was, Robert C. Winthrop, the Chairman of the Board of Trustees of the Peabody Museum at Harvard, wrote to Jeffries Wyman, the Museum's first curator, upon receipt of donated collections that "we shall be in a condition to defy all competitors on our own soil, and shall be equal to almost any collection abroad" (letter from Winthrop to Wyman, Sept. 10, 1868, Peabody Museum Archives, cited in Hinsley 1988:53). This late 19th century challenge was an important motivator for Curator Frederic Ward Putnam's early support of Charles Conrad Abbott's acquisitions, often by purchase, of finely made or unusual archaeological artifacts despite Abbott's unprofessional methods and lack of accurate provenience data, a collecting practice that later, along with his stubborn adherence to an American Paleolithic, tarnished Abbott's reputation.

However, despite his shortcomings, Abbott's work on early humans in the Delaware Valley was consistent with the scope and intent of the Museum's benefactor. The Peabody Museum at Harvard University was founded with an emphasis on the archaeology of the Americas, and formative collections consisted primarily of Native American artifacts. In line with many of the attitudes of the mid- to late-19th century, Peabody's gift stated that "in view of the gradual obliteration or destruction of the works and remains of the ancient races of this continent, the labor of exploration and collection be commenced at as early a day as practicable; and also, that, in the event of the discovery in America of human remains or implements of an earlier geological period than the present, especial attention be given to their study, and their comparison with those found in other countries" (Trustees of the Peabody Museum 1868:26).

Jeffries Wyman, a naturalist and anatomist, was appointed the Museum's first Curator and served until his death in 1874. Under his direction, the Museum grew its collections largely through donations from wealthy Bostonians, but also through contributions from other natural history museums, who found their archaeological collections to be secondary to their evolving natural history emphasis (Wyman 1868). The first exhibits—about fifty specimens—were displayed temporarily in Boylston Hall, which also housed the Museum of Comparative Anatomy at Harvard, prior to and during construction of the Peabody Museum facility, which was completed in 1877. New archaeological donations followed, with collections of stone tools found along the Merrimac River, and collections transferred to the nascent Museum from the Smithsonian Institution, the Boston Athenaeum, and the Massachusetts Historical Society. In all, by the end of 1868, the Peabody Museum held 1,190 specimens, mostly from North America (Wyman 1868:10).

A mere four years later, the Museum was experiencing growing pains. Collections numbered well over 5,000 artifacts. Expansion of Boylston Hall permitted more extensive exhibits, but due to space constraints, many of the collections were still unable to be displayed to the public. After Wyman's death in 1874, Harvard Professor Asa Gray served briefly as Curator *pro tempore* and hired Frederic Ward Putnam to assist in managing the collections and making sense of Wyman's papers. Putnam capably handled both Wyman's notes as well as incoming collections, and the following year was appointed Curator of the Peabody Museum, a position he held for almost thirty-five years (Tozzer 1936). An Assistant Curator, Lucien Carr, was added to the Museum staff the following year.

In 1876, investments of Peabody's donation towards the building fund had grown to approximately $100,000, which meant that money was available to break ground for the building on Divinity Avenue in Cambridge that still houses the Peabody Museum of Archaeology and Ethnology today. Museum exhibit and collections space was designed under the guidance of Alexander Agassiz, an ichthyologist and son of Louis Agassiz, a prominent biologist and geologist on the Harvard faculty; Theodore Lyman, a member of the Board of Trustees; and Professor Asa Gray. Their design followed the most advanced practices for museums of the late 19th century. The first, and main, section of the Museum measured 87ft. by 44ft., constructed of brick and brownstone; with a basement for storage, utilities, and workrooms; and three upper levels of exhibit space. Each of the first two main floors had an upper gallery containing additional display space, while the attic level had two rooms that could be used as workspace or for collections display. Engineering for the building faced significant challenges, since it was designed to carry not only the structure and visitors, but also heavy collections of stone artifacts and required excessive fireproofing to protect valuable items (Slack 1878:187). The building's construction proceeded in stages, with the first of five planned sections complete and occupied by collections by the end of 1877. In the introductory remarks of the annual meeting of the Board of Trustees that year, the Chairman proudly welcomed the group by stating "We meet now, for the first time, in our permanent home, over the entrance to which—carved legibly on the free-stone block above the door—is the inscription Peabody Museum of American Archaeology and Ethnology" (Winthrop 1878:177).

As Curator, Putnam arranged the new galleries primarily by geographic region, and then, particularly in the instance of Abbott's New Jersey collections, by chronology to show cultural and technological development through time. This was different from the exhibit design of many other archaeological museums of the 19th century that frequently organized collections typologically, with for example, all of the spear points displayed together, and all of the axes displayed together, regardless of geographic origin. However, Putnam followed new trends in 19th century museum exhibitions and incorporated evolutionary themes that were geographically specific (Chapman 1988). Putnam outlined the rationale for the arrangement of collections as "to exhibit, as far as possible, the present condition of a people, and to trace its history, its connections and, if possible, its origin in far distant time by the records which we have of its life, its arts, and its industries" (Putnam 1881.7).

Abbott's Delaware Valley exhibit occupied the northern wall and long front table case of the third floor of the Peabody Museum's main building. Artifacts were arranged chronologically to show three periods of occupation: stone implements representing what he interpreted as early Paleolithic occupation from the glacial gravels at Trenton; argillite tools, flakes, and spear points of what later became known as the "argillite culture" (Abbott 1907); and arrowheads, celts, pestles, axes and other objects showing more recent Delaware village occupations (Putnam 1898). The *Guide to the Peabody Museum* included a statement supporting Abbott's erroneous belief that the earliest occupation represented "glacial man on the Atlantic coast of America" (Putnam 1898:17).

FREDERIC WARD PUTNAM

Frederic Ward Putnam was born and raised in Massachusetts and attended Harvard University's Lawrence Scientific School from 1856 to 1864 to study under Louis Agassiz. Scientific education at the Lawrence Scientific School during Putnam's years at Harvard was conducted as an apprentice-style system designed for students seeking careers as scientists or engineers, not necessarily as academics (Green 1948). Students worked with a single professor, rather than attending lectures or completing exams, though Putnam was also influenced by other faculty including Jeffries Wyman and Asa Gray (Browman 2002a:510; Browman and Williams 2013). Putnam's student contemporaries went on to become prominent scholars in anthropology, geology, and natural history, including Alexander Agassiz, Edward S. Morse, Nathaniel S. Shaler, and Theodore Lyman (Browman 2002b).

Though biographical sketches of Putnam, particularly upon his death, lauded the relationship between Professor Agassiz and Putnam, for example according to Alfred Kroeber, "Professor Putnam esteemed the influence of the great naturalist upon himself as of the deepest; and he never wearied of telling his own students, in a manner which could not fail to impress as well as to charm, the story of how his guide put him to work at his first problem" (1915:711, 713), Putnam and Agassiz parted ways when Putnam led a student rebellion against Agassiz resulting from Agassiz's resistance to Darwinian evolution (Hinsley 1988). Agassiz did not accept that species could evolve into other species, but instead believed that each species was individually created by God. He further applied this to humans, stating that each human "race" was created in its own environment, resulting in modern-day accusations of racism that have tarnished his legacy (Gould 1980; Jackson and Weidman 2004:49–52). In addition to his views on evolution, Agassiz further alienated his students by demanding that they decline appointments at competing institutions and prohibiting them from publishing their work (Browman 2002b; Dexter 1965). By 1864, almost all of Agassiz's students had left Harvard (Browman 2002b:213–214). As ringleader, this dispute may have affected later career opportunities for Putnam, including delaying his appointment to Professor at Harvard, when Agassiz's son, Alexander, influenced the candidate selection for the position (Hinsley 1988:61).

Charles Conrad Abbott's initial interactions with Putnam occurred when Putnam was Director of the Peabody Academy of Science in Salem, Massachusetts. Putnam worked first as Curator of Vertebrates from 1864 to 1866 for the Essex Institute, then as Superintendent of the Museum of the East Indian Marine Society, from 1867 to 1869, and then as Director of the merged Peabody Academy of Science from 1869 to 1873 (Browman 2002b; Tozzer 1936; Trustees of the Peabody Academy of Science 1869:8, minutes of April 13, 1867). The Peabody Academy of Science included collections from both prior institutes and primarily held natural history specimens, but some archaeological collections were also donated, including quite a few from Abbott. These were later transferred to other archaeological museums such as the Peabody Museum at Harvard University in the late 1870s.

By 1869, Abbott was sending fish specimens for the Academy of Science collections, and by 1871, he had received recognition for his donation of stone artifacts from New Jersey, which were among those later transferred to Harvard. Putnam favorably referenced Abbott's forthcoming article to be published in *The American Naturalist* in his annual report that year: "Dr. C. C. Abbott, of Trenton, N.J., has sent us a fine collection of about a hundred typical specimens of the various stone implements found in New Jersey. These are specially interesting to our collection as they are the specimens now in course of being engraved for an article by Dr. Abbott on the 'Stone Implements of New Jersey,' and were selected by him as typical of the various forms found there" (Putnam 1872:8). The next year, in the annual report for 1872, he wrote:

> It is, however, to Dr. Charles C. Abbott, of Trenton, N.J., that we are under lasting gratitude for the great liberality of presenting to our Museum probably the finest collection ever made in this country of the relics of the stone age people of a single locality. The Abbott collection, which now numbers nearly three thousand specimens of stone implements, and is rapidly increasing by the active work of the indefatigable collector and student who has made us the recipient of his treasures, is of the greatest importance for study and comparison with other specimens, as it contains so many varieties of implements of almost every known type, all collected in one of the very richest localities of which we have record (Putnam 1873:8).

Despite his stated gratitude for the donation of thousands of artifacts, Putnam referred to Abbott as "collector and student" and did not ascribe the status of a professional peer. His report specified that Abbott was a collector, who handed over important artifacts for study by professionals.

Abbott was not unique in a "student" role to Putnam. Putnam corresponded with a number of fieldworkers who provided archaeological collections while he was Curator of the Museum at Harvard, but all were untrained amateurs like Abbott. Putnam used his letters to guide and instruct these enthusiastic collectors, who greatly increased the Museum's North American holdings. Fieldworkers gained recognition for their work from a prestigious institution, and Putnam in return served "as mentor, critic, financial source, and doorkeeper to their ambitions" (Hinsley 1992:127). Abbott was arguably one of the longest-serving in this role—as student of what Hinsley has termed Putnam's "correspondence school" of archaeological training (1992:127)—but Putnam's instructions, corrections, and guidance seem to have had few measurable effects on Abbott's substandard field methods, which consisted mostly of surface collection without any record of archaeological provenience. By referring to Abbott as "student", who donated artifacts for study by professionals at the museum, Putnam underscored Abbott's amateur status.

Putnam further engaged amateurs as one of the founders of the journal *The American Naturalist,* in 1867, along with several of his classmates from Harvard, and continued to serve as co-editor through 1875, succeeded by Edward Drinker Cope (Browman 2002b). *The American Naturalist* published Abbott's "Stone Age in New Jersey" (1872), which first brought Abbott to the attention of the archaeological community, and other articles on archaeology and nature (Abbott 1870a, 1870b, 1871, 1874, 1876a, 1884b, 1885a), but it was designed as a popular journal, rather than for a professional audience. In the introduction to the first issue, the editors wrote "We trust the Magazine will be equally welcome to the Farmer, Gardener and Artisan" (The American Naturalist 1867:2). Soon after its founding, the journal was referenced by the Trustees of the Peabody Academy of Science as "devoted to the popular exposition of scientific topics in such a manner as to avoid those technicalities which often render the mass of such reading tedious and difficult; a work of this character supplies a long existing demand, and cannot fail of proving a great aid to the student, the amateur, and the general reader" (1869:22, minutes of January 13, 1868). Though *The American Naturalist* distributed articles with scientific rigor, Abbott's publication outlets, with Putnam's support, were still intended for popular, not professional, consumption.

In 1874, Putnam accepted his first salaried position at the Peabody Museum at Harvard and was tasked with assisting Professor Asa Gray in cataloging collections following Wyman's death. Gray stated that Putnam "is better acquainted than anyone else with the Museum, and with Dr. Wyman's method and arrangements, having been much associated with him both in exploration and publication" (1875:11). Putnam's role during his early years as Curator was largely a collections management one. He catalogued and inventoried archaeological and ethnographic collections, and managed donations to the anthropology library. However, until the construction of the new Museum building was complete, many of the collections remained in temporary storage in Boyleston Hall.

Some of the challenges Putnam faced were curatorial, and he had to learn artifact conservation on the fly. For example, in 1875, he noticed that some of the Peruvian vessels in the collections were suffering from the crystallization of salts within the clay matrix. This resulted from temperature and humidity fluctuations in the storage rooms and caused the pottery to crumble and spall. Putnam recommended treatment with a dilute adhesive to stabilize the ceramics and halt their degradation (Gray 1875:12–13). The collections also suffered from insect infestations in the Boyleston Hall display cases, which Putnam treated with insecticide and then removed to sealed tin boxes for storage until proper display cases could be prepared for the new Museum building (Putnam 1876:7). But Putnam's role widened as the Museum grew, and he found himself spending more time courting donors, negotiating collections purchases, and managing amateur archaeologists such as Abbott, instead of conducting fieldwork or curating collections. Many of the decidedly hands-on tasks fell to his capable assistant, Lucien Carr who worked for many years on a volunteer basis. Though the Museum was founded through a large gift from George Peabody, these funds did not fully support the day-to-day activities of the Museum. Putnam gave numerous formal and informal lectures to the Cambridge and Boston elite in an effort to raise funds for fieldwork and salaries. Carr's salary, when he received one, and the salary of the Secretary of the Museum were both paid by Putnam personally, because there was not enough money in the Museum's budget to cover the expense (Putnam 1900:272).

Abbott's employment at the Peabody Museum was unpaid, as Putnam was unable to support the salary of another employee through his meagre budget nor was he willing to use personal funds for additional personnel, particularly for a man as exasperating as Abbott, but Abbott received some money to purchase collections and for personal expenses incurred as part of his Museum activities. The shortage of funds was a never-ending source of irritation for both men. Abbott did not believe that Putnam was truthful in his claims that additional money was unavailable, evidenced by Abbott's almost-daily letters to Putnam pleading for more money:

> March 13, 1882: I am almost daily getting some good things, all of which means, that by April 1st my $25 will be expended, if not before, and the "quarter" ended....Now please don't put me off on the plea of being busy, but let me know about this right away. I anticipate a splendid season, for many reasons, but will be powerless unless I can have about that sum to meet expenses (CCA-FWP/HPM Box 4, Record 51).

And he exhorted Putnam to use any means necessary to obtain funds, imploring him to find money to purchase artifacts for the "Abbott Collection":

March 24, 1886: Do not put this matter by, without consideration. I beseech you by all the powers of Heaven and Earth to do this for me, for I shall consider it a personal favor if you would secure this collection that I may complete the labor of years in showing what Jersey has in prehistoric times. Can you not turn to someone and beg or borrow and get these gatherings of a naturalist, not a mere collector for with them goes field notes that will be of great value to the student of archaeology hereafter. I am not unduly enthusiastic. It is a grand chance that can by no probability again occur. Secure them by all means and I'll prove my devotion in many ways hereafter. Whatever is done must be done promptly (CCA-FWP/HPM Box 4, Record 343).

Though at times, his letters verged on the comical:

April 6, 1894: I am now desperately poor and will be until September but hope not to die of starvation and nakedness before the day of relief (CCA-FWP/HPM Box 13, Record 724).

In dealing with Abbott and other amateur archaeologists, Putnam walked a fine line between creating a museum that rigorously conducted scholarly science and one that presented merely a display of archaeological curios. He hoped to achieve the former, but North American archaeology in the 19th century was in many ways "a combination of backyard scrabbling and high aspirations" (Hinsley 1988:60). Because North American archaeology had neither the cachet of classical Greece and Rome, nor the funding to explore North American sites that Putnam felt held promise, such Ohio's prehistoric mounds or the American Southwest (Putnam 1877:11), Putnam found himself caught in a bit of a conundrum. Should he pursue expeditions in popular locales in Europe and the Mediterranean to appease potential donors? Or, should he conform to the stated goals of the Museum's benefactor, George Peabody, and continue as an Americanist institution, running the risk of Boston's philanthropists donating elsewhere?

Abbott and other amateurs that Putnam coddled and courted provided one solution to the problem. Abbott's research, particularly on the topic of early humans in the New World, aligned with the stated charge laid out by Peabody at the Museum's founding (Trustees of the Peabody Museum 1868:26). Furthermore, Abbott worked for free. He presented a potential way out for Putnam, which may explain why Putnam was supportive of Abbott's work (Browman and Williams 2013), at least in the beginning, often indulging Abbott despite his acerbic personality, even when questions arose about Abbott's slipshod collecting methods and the veracity of his conclusions regarding early humans.

ARCHAEOLOGICAL FIELD ASSISTANT, PEABODY MUSEUM, HARVARD UNIVERSITY

Abbott began sending artifacts to the Peabody Museum at Harvard University as early as 1872, even before Putnam's employment there, when he donated "a very valuable gift of more than eight hundred specimens of implements of stone obtained from the immediate neighborhood of Trenton" (Wyman 1872:27). The curator's report for the Museum in that year stated that the collection included artifacts that "very closely resemble the celts of the drift period of Europe, especially those found at St. Acheul, two or three of which, except for their material, could hardly be distinguished from them" (Wyman 1872:27). This donation occurred contemporaneously with Abbott's 1872 publication and included some of the material described in his article (Fig. 3.1), which he was using as evidence of nascent theories about early, possibly Pleistocene, humans in the Delaware Valley. Three years later, Abbott was in regular correspondence with the Museum's new Curator, Fredric Ward Putnam, and frequently sending archaeological collections. Putnam acknowledged not only his material contribution, but also his evolving theories about humans in the New World: "These implements from the gravel Dr. Abbott believes to be of paleolithic age, and made by a race inhabiting the country before the present Indians reached the Atlantic coast" (Putnam 1876:13).

By 1876, Charles Conrad Abbott was provisionally appointed as an unsalaried field assistant to the Peabody Museum. He was not an official employee but delighted in the affiliation and job title. The annual report of the Museum for that year contained the following announcement: "Probably the most important result attained in American archaeology during the year is that secured by Dr. C. C. Abbott of Trenton, New Jersey, to whom a small appropriation was granted to enable him to continue his researches.... Dr. Abbott has probably obtained data which show that man existed on our Atlantic coast during the time of, if not prior to, the formation of the great

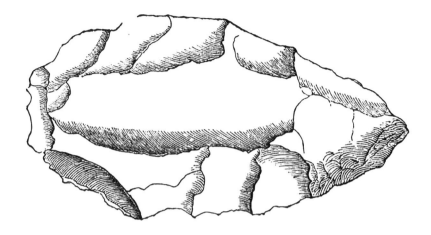

3.1 "Rude" stone implement published in "The Stone Age in New Jersey" (Abbott 1872: fig. 8), that led Abbott to question "if a people as rude as they who fashioned the wrought flints found at St. Acheul, near Amiens, France, once dwelt on the shores of the Delaware, and the relics are as rude as those mentioned above, were not such a people too primitive to wander from another continent?" (1872:146).

gravel deposit which extends towards the coast from the Delaware River near Trenton, and believed to have been formed by glacial action" (Putnam 1877:11). This made a bold statement and would completely re-write the understanding of human antiquity in North America, if true, though Putnam hedged his bets by carefully stating he "probably" has demonstrated ice age occupation of the Delaware Valley. Putnam was not willing to put his own professional reputation on the line in support of Abbott's unproven ideas based merely on a handful of surface-collected artifacts.

Putnam's reluctance to throw his support wholly behind Abbott's American Paleolithic must be viewed within the context of a fast-evolving scientific milieu. For amateur collectors like Abbott, their models of scientific achievement—the career trajectories of men such as Abbott's grandfather and uncle—no longer represented viable paths towards scientific respectability. Hinsley, in his historical analyses of the early years of anthropology at Harvard, has commented that many amateurs and members of the public held the belief that in sciences, and particularly fields drawn from natural history, "observations in the field are not merely important to the scientific process—they surely are—but that such observations themselves constitute science" (1992:124). Abbott held firmly to this belief—that by collecting artifacts and submitting them to the Peabody Museum, he was a valuable member of the scientific team. Putnam's attempts to persuade Abbott to conduct more rigorous study led to little improvement in Abbott's methodology. Yet as Hinsley has also noted "Mr. Peabody's museum occupied the difficult and ambiguous position of offering encouragement without formal accreditation or the promise of a position...the early Peabody stood at a point of conflict between individual aspiration and longer-term institutional goals" (1992:124). Abbott's work for the Peabody Museum, despite his amateurish methods, helped to achieve part of the Museum's institutional goals by acquiring artifacts from North America (Browman and Williams 2013). Putnam, on the other hand, held the unenviable role of reining in Abbott's individual aspirations.

The "paleoliths" that Abbott collected from the Trenton gravels made up only a small fraction of the material Abbott collected for the Peabody Museum, though they received the largest amount of attention, and ultimately the largest amount of criticism. Instead, Abbott's submissions more commonly included assemblages like described in Carr's annual report as "A collection of stone implements from the surface near Trenton, New Jersey, consisting of axes, celts, scrapers, knives, pestles, sinkers, slickstone spearpoints, arrowheads and drills, fragments of pottery" (Cat. Nos. 10145–10211, Carr 1877:17), many of which were found on his farm or on neighboring properties, but others were part of larger lots purchased from collectors elsewhere. Abbott often purchased mundane as well as more unusual items, such as the pendants (Fig. 3.2) that later got him into trouble as alleged forgeries.

Typically, the provenience records for these artifacts were quite poor, and the curator's reports aggregated items into single descriptive entries. For example, catalog numbers 19021 through 19425 were described as "A collection of about 5500 articles, consisting in part of 74 grooved stone axes, 16 celts, 8 paleoliths, and a large variety of mortars and pestles, hammers and polishing stones, sinkers, hoes, drills, ornaments of different kinds and hundreds of knives, arrowheads and spearpoints in jasper and argillite with fragments of pottery and clay pipes." Provenience was listed as "from Morris, Gloucester, Camden, Cape May, Salem, Mercer and Cumberland Counties, New Jersey" (Carr 1880:737). The official artifact catalogue, which was based on the information Abbott provided with the collection,

3.2 Slate ornaments from Gloucester County, New Jersey, purchased from Klingbeil and later presumed by Abbott to be forgeries. Peabody Museum Catalog Numbers 79-42-10/19212 and 79-42-10/19213. Photo by the authors.

presented minimal additional provenience data, and usually just located artifacts to county and state.

In his new position as Curator for the Peabody Museum, Putnam was under increasing pressure to ensure that Museum activities were conducted in a scientifically rigorous manner and this meant that Abbott needed to provide better documentation of artifact and site provenience. In 1876, Putnam took the opportunity to evaluate Abbott's work in the field by visiting him in New Jersey. During early September, Putnam and his family spent twelve days with Abbott at Three Beeches farm to inspect the Trenton gravels and see the area where artifact collections were being made, as well as to offer suggestions for improving field methods.

Putnam's visit also corresponded with the Centennial International Exhibition in Philadelphia. This event marked the first official World's Fair in the United States and included a display of some of the Peabody Museum's artifacts as part of the National Exhibit of Archaeology and Ethnology under the direction of the Smithsonian Institution (Putnam 1877:7). It was the first real demonstration of the Museum to the public and the scientific world, with attendance counted as 8,004,325 paid admissions, with an estimated total of 8,200,000 entering the Centennial (Pennsylvania Historical and Museum Commission 1969:4). Putnam dragged Abbott to many events and introduced him to scientists from around the world. In his diaries, Abbott recorded the trip: "September 4, 1876: Went to Philadelphia to attend a Centennial Celebration of Archaeology and of course there was the meeting of a lot of strangers and a deal of mechanical chatter and that was about all there was to it. Some men I met were really very nice, but others like a fellow named [Stephen] Peet, were fools" and he continued the following day with further introductions and events. "September 5, 1876: At the archaeological meeting all day and at Academy of Natural Sciences in the evening. Then a lot of congenials went to a beer saloon and sat there for an hour and we had a very pleasant time" (CCA/PU Box 2, Folder 2).

Abbott's overall cantankerous personality and his lack of patience for social events were soon evident in his reaction to the people he met at the Centennial: "September 6, 1876: At Centennial all day. It was very much of a bore. Most of the time I was in the Ohio building, but there was nothing to be learned about American Archaeology, as so little is really known and so little scientific work been done. Of course, I met again many people and how very uneven is humanity in the mass. If Putnam were not here, would not think of going" (CCA/PU Box 2, Folder 2). Putnam, too, appeared to become exhausted by the Centennial events. Abbott recorded a few days later "September 10, 1876: Putnam sick a bed, or at least in bed, until noon. As Uncle Tim Conrad came out to see him, I had him get up, which he did. Down stairs in afternoon, to see Uncle Tim and talked about glacial geology in this region. Then, Uncle Tim leaving, Putnam went back to bed. Day otherwise without incident" (CCA/PU Box 2, Folder 2).

However, Putnam's trip to Trenton was a positive development for Abbott's relationship with the Peabody Museum. Upon returning from the visit, Putnam reported to the Museum Trustees that "From a visit to the locality, with Dr. Abbott, I see no reason to doubt the general conclusion he has reached in regard to the existence of man in glacial times on the Atlantic coast of North America" (Putnam 1876:12). Furthermore, the two men spent a portion of the visit walking over the fields where Abbott collected many of his other archaeological specimens. Abbott recorded "September 2, 1876: It was after dinner that I enjoyed myself. Putnam and I took a walk to Seeds' and DeCous' [neighboring farms] where so many relics are found. He got a good idea of the lay of the land and why it was attractive to Indians as to white people now" (CCA/PU Box 2, Folder 2).

Merely a few months after Putnam's visit to Trenton, Abbott spent ten days in Cambridge with Putnam for an introduction to the Museum's staff and local Boston and Cambridge intelligentsia. The Museum building itself was not yet open, so most of Abbott's donated artifacts remained in storage pending the construction of display cases in the new building. During the visit, Abbott socialized with Putnam, Lucien Carr, Asa Gray, and Nathaniel Shaler, who was a Harvard paleontologist and geologist, and had studied alongside Putnam under Agassiz. Though his first interaction with Shaler was not positive, as Abbott wrote, "Prof. N. S. Shaler called and we had a talk about the geological conditions at Trenton. He gave me the impression of being erratic and in no way convincing" (CCA/PU Box 2, Folder 2; November 22, 1876), he later softened towards him because "Shaler is interested in my archaeological work" (CCA/PU Box 2, Folder 2; November 24, 1876), and in 1877, Shaler visited Abbott to examine the Trenton gravels. Yet Abbott—perpetually grumpy—recorded in his diary that "All day, as yesterday, and why I stay here and not be at home is a good deal of a question. It seems absurd to be standing about idle for the greater part of the day and it is not an attractive time of year to go out sight-seeing, which I dislike anyhow" (CCA/PU Box 2, Folder 2; November 21, 1876).

Abbott made trips to Cambridge several times each year during the late 1870s and 1880s in order to meet with Putnam and others, as well as to study, catalog, and arrange his collections in display cases. He developed a working relationship with Lucien Carr that permitted him to occasionally bypass Putnam in everyday Museum matters, which proved to be an advantage when Putnam was preoccupied with fundraising and administrative responsibilities. Furthermore, Carr, who was officially acknowledged as a member of the Museum staff, unlike Abbott, handled many of the daily responsibilities of collections management as the institution grew. Abbott was jealous of Carr's official position, but the affiliated status with the Peabody Museum was a boon, and Abbott grew conceited: "There is just one bother, above all others, that gives me all this annoyance and that is the miserable imprudence of others in New Jersey daring to make collections. I say so freely off hand and have made some enemies by so doing, but I can't always hold my tongue when people having specimens will not deliver them up on demand" (CCA-FWP/HPM Box 1, Accession 78-26, Record 2999; July 2, 1878).

GROWING THE "ABBOTT COLLECTION" AT HARVARD

Many of the early collections submitted to the Peabody Museum by Charles Conrad Abbott were obtained through casual excursions and field-walking in ploughed farm fields surrounding Three Beeches. No controlled excavations occurred; all artifacts were surface-collected. His first official donation to the Peabody Museum, an assortment of flaked and ground stone tools and pottery (Wyman 1872:27), Abbott interpreted as a lithic workshop, which probably indicated that the artifacts donated in this batch all originated in the same general locality although there's no way of knowing that for certain. Wyman wrote of the arrowhead collection that it "is unusually rich, and comprising some fourteen or fifteen types. Besides these there is a large collection of broken arrow heads found near together on what was evidently an arrow maker's working place, and as Dr. Abbott suggests, were undoubtedly broken during the process of manufacture, showing a considerable percentage of loss from breakage" (Wyman 1872:27). These artifacts remain in the Peabody Museum's collections (Peabody Cat. Nos. 71-18-10/4765 through 71-18-10/4779).

New material was soon forthcoming from Trenton, though despite increasingly rigorous field methodologies gaining traction in archaeology, Abbott continued to surface-collect specimens rather than conduct measured excavations of any kind. We know he was aware of newly emerging methods, which were publicized through the annual report of the Smithsonian Institution, which included methodological advances such as controlled excavations, recording, and stratigraphy (McKusick 1970, 1988;

Trigger 1989:128), since Abbott recorded in his diary that he indeed read but largely dismissed, these reports. For example, "October 17, 1875: I staid home reading the Smithsonian Annual Report for 1874. It was instructive in parts, but very heavy" (CCA/PU Box 2, Folder 2).

In 1875, Abbott donated a large lot of artifacts including arrow points, spear points, knives, scrapers, and pottery sherds (Peabody Cat. Nos. 76-8-10/8994 through 76-8-10/9033) that were described in the annual report as "an important collection from the surface and from the soil at various depths. It also contains a number of rude stone implements obtained from the gravel bed, at a depth of from three to seven feet from the surface" (Carr 1876:19). Despite indicating depth of the deposits, Abbott was retrieving these "rude implements" from erosional facies and presuming them to be in situ. The following year, he sent several scrapers that he had recently published (Abbott 1876b; Peabody Cat. Nos. 76-8-10/9595 through 76-8-10/9598), and a jasper biface (1875a; Peabody Cat. No. 76-8-10/10151). Never one to conservatively interpret an artifact when a sensational pronouncement could be made, Abbott seized upon these bifacially-worked lithic artifacts and alleged them to be "scalping knives," though two years later, he acknowledged that "we have never met with any flint implement which archaeologists have classed as knives used for this particular purpose" (1877a:300).

With some funding available for travel and expenses as field assistant, Abbott greatly increased the volume of artifacts that he submitted, as well as his enthusiasm for the field, though his limited aptitude for work often prevailed. "June 14, 1876: As I got $50 from Putnam for archaeological work about here, the day opened with a business-like flavor and I was roused to some activity, but it does not warrant my giving my whole time to the subject" (CCA/PU Box 2, Folder 2). He arrogantly believed Harvard a good fit for his efforts and his archaeological collections, not recognizing that he was one of many unsalaried amateur collectors in correspondence with Putnam who provided artifacts. "November 28, 1876: Of one thing I am assured and that is that I am sending material to a place where it will be appreciated. To think that in all New Jersey there is no institution that would accept it as a gift" (CCA/PU Box 2, Folder 2).

However, with a renewed energy for archaeology and newfound funds, Abbott still did not heed Putnam's gentle instruction nor the Smithsonian's newly publicized field methods, but instead intensified his efforts to purchase artifacts, above all seeking interesting and unique items from amateur collectors throughout New Jersey. Though this vastly increased the number of artifacts he could send to the Peabody Museum, it meant that little to no provenience information could be provided, other than occasional notations about township or county. As a result, Abbott's daily personal journals and the archives of the Peabody Museum hold scant data regarding the sites where these artifacts originated. As an example from a typical collection, there are a series of artifacts with a provenience recorded as "Glassboro, New Jersey." Abbott noted in his personal diaries "April 18, 1878: Went to Glassboro at 8:15am and there until 6:36pm. Met Mr. Beckett and Dr. Heritage, and had a good hunt near Hurffville, four miles east of Glassboro. Got some very good relics, also marl fossils" but about a month later he also noted "May 14, 1878: Got a box of relics by mail from Glassboro" (CCA/PU Box 2, Folder 2). Unfortunately, despite noting that he collected near Hurffville, not Glassboro proper, Abbott never recorded a Hurffville provenience when the artifacts were placed in the Peabody collections. Furthermore, his correspondence to Putnam regarding the locality requested permission and funding to return with a telling question about paying collectors "it is desirable to make a second and more prolonged hunt in Glassboro where my board, etc. will cost nothing. This trip will require about $20 to meet the purchasing of specimens found by boys now on the lookout for them" (CCA-FWP/HPM Accession 78-26, Record 2998; May 15, 1878), suggesting that this fieldwork was often being done by others (Peabody Cat. Nos. 78-26-10/14679 through 78-26-10/14680 and 78-26-10/16124 through 78-26-10/16131).

In other instances, lots of commingled artifacts were sent as a result of Abbott's purchases from a variety of amateur collectors. For example, the annual report recorded "stone implements and ornaments and fragments of pipes and other articles of pottery from Trenton, Crosswicks Creek, and Lake Hopatcong, New Jersey" (Peabody Cat. Nos. 80-57-10/23561 through 80-57-10/23764; Carr 1881:35); as well as a "Grooved stone axe from Bainbridge, Penn., and stone implements and a brass arrowhead from Lancaster Co., Penn—Collected by the late Dr. S. S. Haldeman, a large series of stone implements and ornaments of the usual Ohio valley forms, from Butler Co., Ohio, together with flint points from California, Iowa, Indiana, and Kentucky, all collected by Mr. R. T. Shepherd of Monroe, Ohio, a small carved stone from Burlington Co., New Jersey, collected by Mr. Herbert Coffman—Presented by Dr. C. C. Abbott" (Carr 1881:35).

Abbott continued amassing artifact collections from the fields around Three Beeches and purchasing occasional collections, but recognition may have been dawning that his work was not exactly scientifically rigorous— a concern that Putnam obviously shared. He questioned Putnam about whether a map of his artifact surface finds might be helpful in document- ing archaeological sites along Crosswicks Creek and the nearby fields. In a letter to Putnam on October 6, 1878, he asked "The idea I have in view with reference to this sort of work is to prepare a good sized map of the local- ity, say from grand bluffs at the Cemetery which is the commencement of the good collecting grounds, I have gone over as far south as the mouth of Crosswicks Creek. Such a map, I think I could make and have made, that would be accurate in survey and then I would indicate so far as I can deter- mine them, village sites, work shop sites, graves, cultivated ground, i.e. their corn ground, etc. etc. Do you think such a map would be desirable? If so, I'll do what I can at getting it up" (CCA-FWP/HPM Box 1, Record 3006, Ac- cession 78-26; October 6, 1878). Putnam's reply to Abbott's question has not been located, and it's unclear if such a detailed map was ever made. Abbott did make map of the area south of Trenton showing site locations, though this was presumably produced much later as it is in the archives of the Penn Museum and not at Harvard.

Indiscriminate purchases of collections ultimately landed Abbott in trouble when he bought items from a collector named William Klingbeil in Gloucester County, New Jersey, that were later proven to be forgeries. He first met Klingbeil in the spring of 1879, and wrote to Putnam enthu- siastically: "Klingbeil who had the $25 lot is not a dealer but uneducated collector who feels that [William S.] Vaux and [Michael] Newbold [also pur- chasing collections in the region] don't treat him fair and he now proposes to let them slide and 'cotton to me' and I propose to let others about home slide and give my time to him. It is simply wonderful what treasures he has already secured for me and what wonderful things he sold to Newbold and Vaux. The $25 lot is well worth $100—you would say so at a glance and I was incredibly lucky to get them" (CCA-FWP/HPM Box 2, Accession 79-52, Record 3139; April 27, 1879).

Yet only a few months later, it was starting to become apparent that Klingbeil was selling forgeries, though Abbott was reluctant to admit it: "One thing is certain it can never be proved that Klingbeil is a fraud and his method of working in collecting etc. is such as to render the idea that he is

such, very improbable....I hope you have again examined the Klingbeil specimens you have and greatly desire to know your present opinion of them"
(CCA-FWP/HPM Box 2, Accession 79-42, Record 3145; June 29, 1879). He
reiterated his support for Klingbeil only a few days later: "I find nothing but
what seems to confirm the genuineness of Klingbeil's finds" (CCA-FWP/
HPM Box 2, Accession 79-42, Record 3146; July 2, 1879). And a few months
later was still more hesitantly supporting the veracity of Klingbeil's collections "I have been doing some work by correspondence, almost of a detec-
tive character, about the Klingbeil matter, and cannot get any evidence to
show specimens are not genuine—but why bother you with it! You're not
interested as of old, in NJ archaeology" (CCA-FWP/HPM Box 2, Accession
79-42, Record 3159; October 18, 1879), but Putnam did not reply. In despera-
tion, Abbott wrote to Lucien Carr about the Klingbeil artifact collection,
finally acknowledging that he had been deceived.

Dear Mr. Carr

I have been intending to write you about the Klingbeil specimens for
several days, but kept putting it off in hopes of getting some additional
information. As a result of investigations, very quietly conducted, and
continued for some time, by the aid of friends in South Jersey, I am convinced that *all steatite* implements from Klingbeil except a small pea-
green pipe, that has been broken, are *unsafe* to be cataloged as *Indian*
relics; and a doubt hangs over the two 'necklace pendants' of semi-lunar shape which are *slate* [Fig. 3.2], I think. As you have the catalogue
in charge, I thought it well to let *you* know about it, as soon as I felt that
I *knew* anything about it, myself. Of course, I should not like to have
these specimens placed with such as I have gathered, without some
mark upon them indicating that a doubt, at least, was maintained as to
their being genuine. The whole subject has been a great shock, I may
say, to me; and I am not a little bored by the thought, that an ignorant
shoe-maker should so effectually put a quietus on my collecting. I shall
not be troubling you with impatient new questions, however, so you
will be relieved; but let me ask as a favor, that this fraudulent stuff may
not be so recorded, that I am supposed to consider it genuine. I have
yet, therefore, to get for you some unquestionable 'Shawnee' implements. Rather, I should say, the task is set for those who will pitch in

to the work; and I only hope my successors will be equally interested in the P.M.

Yours ever truly,
Chas. C. Abbott
(CCA-LC/HPM Box 2, Accession 79-42, Record 3162; November 22, 1879, emphasis original)

Carr replied to Abbott with support, as Abbott reflected in his personal diary, but Abbott had been shamed and petulantly indicated an intention to cease his collecting efforts: "November 29, 1879: Carr writes, it is childish for me to worry about Klingbeil, but I am as well pleased to have it a reason for not continuing collecting" (CCA/PU Box 2, Folder 2). Putnam offered Abbott an invitation to visit Cambridge later that winter, which he ultimately accepted, and their relationship continued, but his status had weakened, in part as a result of the Klingbeil debacle, and Putnam frequently did not reply to Abbott's correspondence. In a letter to Putnam the following year, Abbott wrote "I am charitable enough to suppose that your failure to take notice of any of my letters is due wholly to being very busy, or sick" (CCA-FWP/HPM Record 2575 [no accession #, no box #]; December 1, 1880). Furthermore, Abbott's artifact purchases during his tenure as a field assistant with the Peabody Museum potentially harmed his personal and professional reputation locally in New Jersey too, as rumors circulated that he was earning a hefty income by buying and selling collections. A letter he sent to Putnam appealed for help in countering this rumor:

February 23, 1882

Dear Putnam,

In my efforts to induce people to give me specimens, I mention sometimes that I present them to the P.M. and all is done for good of our beloved science etc. etc. I have very recently found that the statement is contradicted by people who want these things to go to Princeton College and that I am simply the hired agent of the P.M. (paid a big salary, etc. etc.). Now this lie is being spread in a quarter where I am soliciting gifts of specimens, and I wish you would therefore, please give me a statement in form of a letter, of what the trustees think of the matter. Have the collections I have made been really purchased by the Museum, i.e. has the money paid in small installments been a full price for the collection and therefore that I stand in the legit merely of a "dealer" of whom you have bought a few things. The degraded Presbyterian priests that run Princeton College have said this and I say it is a lie—who is right? Have you not always looked upon it, that I was essentially a friend of the P.M. and one who donated a valuable gift to the Institution. Certainly before I ever was paid a penny, I gave specimens—800 once—to Wyman and often since, and never have the sums noted me at all paid for my time, but merely to help out in purchasing and traveling expenses. You see now, what I want. A letter I can read or show to John Brown or Jack Robinson to prove that I am not making money by selling to you specimens I beg of others. Write soon.

Yours truly ever,
Abbott
(CCA-FWP/HPM Box 4, Record 48 [no accession #])

It's not clear how Putnam responded to Abbott's request, and Abbott did not address a concern for his local reputation in his diaries.

ARCHAEOLOGICAL RESEARCH QUESTIONS

Despite Abbott's indiscriminate collecting and lack of formal training, he attempted to approach at least some of the archaeological materials he obtained for the Peabody Museum with scientific inquiry, rather than merely as curios. In an early example, Abbott tested the way in which stone drills were used and described his experiments in *Primitive Industry* (1881:109–110, fig. 92). He attempted to replicate the biconical hole drilled in a prehistoric stone gorget (Peabody Museum Cat. No. 52-2-10/33498) by drilling nine additional holes in the same artifact using a prehistoric jasper drill. He noted "a glance will show that the one perforation, made by the Indian, was in all probability made with a similar tool" (1881:109). In his experiments, however, he observed that the drill dulled quickly, after merely one perforation. He altered his methods by placing the gorget in water for subsequent holes and concluded that prehistoric people may have also used water when drilling stone, leaving a polished tip to the artifact. When water is not used, "the friction of *dry*, rapid rotation causes a steady splintering and keeps the drill in a newly chipped condition" (1881:109). Abbott's replicative experiments helped him explain the polish, or lack of polish, on some prehistoric jasper drills. Unfortunately, his experiments were conducted on actual artifacts—specifically the gorget, which is still housed in the Peabody Museum (Fig. 3.3).

3.3 Stone gorget drilled by C. C. Abbott as an experiment to understand prehistoric jasper drill use. Single biconical hole in upper right corner is prehistoric in origin; nine holes drilled by Abbott in the center of the artifact. Peabody Museum Catalog Number 52-2-10/33498. Photo by the authors.

He also recognized that materials such as obsidian and copper were rare and questioned the provenance of such objects. For example, two obsidian artifacts were found by Abbott on Three Beeches (Peabody Museum Cat. Nos. 86-10-10/38925 and 98-1-10/50824.1). Abbott proposed that they either came from Utah or Oregon, though he did not discuss how he arrived at this alleged geologic provenance (Abbott 1907:57, 1908:72–74, 1912:28). He knew obsidian was rare in eastern United States archaeological contexts. In his correspondence with Putnam, dated April 11, 1886, Abbott wrote: "Now don't go on wild. I found an obsidian flake or piece of one, yesterday. The spot has a curious history, which I'll tell you if you stop over" (CCA-FWP/HPM Box 7, Record 344, Accession 86-10). Unfortunately, the "curious history" of the site was not disclosed in his correspondence or personal diaries. On May 6, 1886, Abbott further elaborated on his obsidian find in a letter accompanying a shipment of artifacts to the Peabody Museum. He wrote that "I have also the pleasure of announcing the 'surface find' of a fragment of obsidian, found on the brow of the plateau upon which my house stands and about 200 yards east of it. I believe it is the first incidence of this mineral being found in New Jersey" (CCA-FWP/HPM Box 7, Record 345 [no accession #]).

Modern X-ray fluorescence analysis of these two obsidian artifacts indicated likely geologic provenances of Blue Spring, California, and Valles Rhyolite, New Mexico, obsidian sources (Dillian et al. 2010). Abbott would have had no way of determining the geologic origin of obsidian in the late 19th and early 20th centuries but understood that obsidian artifacts found in the mid-Atlantic were from the far west and represented long-distance trade. "It is something more than barter. It is distinctly a feature of fixed conditions and that have been long-fixed and are generally known" (Abbott 1908:73), and further that:

> That obsidian, that is not found east of the Mississippi, should find its way to the middle country, and from there occasionally to the Atlantic coast, is not an unthinkable proposition, however, improbable it may seem at first. The fact, however, remains that these foreign productions do occur here and that the Indian brought them. They have been found under circumstances that set aside all possibility of their presence being attributed to even the earliest European travelers (Abbott 1908:75).

Interestingly, and perhaps ironically given that he purchased collections with little first-hand knowledge of their archaeological provenience, Abbott voiced an awareness and concern that unprovenienced obsidian specimens could be incorrectly attributed to eastern United States archaeological sites. He stated in his correspondence that he received obsidian specimens from other collectors, but that they had little research value because he did not know where they had been found. He wrote to Putnam on February 10, 1887, for example: "By the way, Berthoud has sent me some exquisite obsidian points, etc. (one mounted and poisoned) etc. etc. Do you want them, my dear boy? Or shall they be turned into scarf-pins, etc." (CCA-FWP/HPM Box 7, Record 398 [no accession #]).

Abbott had an analogous interest in copper artifacts from New Jersey and Pennsylvania, although it did not appear that any of them were found directly on Three Beeches farm, at least not by Abbott. Prehistoric copper artifacts, like obsidian, were exceptionally rare in central New Jersey archaeological sites. Later, during the Contact period, Native American people more commonly used copper and brass acquired through trade with early colonists (Veit et al. 2004). Abbott noted copper in many collections. In 1881, he proposed that all copper in New Jersey was obtained through trade with western copper-producing regions. However, he changed his mind a few years later "A careful resurvey of many localities where ordinary Indian stone implements occur in abundance; and correspondence with collectors in various portions of New Jersey and Eastern Pennsylvania now convince me that the use of copper, as implements and ornaments, was much more common than I supposed, and that among our Delaware Indians were many coppersmiths" (Abbott 1885a:774). In a published article in *The American Naturalist*, Abbott referenced 128 copper artifacts in the Peabody Museum collections, which included arrowheads and bracelets that were most likely Contact period copper artifacts derived from European trade, and not prehistoric indigenous copper, though Abbott would have not known that at the time. However, he felt that, though rare, copper was more ubiquitous than previously thought "I find that one or more celts, spears, arrow-points, bracelets, rude beads, or fragments of sheet copper are sure to be found" (Abbott 1885a:776).

He referenced a collection that he reviewed and later purchased for the Peabody Museum that contained "narrow bands of hammered copper, and some large crescent-shaped ornaments were also found....[and] a nodule of native copper weighing thirteen ounces" (1885a:776). He told Putnam more about the collection in an accompanying letter "They were found in Pennsylvania, but in the Valley of the Delaware, not as the crow flies, more than six miles from where I live and about opposite my house, so they can be labeled Bucks County, Pennsylvania, Valley of Delaware, near Trenton, and go in my collection. They were found in 1832—54 years ago. The copper was rubbed clean by a file, as you will see, but not so as to hurt it as a specimen in any way. Is it pure copper. By testing its weight I thought it seemed heavier, as though it had a percentage of gold in it. I hope you will be pleased with it" (CCA-FWP/HPM Box 7, Record 347 [no accession #]; December [n.d.] 1886).

With a view different from other archaeologists in the region, who favored trade over local copper production (Abbott 1881; Putnam 1882; Schrabisch 1917; Skinner and Schrabisch 1913; and summarized in Lattanzi 2007), Abbott argued for in situ manufacture of copper objects. "Among the fragments, so called, of hammered copper, are several which have every appearance of being unfinished objects....It would appear, then, from an examination of the copper objects found in Pennsylvania and New Jersey that the weight of probability is strongly in favor of their home manufacture" (Abbott 1885a:777). However, the source of native copper remained uncertain. We know today that there are more than twenty locations where copper can be found within the state, mostly in the Watchung and Kittatinny Mountains in northern New Jersey, but these tend to have small deposits. Historic copper mines were not commercially successful and mining efforts quickly abandoned due to the paucity of copper deposits compared to other large and much more profitable mines in the western United States (Veit et al. 2004).

Interestingly, the largest collection of copper artifacts in New Jersey come from the Three Beeches farm and surrounding sites but were not excavated by Abbott. Instead, these artifacts were found during excavations in the 1930s by Dorothy Cross, who found beads, a disk, a hemispherical object, a copper wire, and a 14-inch long copper pin recovered from a well-provenienced, excavated cache of 127 argillite Fox Creek blades. The pin has a loop at the head, which is attached to the shaft with a thin band of copper wrapped around the base of the loop (Cross 1956). These copper artifacts are currently part of the archaeological collections at the New Jersey State Museum.

More recent research into the geologic origins of prehistoric copper from New Jersey used technology not available to Abbott in the 1880s. Laser-Ablation Inductively Coupled Plasma Mass Spectrometry (LA-ICPMS) yields elemental composition data down to parts per million and has demonstrated that many of the Delaware Valley copper artifacts, including those discovered by Dorothy Cross in the area around Three Beeches farm, do in fact likely originate with local, Pennsylvania and New Jersey sources of copper, perhaps Franklin Mine in New Jersey, or the Cornwall Mine in Pennsylvania (Lattanzi 2007:131–132). These data suggest that Abbott may have been correct in his assessment of a local copper industry in the Delaware Valley, and place him among others asking scientific questions of archaeological data.

ABBOTT AND THE SCIENCE OF HUMANITY

Even though the field was rapidly changing from one of amateur collecting to professional archaeological science, public attitudes about archaeology evolved much more slowly. Among the late 19th century Boston elite, who were the primary source of monetary donations to support the Peabody Museum, persisted the belief that museums should educate the public about the Classical world instead of local, Native American prehistory, because it marked the apex of human cultural development and served as a model for modern civilizations to follow (Hinsley 1988). Putnam, in order to remain consistent with George Peabody's bequest, needed to instead reveal the importance of North American archaeology. To do this necessitated an educational bias towards the science of humanity, not the display of Classical art history. As Hinsley has pointed out, this demanded exhibits that demonstrated "the many rather than the few, the common rather than the exceptional, as the keys to cultural understanding" (1988:60). Abbott's American Paleolithic was a chance for the Peabody Museum to situate North America within larger conversations about the history of humanity.

In 1881, Abbott published *Primitive Industry*, which included his essay on the "paleoliths" of the Trenton gravels, alleged by Abbott to be evidence of human occupation of great antiquity, however, this did not lead to additional income, and Abbott was forced to take a job in a Trenton bank, which he despised and deeply resented. "November 9, 1881: My days of scientific work are rapidly drawing to a close, if indeed, they are not now quite over"

(CCA/PU Box 2, Folder 2). Fortunately, his bank employment was relatively brief, and with the publication of additional naturalist volumes, and the support of Putnam and the Peabody Museum, Abbott was able to return to the farm and his archaeological pursuits. With *Primitive Industry*, the last two chapters of which were devoted specifically to an explanation of Abbott's theories and alleged evidence for early humans in the New World, Abbott soon found himself part of a much larger debate not only about human antiquity, but also involving glacial geology, human evolution, and rigor in archaeological methods.

4

Champion of the American Paleolithic

Just as there is abundant evidence of the presence of man dwelling at the foot of the great glacier that occupied the valley of the Delaware, when boulders, gravel and coarse sand were being deposited in vast quantities in the open sea, in which the southern terminus of the ice ended, so, as the glacier gradually left the valley of the present river, melting rapidly, the flood of waters, flowing southward, were surcharged with sand and mud, which, as the waters spread, and flowed more quietly, settled on the bottom of the then shallow sea, and here also, have we traces of this same race, who, as before, continued to lose in the depths of the once deeper and now shallow waters, those implements of stone which tell the story of their sojourn here.

--Abbott (1878:245)

In 1872, Charles Conrad Abbott published his first widely-disseminated archaeological essay with "The Stone Age in New Jersey" in *The American Naturalist*. In this relatively brief, descriptive article, he defined the various types of prehistoric stone artifacts in his collection, including specimens that appeared very crudely flaked, leading Abbott to surmise "either that there were many execrable workmen among their tool makers; or that the age of the crude specimens far exceeds that of finely wrought relics" (1872:146). Discarding the theory that some flintknappers were just more poorly skilled than others, he suggested instead that these roughly flaked artifacts represented an earlier period of time, "there is always a gradation from poor (primitive) to good (elaborate), which is an indication, we be-lieve, of a lapse of years from very ancient to more modern times, from a palaeolithic to a neolithic age" (1872:146).

Based on their physical appearance, and using published illustrations in John Lubbock's *Pre-Historic Times* (1865) for inspiration, Abbott drew an immediate connection between these roughly flaked artifacts and those from Paleolithic sites in Europe. He surmised that the makers of these artifacts must have been an unsophisticated, "primitive" people, and asked "were not such a people too primitive to wander from another continent?" (1872:146). If so, he concluded "the first inhabitants along our Atlantic coast and inland to have been autochthones" (1872:146), to mean that they evolved in situ along the eastern coast of North America. However, in a footnote, Abbott clarified that "we say autochthonic, but if all mankind sprung from some catarrhine ape of the Old World, a migration to America must have occurred; but this is going so far back into the past, that the relative positions of continent and ocean may have been widely different from what now exists" (1872:147). Throughout his career, he clung tenaciously to the idea that these "rude implements" were evidence of ancient human occupation of the Delaware Valley documenting a New World Paleolithic analogous to that in Europe.

THE BACKGROUND TO A THEORY

During the 19th century, many Christians adhered to a chronology of the natural and human world reflected in the work of James Ussher, a 17th century Anglican archbishop who used Biblical references to calculate that creation occurred in 4004 BC. It followed then that all plants, animals, and humans must have had a very brief history, supporting the idea of a divine creation that left little time for evolution to transpire. By the middle of the 19th century, this chronology appeared increasingly unlikely, as undeniable evidence for human antiquity mounted. For example, in his 1865 tome, John Lubbock wrote, "Historians, philologists, and physiologists have alike ad-mitted that the short period allowed could hardly be reconciled with the history of some eastern nations, that it did not leave room for the develop-ment either of the different languages, or of the numerous physical pecu-liarities, by which the various races of men are distinguished" (313).

In addition to linguistic, cultural, and physical diversities that could only be the product of deep time, 19th century collectors, both amateurs and professionals, found fossils of extinct animals (Grayson 1983; Hinsley 1981; Rudwick 2008:5; van Riper 1993), which further countered creationist teachings of a recent past. Some biblical followers dismissed the fossil evidence and stated that scripture documented multiple complete extinction and creation events, and fossils therefore simply represented a pre-human period (Bowler 1988; Grayson 1983; Montgomery 2012; Ruse 1979; Symondson 1970). But, if that was indeed true, no evidence of humans could be expected alongside extinct forms of animals (Grayson 1983; Hinsley 1981; Rudwick 2008:5; van Riper 1993). However, a preponderance of evidence was accumulating, including fossils that were sometimes in direct association with humans, or at least humans' stone tools. By the 18th century, most scholars accepted that the earth's history was considerably older than 6,000 years (Grayson 1983; Hinsley 1981; Rudwick 2008:5; van Riper 1993). In the early 19th century, Paul Tournal, John Frere, Jules de Christol, Philippe-Charles Schmerling, John MacEnery, Jacques Boucher de Perthes, and Thomas Henry Huxley all documented European sites containing human remains and associated artifacts in situ adjacent to the fossils of extinct species (Boucher de Perthes 1847, 1857; Grayson 1983; Huxley 1863; Meltzer 2015; van Riper 1993). However, because evidence of humans was not expected in association with extinct animals, such finds were often discarded as either intrusive from later deposits or as part of disturbed geologic strata. For example, in the early 1830s, Philippe-Charles Schmerling recovered extinct mammal bones alongside hominin skeletal material and stone tools in a cave near Liége, Belgium, but the association was questioned by geologist Charles Lyell for containing mixed stratigraphic levels (Grayson 1990; Lyell 1881). More than a century later, these hominin bones were identified as the broken skull of a Neanderthal child (Grayson 1990:7–8).

In the 1830s through 1840s in the Somme Valley of France, Jacques Boucher de Perthes collected stone tools and Pleistocene fossils in his free time. The wealthy Boucher de Perthes was an amateur geologist and archaeologist who explored and excavated prehistoric sites in the company of members of the local learned society, an amateur société d'émulation near Abbeville. Members of the local société mostly collected mammalian fossils, but as early as the 1830s, handaxes were found, first by local physician Casimir Picard, and later by Boucher de Perthes. In 1847, Boucher de Perthes published these finds as *Antiquités Celtiques et Antédiluviennes* in which he described stone tools representing the work of the ancestors of modern people, which he attributed to a founding Celtic population, as well as what he interpreted as much older stone tools recovered with fossils of extinct elephants and rhinos found at the sites of Menchecourt, l'Hôpital, and Moulin Quignon, in sedimentary deposits of Pleistocene glacial outwash. He emphasized the stratigraphic context of the gravel deposits and documented the positioning of artifacts and fossils within those strata (Fig. 4.1). Boucher de Perthes concluded that his "antediluvian man" lived in a time contemporaneous with these extinct species (1847, 1857).

At the same time, in Britain, Charles Lyell and other geologists who had previously discounted evidence of humans during the Pleistocene, experienced a profound paradigm shift resulting largely from participation in excavations of Brixham Cave in southwestern England (Grayson 1990, 1983; van Riper 1993). Lyell, along with other established British scientists, carefully excavated cave deposits with the goal of documenting the chronological sequence of Pleistocene fauna, not humans, in the region. However, a total of 36 possible stone tools were found during the excavation in 1858 and 1859, of which fifteen were believed to be indisputably of human manufacture, and all from secure stratigraphic contexts. Given the status of the scientists participating in the excavations—Lyell was well-known in the discipline for his publication of *Principles of Geology* thirty years earlier, and the project was sponsored by the Geological Society of London (Trigger 1989:93)—the carefully documented stratigraphic sequence, and the stone tools found in situ, Brixham Cave offered irrefutable evidence of human association with extinct Pleistocene mammals and, therefore, a greater human antiquity than previously believed (Grayson 1983, 1990:10; van Riper 1993).

Prior to the publication of the Brixham Cave specimens, Boucher de Perthes's theories were widely dismissed, in part because the intellectual milieu was simply not receptive to a great human antiquity. Despite the recognition by geologists that the earth's history extended beyond 6,000 years, the belief persisted—even among professional scientists— that humans were a relatively recent addition to that history (Daniel 1981; Grayson 1983). However, his work was also dismissed because Boucher de Perthes provided some innovative analyses of his artifacts. He argued that many of the stone tools represented symbolic and religious items, some of which he felt were stones purposefully shaped into animal figures such as horses, cattle, elephants, rhinoceroses, and human figures (1847; Grayson

4.1 Description reads, "Workman holding up Drift mans' [*sic*] blades where he says he found them in the upper stratum Limon rouge at the Chemin de Poste Quarry, Abbeville. December 1892　H.C.M." Paleolithic implements at their findspots in France. Photograph by Henry Chapman Mercer in 1892, possibly in support of his friend Abbott's Trenton finds Image no. 22872 courtesy of the Penn Museum.

1983:126). As a result of these fanciful interpretations, review of his work was extremely negative and the entirety of the manuscript viewed with skepticism by the scholarly community. Yet after the discovery of Brixham Cave, Boucher de Perthes's sites and collections gained renewed attention from respected geologists and archaeologists throughout Europe—Lyell, John Evans, and geologist John Prestwich all visited archaeological localities within the Somme Valley in 1859 (Trigger 1989:93)—and this was soon followed by Lyell's *The Geological Evidences of the Antiquity of Man* in 1863. However, problems persisted with Boucher de Perthes's data. In 1863, for example, a human jaw was allegedly found by a worker at the quarry site of Moulin-Quignon, where Boucher de Perthes collected many fossil and stone tool specimens. Initially, French and British experts pronounced the specimen authentic, but it later was proven a scam by a worker seeking the 200 francs that Boucher de Perthes was offering in reward for hominin fossils (Bonanno 2009:108). Boucher de Perthes was vindicated when Charles Lyell and other prominent geologists visited sites near his home in Abbeville, France, and confirmed the glacial context of Pleistocene fossils and stone tools, but not the fraudulent human jaw, which quietly disappeared from the record (Lubbock 1865:281). Nevertheless, Jacques Boucher de Perthes gained worldwide fame for discovering humankind's great antiquity (Grayson 1983, 1990; van Riper 1993). With these discoveries, and great fanfare, human antiquity breached the ice age barrier in Europe.

THE BEGINNING OF A NEW WORLD THEORY

In "The Stone Age in New Jersey" (1872), Abbott presented a series of stone artifacts that bore a remarkable resemblance to the artifacts described by Boucher de Perthes (Fig. 4.2). Though Abbott claimed he was not explicitly seeking Pleistocene artifacts, he felt the resemblance was undeniable. "While pursuing my collecting of Indian relics, it was gradually forced upon my mind that these rude implements were more intimately associated with the gravel than with the surface of the ground and the relics of the Indians found upon it" (1883b:126). Abbott theorized that these roughly flaked artifacts were different from the Native American artifacts found nearby and instead represented ancient ice-age humans in the Delaware Valley, drawing direct parallels to the stratigraphic context and lithic technology of discoveries in England and France.

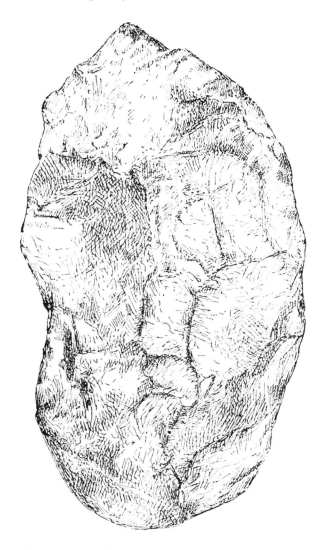

4.2 Stone artifact argued by Abbott to be a Paleolithic artifact "so remarkably similar to the European patterns of Paleolithic implements" (1878:230–231, fig. 2). Sketch by C. C. Abbott. Peabody Museum Catalog Number 77-2-10/11539.1.

By 1872, fortunately for Abbott, such finds were more widely accepted by the scientific community, at least in Europe, thanks to the support of Lyell and other geologists. In North America, a similar glaciation was also established, as a result of geological research by scholars who included Abbott's uncle Timothy Abbott Conrad. The timing and sequence of one or more glaciation events had yet to be determined, but most believed that an ice age similar to that identified in Europe had occurred in North America (Agassiz 1840; Conrad 1839; Dana 1863; Hitchcock 1857). Abbott's publication referenced the work of John Frere, Jacques Boucher de Perthes, and Charles Lyell, but relied very heavily on John Lubbock's highly popular 1865 publication, *Pre-Historic Times* for descriptions and assessment of the "crude" argillite bifaces he believed dated to a great antiquity (Abbott 1872). Further, he applied many of Boucher de Perthes's assessments directly to the Delaware Valley, similarly arguing that roughly flaked stone tools at deep stratigraphic levels represented early ice age hominins, and that more shallowly buried and surface finds including lithic spearpoints and knives were made by the ancestors of present-day people. In fact, the parallel between the two men's work was so strong that Alfred Russel Wallace later commented that Abbott "appears to stand in a somewhat similar relation to this great question in America as did Boucher de Perthes in Europe" (Wallace 1887). In Abbott's case, he alleged that the artifacts that appeared more modern were made by Native Americans versus Boucher de Perthes's Celts, but for presumed older specimens, Abbott attempted to duplicate Boucher de Perthes's famous Old World examples in New World contexts. As a result of perceived similarities, Abbott argued there must have been a sequence in the New World identical to that found in Europe, in which prehistoric populations passed from the Paleolithic to the Neolithic and that "in the rude weapons, now deep down beneath the grassy sod and flower-decked river bank, we learn, at least, the fact of the presence, in the distant past, of an earlier people than the Indian" (Abbott 1883b:126). Acknowledging little historical information by which to draw conclusions about these artifacts, Abbott noted "conjecture must go a great way in deciding upon their use" (1872:148). Due to the apparent disparity in manufacture between the two groups of implements (crude and finely crafted), Abbott concluded, "we can scarcely imagine that a people who could fashion the latter, would deign to utilize the former" (1872:146). He further believed that since they "are usually formed of the mineral that characterizes the locality where they are found," they must have been made expediently, with little planning and no desire for a higher-quality stone (1877a:247). Regrettably, Abbott did not have sites with the same secure stratigraphic sequence as was demonstrated in Boucher de Perthes's sites in France, and questions soon arose about his inexpert documentation of their archaeological provenience in alleged glacial gravels of the Delaware Valley.

Ironically, arguing for restraint, something Abbott typically possessed very little of, he stated that "I purposely referred to these chipped stones as *supposed* Paleolithic implements" (1883b:127, emphasis original). Abbott realized that if his ideas were to be accepted, he needed to answer two important questions: first, were the "rude implements" he found in the Delaware Valley actually artifacts, and not naturally-formed river-tumbled rocks? And second, were these artifacts truly ancient, specifically of Pleistocene age? This second question hinged on two important issues: whether the sediment within which the artifacts were found was actually Pleistocene in age, a geological question Abbott was not qualified to answer; and whether or not the artifacts were deposited with those presumably Pleistocene sediments, or were intrusive into older sediments, a question that centered on archaeological rigor and careful excavation, which were typically lacking in Abbott's self-taught field methodology.

THE ARCHAEOLOGICAL EVIDENCE

Abbott struggled to convince disbelievers that not only were his specimens truly artifacts, but that they also were exceptionally old. He based his understanding of lithic technology on the work of Sir John Evans. In 1872, Evans published *The Ancient Stone Implements, Weapons, and Ornaments, of Great Britain*, which quickly became the standard reference for lithic artifacts of the European Paleolithic, and Abbott adapted these descriptions in his own interpretations of "paleoliths" in the Delaware Valley. In this volume, Evans discussed the way in which stone tools were made, using observations of gunflint manufacture from the 1850s, as well as others' ethnographic descriptions of people who still used stone tools, as an initial point for gaining greater knowledge about flintknapping (Evans 1872; Roberts and Barton 2008; Lamdin-Whymark 2009).

Evans wrote that in order to understand stone tool production "we cannot, in all probability, follow a better guide than that which is afforded us by the manner in which instruments of similar character are produced at the present day" (1872:13). He also outlined his own flintknapping attempts, and wrote that "I have found by experiment that taking a flake of flint (made, I may remark, with a stone hammer, consisting of a flint or quartzite pebble held in the hand), and placing it, with the flat face upwards, on a smooth block of stone, I can, by successive blows of the pebble, chip the end of the flake without any difficulty into the desired form" (1872:33). Evans used his flintknapping knowledge to provide detailed descriptions of archaeological artifacts, which Abbott then employed to substantiate his own claims for an American Paleolithic.

In some of his earliest writing on the "paleoliths," Abbott defended his claims of human manufacture against suggestions that the stones simply exhibited natural breakage from tumbling in the Delaware River. He carefully described flake scars visible on the artifacts' surfaces: "the edges still remain sharp, regular, and exhibit an amount of skill in 'flint-chipping' about equal to that of the ordinary slate lance-heads, spear and arrow points" that had been "worked into its present shape by a series of powerful blows, or by pressure" (1877a:248). If they were the result of natural tumbling, Abbott argued:

> they would assuredly have happened at various periods, and, besides leaving different degrees of weathering on the fractured surfaces, would also exhibit traces of the causes that produced the breakage, as in scratches where a flinty rock had graved and cut the underlying pebble, in ground-off angles where some huge mass had been rolled upon and crushed off the weaker projecting portions left by a previous altering agency. It is needless to state no traces of occurrences like these are discoverable (1877a:248).

Abbott initially faced concern from Frederic Ward Putnam about the veracity of his Paleolithic claims. Putnam wrote cautiously of Abbott's finds that "Among these are numerous rude forms obtained from the gravel bed at a depth of from three to seven feet from the surface. These implements from the gravel Dr. Abbott believes to be of palaeolithic age, and made by a race inhabiting the country before the present Indians reached the Atlantic coast" (1876:13). Abbott commented in his diary, "December 14, 1876: I went to town in afternoon and sent to Putnam what I believe to be four palaeolithic implements. I think Putnam is skeptical still in the subject but I am not" (CCA/PU, Box 2, Folder 2).

Abbott's declaration of a New World Paleolithic was new, but not earth-shattering. Other scientists had been fighting to gain acceptance for similar hypotheses in Europe for several decades, and once their work gained widespread acclaim, Abbott simply followed in their wake. Abbott asserted that if Pleistocene humans were possible in Europe, they also could have existed in the New World. However, he was still forced to support the argument through archaeological data and relied exclusively on specific stone tools in order to do that. The lithic artifacts that Abbott often referred to as "rude implements" or "paleoliths" or sometimes as "turtle-backs" (1877a:248) bore striking resemblance to the Acheulean handaxes found in Europe, first publicized by Boucher de Perthes and described as the "axe of the type of St. Acheul" after the sites in the Somme Valley where they were found (Haynes 1883). When compared side by side, there was little obvious difference other than raw material type between the Paleolithic artifacts of Europe and those of the Trenton gravels in New Jersey. The visual evidence "will clear away all doubts as to the importance and reliability of Dr. Abbott's discoveries and investigations, which have proved the former existence of palaeolithic man in the valley of the Delaware" (Putnam 1883:149).

Abbott's Paleolithic attribution of the artifacts in New Jersey hinged upon three central archaeological arguments: first, and most importantly, that there were strong morphological similarities between his artifacts and the handaxes found in clear association with Pleistocene vertebrates in Europe. Second, that the artifacts were rough and poorly made, indicating a more "primitive" flintknapping technology. And third, that extensive weathering present on the argillite artifacts was indicative of great antiquity.

The morphological similarities between Abbott's Delaware Valley artifacts and the Acheulean handaxes of Europe were heralded as the most compelling evidence of a similar occupation during or at the end of the last ice age in both regions. Because European handaxes had recently been demonstrated to have a strong association with Pleistocene fossils, Abbott conjectured that the American artifacts must date to the same period. "In its shape and size, as well as the circumstances under which it was found, it is a repetition, in America, of the hundreds of such finds, that are so common in many of the river valleys, both of France and England" (Abbott 1881:491). In several publications (for example, in Abbott 1873, 1877a, 1881), Abbott explicitly cited John Evans (1872) in support of these claims. Abbott had been corresponding with Evans since at least 1874 and sending artifacts, including a sample of those he considered Paleolithic in origin. On September 28, 1874, he sent a package of 56 artifacts collected from Three Beeches, and referenced a future shipment "I shall quite soon send you a series of 'rude implements,' which I distinguish from surface found forms, for reasons I will state, when I next write. In my, I fear, never to be printed monograph, I have called them 'turtle backs.'" (CCA to John Evans, Related Documents File, Pitt Rivers Museum 1928.68). Ultimately, Abbott sent Evans at least 60 artifacts, which are now housed at the Pitt Rivers Museum at Oxford University. Correspondence between the two men greatly bolstered Abbott's ego and confidence in claiming a New World Paleolithic attribution for his archaeological finds.

The alleged Paleolithic artifacts were described as "flat-bottomed, peak-backed, stones" (Abbott 1877a:248) with visible flake scars and were made of locally available lithic material later identified as argillite. These artifacts typically ranged four to six inches in length, two to four inches in width, and approximately one to two inches in thickness (1877a). And furthermore:

> Convinced that the so-called "turtle-back" celts, which are the most primitive form of the chipped implements of the gravels, really are of artificial origin, many of them being identical in shape with the ordinary forms of European drift implements, and furthermore, since among the specimens found, are several spearhead-like implements, there can be but little doubt that, unassociated as they are with the common forms of surface-found relics, they are remains of an earlier and a ruder people, who occupied the eastern shores of this continent prior to the advent of the Indians, or are their immediate ancestors, as the case may be (Abbott 1881:490).

Abbott felt that this argument was incontrovertible—one could simply *look* at the artifacts from Europe and the artifacts from America and *see* that they were identical. And, if they were identical, they must have been created by a similar primitive human and in a similar ice age setting. Others seemed to agree. Gabriel de Mortillet, who was most well-known for classifying the Paleolithic into the epochs still used today, indicated that the primary difference between the artifacts from the Trenton gravels and those from St. Acheul was that the Trenton artifacts were made from argillite, which was harder to flake and therefore yielded artifacts that appeared less sophisticated than those from France (de Mortillet 1879).

The poor workmanship of the Trenton artifacts was key to their antiquity, according to Abbott. In a similar vein to theories about a linear evolution of species, Abbott asserted that there must have been a linear development of flintknapping skill through time. Therefore, roughly flaked artifacts were older than more finely made ones (1872). Some New Jersey specimens exhibited only negligible flaking around their perimeter, in some cases only unifacially. This did not faze Abbott, who argued that a range of variation simply reflected insignificant differences within the series. "The flat under surface does not give to these 'turtle-backs' as good cutting edges as are found on those specimens that are chipped on both sides" (1881:496). Others were bifacially flaked and superbly made. An example, illustrated in *Primitive Industry*, was argued to represent "an excellent connecting link between the ruder forms...and those that are of higher design and better finish" (1881:496, fig. 418). Yet by definition, none of the alleged Paleolithic artifacts found in the New World exhibited technological skill indicative of later Native American occupation.

According to Abbott, the Paleolithic artifacts presumably served as hunting weapons and cutting or chopping tools for butchering the large Pleistocene mammals that lived in a glacial environment. The tools "might readily be mounted in a handle, or, having a blunt base, be held in the hand and wielded with terrible effect" (Abbott 1881:496). And, even the more roughly flaked artifacts could be used as tools. "The edges are sufficiently sharp to be available for cutting flesh and similar yielding substances. For some such purpose, they were probably used" (Abbott 1881:496). Some, he argued, may have even been hafted as ice picks. "If we are warranted in supposing that the people who made and used these palaeolithic implements lived here during the prevalence of an arctic climate, then they must have had some means for cutting holes in the ice....If used in this manner, they would be peculiarly liable to be lost through the holes cut in the ice" (1881:503), which would explain how these artifacts were deposited in river gravel sediments.

In *Primitive Industry* (1881), Abbott was careful to document not only the form and condition of the artifacts used to support his argument, but also what he assessed as their provenience and context, specifically indicating finds that occurred in situ in presumably undisturbed sediment. This

was important in establishing that the Paleolithic artifacts came from Trenton Gravel sediments, and not from deposits that were mixed with other,
presumably later, occupations. For example:

> The specimen was twenty-one feet from the surface of the ground, and
> within a foot of the Triassic clays that are here exposed. Directly over
> it, and in contact, was a bowlder of large size, probably weighing one
> hundred pounds; while at a distance of five feet above was a second
> much larger bowlder. The character of the mass, which was that of the
> bluff on the bank of the river near Trenton, was such as to render it
> impossible that this specimen could have reached this position subse-
> quently to the deposition of the containing bed (1881:506).

Drawing on the work of Lubbock (1865), Abbott asserted that these early
dwellers of New Jersey and, therefore, their cousins in Europe during the
Paleolithic, were biologically and culturally related to the modern Eskimo
(1878:253). The Eskimo were a useful model, for they also lived in cold environments, and successfully adapted to ice and snow, meaning, to Abbott,
that Paleolithic people in the Delaware Valley could also have used similar technologies and similar adaptations to survive an ice age climate. He
concluded that the environment would not have been a barrier to human
occupation.

However, these Paleolithic occupants were, Abbott believed, an earlier
"race" of people different from later, modern Native Americans. In later
publications, he gave them the genus and species name *Homo delawarensis*
(Abbott 1912:128). He justified this by explaining that the artifacts were different and, therefore, the people who made them must have been dissimilar
too. "These Paleolithic implements, so different from the others in many
respects, remain as the only trace of that still older people, the autochtho-
nous race of these shores who were in sole possession when driven away
by the incoming Indians, whose own stone implements at the time were
but little more elaborate" (1876a:72). Abbott accepted that a later migration
may have interbred with, or replaced, what he referred to as a "pre-Indian
people" (1878:255). He stated that "if an Asiatic people migrated hither, they
drove away or absorbed the primitive race that utilized such rude implements" (1872:147). This later population, Native Americans, was the maker
of a more varied lithic toolkit that included knives, scrapers, arrowpoints,

and other artifacts. His chronology could be summed up as representing three distinct periods of occupation: stone implements of early Paleolithic humans from the glacial gravels at Trenton; argillite tools, flakes, and spear points, signifying the end of the last ice age; and arrowheads, celts, pestles, axes, and objects of more recent Delaware village occupations (Browman and Williams 2013; Putnam 1898).

Because these Pleistocene sediments, and the artifacts that they contained, were deeply buried, they must be old. Abbott calculated that "the freshets of the Delaware River, occurring usually twice a year, deposit about one two hundred and fifty-sixth (1/256) of an inch per annum" (Abbott 1876a:71). By examining the depth of burial, Abbott surmised that the more recent Native American artifacts were probably over 3,500 to 4,000 years old, and, therefore, the Paleolithic artifacts must be considerably older than that, given their depth at times of over ten feet or more (1876a:72). The chronological separation between these sequential occupations, according to Abbott, could also be seen through differential degrees of weathering on the artifacts. The weathering was "of much importance, in its bearing upon both the age and origin of these objects" (1881:486). Paleolithic artifacts of argillite were heavily weathered, while those of presumably more recent Native American settlement, often made of jasper, chert, and quartz, exhibited little evidence of weathering.

Argillite is a solidified mudstone created of silt-sized particles compressed to form a homogenous stone that exhibits conchoidal fracture. When argillite is bedded or layered, it is more commonly called shale. The variety of argillite (analcime/dolomite-speckled [colloidal-chemical]) that is common to the Delaware Valley is part of the Upper Triassic Lockatong Formation of the Central Newark Basin (Albright and Williams 1980; Van Houten 1960, 1964, 1965). This argillite fractures conchoidally or subconchoidally and is good for toolstone manufacture. It is often dark gray or grayish-red in color, though it weathers to a brownish-gray or reddish-gray. Exposed surfaces of argillite weather through both chemical and physical processes to create a chalky, clay-like rind.

Abbott theorized that it was possible to use surface weathering on artifacts as a rough measurement of age. He understood that weathering was not immediately translatable to calendar years but suggested that weathered specimens were older than non-weathered specimens. For example, "is it not safe to conclude that, from the great degree of weathering which the vast majority of the implements made from it have undergone, such specimens are of an earlier origin than those of jasper and quartz." Furthermore, "No jasper specimens have been found showing alteration of the surface. They are as fresh as though chipped but yesterday" (1880:514). As a result, he concluded, the argillite artifacts, with their weathered patina, must be significantly older than artifacts made of other lithic materials found in the same area. Even when found together, it should be possible to distinguish older, Paleolithic artifacts from newer, Native American ones. "Inasmuch as these rude relics that are *intimately* associated with newer relics invariably exhibit a greater degree of weathering and decay than accompanying implements of the same mineral, it is not difficult to separate them" (Abbott 1876a:66, emphasis original).

Unfortunately, Abbott compared argillite specimens to nearby artifacts of jasper and quartz, which do not weather like argillite does. Furthermore, argillite weathering is dependent on factors such as soil chemistry, acidity, and moisture content, all of which can affect the rate at which a weathered rind appears on artifacts. We understand today that the rate of weathering cannot be used as a reliable estimator of age for argillite artifacts, but Abbott did not know this—or did not want to know this. Despite this flaw, the chronology of Abbott's finds was more decisively rooted in the geologic context, similar to the way European artifacts were dated in Boucher de Perthes's examples. However, Abbott, an untrained amateur archaeologist was venturing into a realm of knowledge held by a cadre of highly trained, expert geologists. And unlike Boucher de Perthes's Pleistocene sites in France, the Trenton gravels did not offer secure, undisturbed, ice age strata.

THE GEOLOGIC EVIDENCE

The geologic context was harder for Abbott to interpret than the archaeological data, given that he had very little background and no training in geology. Ultimately, he relied on the visits of friendly geologists and previously published data for his claims of the age of Delaware Valley sediments. He argued that Paleolithic artifacts were found in a stratum identified as the Trenton gravel, which was determined by Pennsylvania State Geologist, Henry Carvill Lewis, to be river deposits derived from the terminal glacial moraine in the upper Delaware Valley. Therefore, Abbott claimed, geologically, these sediments and as a result, the period of occupation reflected by

Abbott's alleged Paleolithic artifacts, must have been towards the end of the last ice age (Abbott 1883b).

Faithfully following Lubbock's (1865) accounts of European examples, Abbott argued that the Delaware River was once a much larger river, as much as fifty feet higher than its current level, and it was in this massive water body that rough stone implements were deposited within glacial outwash gravels. Speaking for Europe, Lubbock wrote "it holds good of most of our rivers, that along the sides of their valleys are patches of old gravels left by the stream at various heights, before they had excavated the channels to their present depth" and that there were two main depositional horizons along European river channels of at least Pleistocene age "one continuous along the bottom of the valleys and rising little above the water level" and a second "occurring in detached masses at an elevation of from fifty to two hundred feet above the valley" (1865:287). Lubbock concluded that "If, therefore, we get no definite date for the arrival of man in these countries [in Europe], we can at least form a vivid idea of his antiquity" (1865:308).

In the Delaware Valley, Abbott used the same logic, again directly applying European examples to his finds. He argued that the artifacts must be from a human living in the ancient past, around the time of the last ice age, though placing a date on that antiquity was difficult. "I do not presume to boldly assert that America's early man, at least on the Atlantic coast was *pre*-glacial; but that he *ante*-dates the Red Indian, *if it be true that the latter is a recent comer*, I do confidently maintain, backed as I am by the unquestionable testimony of the Trenton gravel" (Abbott 1883b:132, emphasis original). But, he needed to proceed with caution. According to Haynes, "Though the objects themselves may present the right type, shape, and general appearance, we must look carefully at the conditions under which they have been discovered before we can pronounce judgement" (1883:135). It was problematic for Abbott that unlike sites in Europe that contained fossil vertebrates in direct association with stone tools, the artifacts he found in the Delaware Valley were not accompanied by fossils. In fact, fossils in the Trenton gravels were exceptionally rare. As a result, the age of the artifacts in New Jersey was much more tenuous than those of Europe, and Abbott faced significant challenges in accurately dating his finds.

Abbott did not claim to be qualified to assess the age of the sediments along the Delaware River that contained his alleged Paleolithic artifacts, though he did semi-jokingly "lay claim to a smattering of gravel-ology" (1892a:271). Instead, he relied on geologists like Henry Carvill Lewis, Nathaniel Shaler, George Frederick Wright, and others. In order to gain their support for a Pleistocene context, Abbott invited these men to visit him in the field and inspect the Trenton gravels for themselves. "February 14, 1877: Got a telegram saying Shaler here today. Met Shaler at 2:50pm and we drove down to Riverview and saw the gravel bank. Shaler pronounced it drift, very slightly modified by subsequent wave action. Found two specimens. Then went upland and saw surface boulders in South Trenton....After supper, talked a long time in his room about geology and other matters, and then I came home. The result in brief is that *I have discovered glacial man in America*" (CCA/PU Box 2, Folder 2; emphasis original).

Other geologists seemed to concur: "September 20, 1878: [Lucien] Carr and [Josiah] Whitney came. We drove down to Riverview and hunted up the gravel matter....Prof Whitney pronounced the formation as glacial drift of the pluvial era of that epoch and was distinctly a part and parcel of the glacial conditions once existing and not of a distinctly succeeding period. This is an authoritative decision on the subject and confirmatory of my previously published views dated Sept. 9th" (CCA/PU Box 2, Folder 2). Notable geologists and archaeologists expressed support for Abbott's claims: "November 19, 1880: [Sir William Boyd] Dawkins gives as his opinion that I have made unquestionably the discovery of Paleolithic man in the Delaware Valley. He enthusiastically endorses my position, and I need no greater authority to express an opinion!" (CCA/PU Box 2, Folder 2). Abbott later related to Putnam that: "Dawkins's visit was a great success, in every way; and not the least result is that he has suggested methods of work next year, which I think will be of much interest, and afford further evidence of the existence here, formerly, of palaeolithic man" (CCA-FWP/HPM Record 2575 [no box #, no accession #]; December 1, 1880). However, Dawkins opinion changed just a short time later when he heard rumors that Abbott had lied about the provenience of one of his finds—passing off an Arkansas artifact as having originated in the Trenton gravels—subsequently, Dawkins became uneasy about the entirety of Abbott's claims of a secure geologic context (Meltzer 2015:61).

George Frederick Wright, a theologian, amateur geologist, and professor at Oberlin Theological Seminary, published extensively on the age of the Trenton gravels (1883, 1889, 1892a, 1893, 1896), placing their date firmly at the end of the last ice age. "The most likely time for this deposition to have occurred was near the very close of the glacial period, when the lower moraines were fresh and when ice fields still lingered in the southern valleys of the Catskills" (Wright 1883:144). He argued that these gravels originated with glacial moraines to the north near the Delaware Water Gap and were transported downstream during flood events, ultimately depositing many feet of unconsolidated gravel and sand at Trenton. Furthermore, supporting Abbott's work, though with no evidence to this effect, this depositional event, or events, at the end of the glacial period was marked by "the presence of the mastodon and other extinct animals with palaeolithic man in the neighborhood of Trenton" (1889:527).

In the larger geological milieu, debate raged about the sequence of glaciation and the qualifications necessary to interpret glaciation events, which affected the interpretation of the chronology of human occupation as well as the definition of professional scholarly authority. Wright, who like Abbott was untrained in his field, believed that there had been a single ice age in the past, and the geologic signatures of extensive ice sheets represented a unique period in time (Wright 1889, 1892a), while others, represented most vociferously by professional geologists from U.S. government agencies, favored multiple glacial advances and retreats, with humans entering the New World during an ice-free interglacial period (McGee 1889a). Abbott presented his Paleolithic implements as deposited at the end of a final glaciation of the Delaware Valley within gravels that were formed by outwash from the melting of a large glacier.

Facing possible critique that the alleged Paleolithic artifacts were intrusive into earlier sediments due to taphonomic processes such as rodent burrowing or erosion, Abbott brought prestigious archaeologists and geologists to the Delaware Valley to see for themselves and relied on their reputations to bolster his argument. Frederic Ward Putnam and Lucien Carr of the Peabody Museum at Harvard University, and Henry Williamson Haynes, an archaeologist from Boston, all found "paleoliths" in the Trenton gravels, and were willing to attest to this at professional meetings and in print (Carr 1883; Haynes 1883; Putnam 1883). Haynes wrote: "I consider it absolutely and incontestably established that these objects have come, as alleged, from the gravel-beds of the Delaware valley" (1883:133). Geologists such as George Frederick Wright documented the sediments and artifacts in situ (Fig. 4.3), arguing that they represented undisturbed glacial

4.3 Charles C. Abbott observing archaeological excavations. The reverse of the photo contains the caption by Abbott "Here I am as an 'archaeologist' in the field—one of a near neighbor's. The head and shoulders of man in trench are those of Prof. G. F. Wright of Oberlin, Ohio; a college professor, and intensely interested in the question of antiquity of man in this region. I am not as 'tough' looking as this makes me appear. C.C.A." Charles Conrad Abbott Papers (C0290), Box 15, Folder 2; Manuscripts Division, Department of Rare Books and Special Collections, Princeton University Library.

sediments (Wright 1883, 1893). Other geologists also offered support: "October 7, 1878: Got a letter from Putnam who says that Whitney [Josiah D. Whitney, Harvard University geologist] says I am right as to paleolithics, but would himself consider the gravels as Pliocene, and my ancient Jerseyman as contemporaneous with Calaveras skull &c, and all will he in detail in his forthcoming volume" (CCA/PU Box 2, Folder 2).

Abbott was confident in the association between his artifacts and the glacial gravels. According to H. C. Lewis "They occur in positions which render it extremely probable that they belong to the same age as that of the deposition of the gravel" (1880a:306). This was partly due to their presence at great depth below the surface, but not so deep as to be earlier than the glacial period. Paleolithic artifacts were never found in older sediments, though they were sometimes found in younger sediments, a fact attributed to soil turbation. "We can easily imagine an earthquake creating a deep chasm or crack in the surface, and inhuming a comparatively modern implement; but there are no traces of such cataclysmic action here, and if such an event had occurred, there would be other evidences than the commingling of objects from the surface with the underlying deposits; but such are wanting" (Abbott 1881:511). Abbott was doggedly certain in his conclusions, yet caution may have been advisable. Words of warning emerged: "Every cautious field geologist accustomed to the study of unconsolidated superficial deposits quickly learns to question the verity of apparently original inclusions" (McGee 1889a:306).

FAME AND (A LITTLE BIT OF) FORTUNE

Abbott reveled in the support and confirmation of well-known archaeologists and geologists. Putnam, who initially had been tentative in his support of Abbott and a New World Paleolithic, gained enthusiasm as evidence mounted substantiating Abbott's ideas. He spoke in scholarly meetings about the veracity of these finds. "Certainly the evidence that has been brought forward tonight will clear away all doubts as to the importance and reliability of Dr. Abbott's discoveries and investigations, which have proved the former existence of palaeolithic man in the valley of the Delaware" (Putnam 1883:149), and directly compared Abbott to Boucher de Perthes: "in 1875, Dr. Abbott made the discovery of palaeolithic implements in America. This place is of the same importance to American archaeology that Abbeville is to European" (Putnam 1888:421). Others also joined the chorus supporting Abbott's discovery: "I do not hesitate to declare my firm conviction that the rude argillite objects found in the gravels of the Delaware River, at Trenton, New Jersey, are true palaeolithic implements" (Haynes 1883:137). Abbott, despite his status as an amateur, had finally achieved scholarly fame.

Abbott's collection went on display at the Peabody Museum at Harvard University to great fanfare. The exhibit arrangement was designed to track human occupation in the region from Paleolithic times to the present day, and chronologically displayed the "rude implements" of the Trenton gravel as the starting point, drawing parallels with early finds in Europe. An announcement in *Science* read: "The Paleolithic implements from the gravel and from the talus include nearly all found, some of them coming from a depth of thirty feet in the gravel; with one exception, a black flint, they are made of a hard, fine-grained argillite; many are but slightly chipped, while others are of well-defined forms, similar to the paleoliths of the Old World" (Anonymous 1886:5). As Abbott's Paleolithic artifacts gained pride of place as a centerpiece of the Peabody Museum's American collections, he was hailed as a visionary scientist. "The collection and its arrangement are invaluable, unique, and of extreme importance to all who wish to study the stone age of our Atlantic coast. It reflects great credit upon the industry and sharp-sightedness of the collector, and exhibits as well the same perspicacity and serious method that is a marked feature of the entire museum" (Anonymous 1886:5).

Abbott's fame as America's Boucher de Perthes ignited a search for other Paleolithic sites in North America. Abbott predicted "I submit that man was preglacial in America, was driven southward by the extension of the ice-sheet, and probably voluntarily retreated with it to more northern regions; and if so, then in Ohio true palaeolithic implements will surely be found, and evidences of man's preglacial age will ultimately be found in the once-glaciated areas of our continent" (1883c:359). His prediction seemed to come true, with Paleolithic artifacts recovered from presumed glacial sediments at multiple sites throughout the United States in subsequent years.

In Madisonville, Ohio, for example in 1885, a bifacially worked flint artifact was found approximately eight feet below the ground surface in gravels near the confluence of the Little Miami River and Mill Creek, about eleven miles northeast of Cincinnati. Geologically, this site was believed to be filled with glacial outwash gravels, similar to those found at Trenton, but capped by a deposit of loess on the surface. The artifact was found during excavation for a cistern on the property of Dr. C. L. Metz, and therefore argued to have been recovered in situ. Dr. Metz found a similar artifact two years later, and it was presented as further evidence of Paleolithic occupation of the New World, and more importantly of the legitimacy of Abbott's discovery a decade earlier (Wright 1889).

An additional bifacially worked artifact similar to those found at Trenton also appeared in Medora, Jackson County, Indiana, about one hundred miles west of Cincinnati, recovered while "digging with a hunting-knife about [a] boulder, in order to ascertain whether there were any glacial scratches upon it, that I found the paleolith" (Cresson 1890a:151). It was discovered by Hilborne T. Cresson, serving as a Special Assistant to the Peabody Museum, who was working in the area. Cresson had previously found an alleged Paleolithic artifact near Claymont, in New Castle County, Delaware, in 1887, and another in the same area in 1888 (Cresson 1890b:141). In these cases, the Trenton artifacts, as well as the Trenton gravels, were upheld as the type specimens for the New World Paleolithic and subsequent finds interpreted in comparison. Cresson cited a communication from Wright about the Indiana artifacts: "From my notes it seems to me most likely that the situation is nearly identical with that at Trenton" and perhaps pushing occupation even further back into prehistory, that "the triangular glaciated space in southern Indiana must have been a favorable place for preglacial man, and its borders present just the conditions for the preservation of his remains" (letter from G. F. Wright as cited in Cresson 1890a:151–152).

In Minnesota, near Little Falls, in Morrison County, additional artifacts were found by Miss Frances E. Babbitt in 1879 (Babbitt 1890). They were interpreted as coming from a "well-defined thin layer in the modified drift forming the glacial floodplain of the Mississippi River" (Wright 1889:544). Like other Paleolithic specimens, these too were directly compared with those from Trenton "These specimens found by Miss Babbitt are all of white quartz, and while some are simply chips, others of these before you are identical in shape as well as material with the specimens obtained by Dr. Abbott in the Trenton gravel" (Putnam 1890:159).

Geologist W J McGee used the Trenton geology and associated artifacts to further his own claims about human antiquity in the Great Basin. He believed that his own research had discovered Paleolithic humans in the American west, and that these went hand in hand with the Trenton examples (1889a). In fact, most archaeologists and geologists, by the late 1880s, unquestioningly accepted an American Paleolithic. As best summed up by Thomas Wilson, curator at the United States National Museum (later the Smithsonian Institution):

> These finds of proved antiquity are in great numbers, and they demonstrate both the existence and the antiquity of a Paleolithic period in America. This cannot longer be doubted. It is the conclusion of all the scientists who have studied the question. I have mentioned Professor McGee. It goes without saying that Dr. Abbott believes it. Professor Putnam was one of its earliest believers. Professors Wright and Haynes have given it their adhesion, and so have all the geologists who have examined the localities where the implements have been found (1889:236).

With the acceptance of the American Paleolithic, Abbott's accomplishments catapulted him to fame and placed him in league with some of the most famous archaeologists of the 19th century. His book *Primitive Industry* (1881) was North America's answer to Sir John Evans's *The Ancient Stone Implements, Weapons, and Ornaments, of Great Britain* (1872), which was the standard reference for the European Paleolithic. Abbott found himself thrust into the scholarly limelight, and it greatly inflated his ego but did little for his wallet. "August 19, 1883: Fact is, I am getting a little tired of these everlasting gravels. Their study cost me a couple of years' hard work and never brought me in a penny. Those who popularize the subject, draw in the shekels. This last article on the subject however is written for pay so I hope it will suit" (CCA/PU Box 2, Folder 2).

Despite this scholarly attention, Abbott felt that the Peabody Museum had abandoned him once they had obtained the artifacts they needed in order to comply with George Peabody's initial goals for the Museum. Abbott lamented in his diary: "July 13, 1883: Putnam is to write me next week about archaeological matters but he can do nothing but try to cheer with hopes of better times and such stuff. I guess that my Cambridge days are about over. The museum has squeezed the juice from the lemon and now throws the skin away. I suppose I am only skin now, to them, but it is the way of the world and no one need complain. He who suffers in silence is a brave man" (CCA/PU Box 2, Folder 2). What was probably more likely was that Putnam, as official Curator of the Museum, and with his sights set on the Peabody Professorship that still eluded his grasp, was becoming increasingly uneasy about Abbott's methods and acerbic personality. Despite many years of schooling under Louis Agassiz, Asa Gray, and Jeffries Wyman at Harvard, Putnam never received an official degree from the University and like Abbott, similarly faced professional discrimination that hindered entry into the field. As a curator, Putnam's skills were more than adequate, but as a *Professor*, fellow Harvard faculty questioned his qualifications (Hinsley 1988:61). Alexander, Louis Agassiz's son, vehemently opposed Putnam's appointment to the Peabody Professorship (Hinsley 1988:61), ostensibly on the grounds of his lack of degree, but may also have harbored resentment about Putnam's split with his father while a student at Harvard.

As a result of his probationary status, Putnam was overly cautious in his leadership of the Peabody Museum, and particularly in his dealings with the Museum's network of amateur collectors (Hinsley 1988:62). Putnam counselled Abbott to adhere to rigorous field methods in obtaining specimens (Hinsley 1988), but as early as 1884, Putnam received warnings that Abbott's Paleolithic implements might not have had the secure provenience that Abbott claimed. Allegations even surfaced that Abbott had been seen planting alleged Paleolithic implements in the Trenton gravels for visitors to find. Putnam quietly investigated and found no proof of wrongdoing but proceeded carefully in his relationship with Abbott (Meltzer 2003:61).

In a letter to Putnam, Abbott addressed this allegation:

> The Philadelphia Academy are mad because Brinton gave a partial adherence to my views so I am told, and that Lcidy and Co. want the academy as an institution to deny the trustworthiness of my work, until corroborated by persons specifically designated by them. This is what down here they call "science." However, it is not a matter of importance to the world at large or to
>
> Yours truly,
> Abbott
> (CCA-FWP/HPM Box 5, Record 249, Accession 84-11, 84-58; May 2, 1884)

Though Abbott continued to write to Putnam regularly, Putnam often did not reply, and Abbott's letters gained a veneer of sarcasm that was readily apparent: "[if] your archaeological mightiness can find time, will you tell me if I can do any active work this fall for you?...Please therefore, if you have any recollection of my existence, let me know if I can be utilized—when and how. I write, because I may be mistaken, but my impression is I am to be or have been quietly thrown overboard. This is all right, however. Simply in accordance with my ordinary luck in life" (CCA-FWP/HPM Box 5, Record 161, Accession 83-59; September 12, 1883).

Worse, Abbott's financial situation was so dire that he was forced to accept a position as clerk in Trenton bank, leaving little time for archaeological collecting and no funding for travel to scholarly meetings or to Cambridge to continue work with the Peabody Museum. For three years, bank employment drove Abbott into a deep depression and in his diary, he simply recorded the routine of everyday life, interspersed with comments on health and his neighbors and relatives. "June 20, 1884: I meditate in damns, awaiting the opening of the bowel. What with sleeping much, reading a little, and diarrhea by way of variety, pulled through one of the most uncomfortable days I ever remember" (CCA/PU Box 2, Folder 2).

Even though Abbott's personal fortunes did not improve, his status in the scholarly world gained new heights in the late 1800s. An anonymously written article in *Science* magazine heralded Abbott's work (1886), and Putnam threw his support behind Abbott in print and in scholarly meetings (Putnam 1883, 1888, 1890). The American Association for the Advancement of Science and the Boston Society of Natural History both held symposia in the late 1880s on the antiquity of humans in the New World (Meltzer 2003), which largely supported Abbott's claims. In recognition of his ascendance to the scientific community, Abbott was elected as vice-president of section H (anthropology) of the American Association for the Advancement of Science (Meltzer 2003). Newspapers and magazines further hailed his success, but it was short-lived and by the winter of 1889, rumors were circulating that something was amiss with Paleolithic man in New Jersey.

CAUTIONARY WORDS

By the late 1880s, most archaeologists and geologists accepted that humans of some form, whether *Homo sapiens* or an earlier species, were present in the New World during the Pleistocene. The argument for a New World Paleolithic was believed to have the same validity as that of the Old World, with almost identical artifacts, environmental conditions, and plant and animal resources. But, if the theory was true, who were these early humans in New Jersey? Abbott argued that they were not the ancestors of modern Native Americans, but instead, an earlier, primitive group that may have been different from later populations: "veritable traces of a people, who inhabited the northern Atlantic seaboard of America, prior to the advent of the Indian; if we accept the current opinion that the latter was a comparatively recent comer to our shores" (Abbott 1881:471), maybe even representing a new species (Abbott 1912:128). Putnam wasn't quite as confident on this point: "Was he of one race on the two continents [Europe and North America]? Has he left descendants or has he passed out of existence with the mammoth and the mastodon? These are questions we hope may be answered in the near future" (Putnam 1888:424).

Though Abbott thought his New Jersey Paleolithic people were autochthons, there were competing theories, with others claiming that they may have traversed the Bering Strait via ice (Dall 1877) or perhaps on a land bridge, retaining connections with Asia through migration or trade (Rau 1882). Furthermore, the specific chronology remained uncertain (Meltzer 1993). Some geologists, such as H. C. Lewis, were hedging their bets as early as 1880. Lewis agreed that the artifacts were found within the Trenton gravels, and that they probably pre-dated the more recent Native American occupation of the Delaware Valley. However, he disagreed with the ice age deposition of the sediments, unless perhaps there was a second, more recent glacial period previously undocumented (1880a, 1880b). He stated instead that these were river gravel deposits and were post-glacial: "the data obtained do not necessarily prove, geologically considered, an extreme antiquity of man in Eastern America" (Lewis 1880a:309). The geological evidence for the Trenton gravels ultimately proved to be unreliable and soon questions arose about the "paleoliths" themselves. Cracks were beginning to appear in the case of the American Paleolithic.

5

Debunking the American Paleolithic

"There is no doubt overshadowing the existence of man in the Delaware valley as long ago as the close of the glacial period: his presence, then is not merely 'a theory advanced by Dr. Abbott,' as you suggest, but a fact susceptible of actual demonstration."

--Abbott (1883d:437)

In the winter of 1889–1890, William Henry Holmes, working for the Bureau of American Ethnology (BAE), began excavations at the Piney Branch site in Washington, D.C. The site was interpreted as an example of the American Paleolithic (Wilson 1889) and contained Tertiary and Cretaceous strata with artifacts that replicated Abbott's "paleoliths" from Trenton. The artifacts were described as "chipped from quartzite pebbles, and the quartzites of the Potomac thus attest the potency of an imported fashion probably set on the Delaware" (McGee 1889b:233). Not only did "The paleolithic implements found in the District of Columbia compare favorably with those collected by Dr. Abbott at Trenton....they are equally if not more like the Chelleen implements found in Europe and Asia" (Wilson 1889:239). Piney Branch was clearly a Paleolithic site—or so it was believed.

But even during the heyday of the American Paleolithic in the 1880s, not all researchers were satisfied with this interpretation of Piney Branch. S. V. Proudfit, an attorney and member of the Anthropological Society of

Washington, was one of the first to propose otherwise. He argued, "My own conclusion as to the relics found at these points is that they are the resultant debris of Indian workshops, where material was roughly blocked out, to be afterward fashioned into knives, spearheads, &c.; and that no good reason is yet apparent for attributing their origin to paleolithic man" (1889:245). Also weighing in on the discussion, Putnam hedged his bets and concluded that more work, including careful excavation, was needed to address questions of Piney Branch's antiquity, though his skepticism did not extend to all alleged Paleolithic sites, and he fully accepted Abbott's Paleolithic claims in Trenton (1889).

William Henry Holmes was a self-taught geologist and an archaeologist, but gained acceptance into the professional scientific community first as an illustrator, sketching specimens for the Smithsonian Institution. His initial foray into the field was as the official artist for Ferdinand Vandeveer Hayden's geologic survey that included the newly-established Yellowstone National Park. His illustrations aptly depicted geologic strata and landscape features that were difficult to capture using new photographic technology, rendering Holmes an essential member of the project team (Meltzer and Dunnell 1992). During this project, and later working for the U.S. Geological Survey (USGS), Holmes also explored and documented archaeological sites such as the massive obsidian quarries of Yellowstone and Ancestral Pueblo villages in the American Southwest. In 1889, Holmes left the USGS and joined the Smithsonian Institution's BAE. With a brief stint as Curator of the Field Museum in Chicago from 1894–1897, he spent the majority of his archaeological career at the BAE.

In 1889, John Wesley Powell, the Director of the BAE and the USGS, sent Holmes into the field to investigate Piney Branch (Meltzer and Dunnell 1992:xv; Powell 1894:xxvi). Powell's motivation was only partly inspired by the need to professionally assess the presence of an American Paleolithic at the locality. More importantly, Powell needed to cement the BAE's position as a leading contributor to American archaeology and a worthy recipient of Congressional appropriations for fieldwork. In order to do this, Powell was forced to establish continuity of Native American occupation of the continent—a goal that continued the aims of Cyrus Thomas's investigations of Midwestern mounds. Thomas's mound research conclusively determined they were the product of Native American engineering, not constructions by others such as lost tribes of Israel or inhabitants of the mythical Atlantis.

Building on this success, Powell directed the BAE's efforts further back into the more distant past with the popular topic of the American Paleolithic (Meltzer 1983).

The importance of a continuity of Native American occupation through deep time was rooted in the methodological approach of the BAE to archaeology—one now known as the direct historical approach, though that term had not yet been coined during the late 19th century. This perspective works from the ethnographic known into the prehistoric unknown, using modern populations, in this case Native American people, to help understand the prehistoric past. The BAE was heavily invested in ethnographic research among Native American tribes, particularly in the western United States (Meltzer 1983:69–70). If Abbott was correct in his assessment that ancient, Paleolithic humans in the New World were a different, now extinct species of people, then this approach was not valid and the BAE would have no claim to archaeological research of the distant past (Meltzer 1983). Given the popularity of Paleolithic research in the U.S. and abroad, this could jeopardize potential funding for archaeological studies by the BAE. The stakes were high for Holmes's investigation of Piney Branch, and he approached the site with his conclusions already in mind—shaped not only by the political environment within the BAE, but also by his prior experiences on surveys with the USGS in the American West, where he recorded lithic quarrying activities similar to what he would later identify at Piney Branch (Meltzer and Dunnell 1992).

By November of 1889, after only a few months of excavation, Holmes was ready to conclude that the Piney Branch site, and by extension perhaps, all of the alleged Paleolithic artifacts found at various localities in the New World, were not evidence of a great antiquity of human occupation of the Americas, nor did they represent an extinct population, but were instead simply quarrying debris left by prehistoric, Native American inhabitants of the region (paper read before the Anthropological Society of Washington on Nov. 16, 1889, published as Holmes 1890). Holmes's conclusions were quickly published in *American Anthropologist*, a publication supported by the Anthropological Society of Washington (which later became part of the American Anthropological Association). Denying what must have been heavy pressure from the BAE for Holmes to demonstrate continuity of occupation from Native American ancestors to modern people, Holmes claimed that "the present exploration has been undertaken, without preconceived notions of what the results should be, and the conclusions are based almost entirely upon facts and arguments pertaining to and derived from my own investigation" (Holmes 1890:1). Citing previous work at Piney Branch by Wilson, McGee, and Proudfit, Holmes stated that the site contained "the material used in implement making, and here they worked, until a mass of refuse of astonishing magnitude had accumulated" (1890:4), but not an American Paleolithic.

As a geologist, archaeologist, and illustrator, Holmes conducted careful excavations and paid particular attention to the location of artifacts within geologic strata. He presented these data in meticulous profile renderings, drawings, and photographs in his publications (1890: plates 1, 2, 3), a level of detail often lacking in Abbott's work, who preferred to collect artifacts from erosional faces exposed by downcutting streams or as surface finds. Holmes carefully documented the depth and provenience of artifacts as well as natural stones and boulders within the associated sediments, using these data to interpret quarrying activity and geologic association. He further invited W J McGee, who had previously upheld Abbott's interpretations of Paleolithic occupation at Trenton (McGee 1889b), to visit the site and offer support instead for Holmes's new interpretations of the geologic strata (Holmes 1890).

The most compelling aspect of Holmes's results rested in his documentation of the lithic reduction strategies represented within the site. He argued that artifacts processed through a series of steps, from minimally worked nodules with only one or two flakes removed from them, to thin, bifacially worked blades that were "straight and symmetrical" and that their "edges should have a bevel as slight and as consistent with needful strength" (1890:13). These finished bifaces "were carried away, and that to destinies that we may yet reveal. Further work, additional shaping, if such there was, employed other processes and was carried on in other fields" (Holmes 1890:13). In his initial 1890 publication, Holmes argued for three reduction stages represented at the quarry: the first stage was unifacially flaked, the second stage was bifacially flaked, and the third stage exhibited additional bifacial thinning and shaping (1890:plate 4), setting the foundation for the way in which lithic analysts still describe bifacial reduction of quarried nodules (Andrefsky 1998; Callahan 1979; Kelly 1988; Ozbun 1991). Holmes concluded with "a pang of regret" that "our utmost effort cannot wring from them a fact or a suggestion of value upon any of the great questions of time, race, and culture" and that "what is true of the rude forms of this particular locality may be true also of all similar forms found throughout the Potomac valley" (1890:14) and clearly by extension, throughout North America. Furthermore, "geologically there is nothing to carry the history of man in this place back beyond the age of the Indian" (1890:21). His conclusion was firm: "it is impossible to show that there exists the slightest trace of any other race than the American Indian" (1890:24).

Hearing the news, at first, Abbott was frantic. He scrambled to obtain a copy of Holmes's *American Anthropologist* publication, puzzled that Holmes was now entering into the Paleolithic arena (Meltzer 1991). However, this argument was not entirely new (Proudfit 1889), and Abbott quickly downplayed the work, stating that, though it might be true for the Piney Branch site, it had no implications for the Paleolithic artifacts found near Trenton (1890a). Abbott had even addressed the question of early stage lithic reduction in a publication on the Delaware Valley more than a decade earlier when he stated that "Careful examination of a series shows that they cannot be merely roughly-outlined pieces intended for future more finished work, inasmuch as the present general character and dimensions of the great bulk of them renders additional chipping impracticable" (Abbott 1877a:248). He refuted these concerns in the past and could certainly do it again. Or so he thought.

Regardless, because the Piney Branch publication impacted Abbott's work in Trenton, he could not simply ignore it. He visited the site in May of 1890 with Holmes as a guide. The archaeological deposits at Piney Branch were impressive, with an "enormous number of 'blocked-out' quartzite and quartz implements that literally cover the ground" (Abbott 1890a:8), but Abbott disagreed with their interpretation. Not only did Holmes's theory seem implausible, because according to Abbott, "an examination of many work-shop sites show clearly that large pebbles were not gradually brought down to small points, but chips and pebbles of nearly the desired size were chosen and worked to the desired shape without that enormous waste of labor characteristic of the Piney Branch workshops" (1890a:10), but the geologic context was different too. Abbott argued that along the Delaware River, stratigraphic associations irrefutably placed the Trenton paleoliths within a Pleistocene chronology. Abbott pointed out that "the confusion that has arisen concerning the evidences of man's antiquity in America is due to the fact that too much stress has been laid upon the character of the implements found, and too little upon that of the circumstances under which they were found" (1890a:10). Whatever Holmes had found at Piney Branch, it was different and had no bearing on the Delaware Valley. And furthermore, if Holmes's allegations were true, it would "remove the paleolithic implements of Europe, Asia and Africa from the prehistoric archaeology of those continents" (Abbott 1890a:10). The unstated question being: did Holmes really want to take on *all* of the archaeological establishment, both in the U.S. and in Europe?

Employed as curator at the Penn Museum beginning in November of 1889, Abbott devoted a mere three pages of his 1890 report for the Museum's American Section (the section was at that time called the Museum of American Archaeology) to the subject of Piney Branch, and believed that that was the end of the problem. In fact, he made only passing reference in his diary that year and noted "August 22, 1890: The meeting of the Anthropological section was interesting as there was much discussion on some points in which I am interested. The evidence of two conflicting views of ancient America, such as represented by Putnam on one hand and National Museum [the Smithsonian Institution's BAE] on the other was quite amusing" (CCA/PU Box 2, Folder 3). Little did he know that this "amusing" conflict would grow into a conflagration that would bring about the demise of the American Paleolithic.

THE WASHINGTON CLIQUE'S CRITIQUE

As the debate over an American Paleolithic accelerated in the early 1890s, participants fell into two opposing camps: professional scholars affiliated with government institutions and agencies, such as the Smithsonian Institution, the BAE, the USGS, and other "Washington men," who generally did not ascribe to an American Paleolithic; and on the other side, archaeologists and geologists, some of whom were employed by academic institutions and museums, who supported the American Paleolithic, but who were often self-taught amateurs like Abbott—highly educated members of the upper class, but with unrelated credentials. The battle was between the big, powerful government and the small, independent scholar. Abbott wrote, "the scientific men in Washington claim a monopoly of knowledge and so occupy a peculiar position, self-assumed, of course" (Abbott 1892a:270), but many resented perceived bullying, criticizing the

USGS and others for "attacking and discrediting the work of individual scientific laborers [whose research] happens to have been conducted on lines
which the ruling spirits of that body do not approve" (Youmans 1893:842).
As Abbott mockingly noted, "The ghost of palaeolithic man has arisen to
plague the geologists at Washington; and those that look upon them as little
gods are all shouting 'Me, too.'" (1892a:270).

This burgeoning debate, at its core, necessitated careful re-assessment
of the evidence, which included a re-examination of the sequence and
timing of Pleistocene glaciations. Here, too, the battle was drawn along
similar party lines. On one side, government geologists, primarily working for the USGS; and on the other, the non-governmental museums, state
geologists, and independent, amateur scholars. The USGS geologists held
that there had been multiple glacial advances and retreats during the Pleistocene (McGee 1889b, 1892), while George Frederick Wright on the other
hand, adhered to the belief that only a single glaciation event occurred, and
the geologic signatures of extensive ice sheets represented a discrete period
in time (Wright 1889, 1892a).

On the surface, the question of many or one glaciation appears to have
little bearing on whether or not humans were present during the Pleistocene. Abbott, for example, did not address how many glaciations had occurred, just that Paleolithic humans were present during ice age times,
"there is abundant evidence of the presence of man dwelling at the foot
of the great glacier that occupied the valley of the Delaware, when boulders, gravel and coarse sand were being deposited in vast quantities in the
open sea, in which the southern terminus of the ice ended" (1878:245), but
whether this was the only glacier or the last glacier was somewhat irrelevant to his overall argument. However, it mattered to the geologists, and
those like Wright who threw their support behind Abbott tended to support a single glaciation, putting them at odds with the USGS geologists and
further widening the rift between the federally supported scientists and the
non-governmental, amateur scholar.

When George Frederick Wright published *Man and the Glacial Period*
in 1892, the spark that was ignited by Holmes at Piney Branch grew into
a raging inferno. Wright, who was Professor of New Testament Language
and Literature (in 1892, he was appointed Professor of the Harmony of Science and Revelation) at Oberlin Theological Seminary, argued vociferously
for a single glaciation and a Pleistocene occupation of North America, with

particular support for Abbott's work in the Delaware Valley and other Paleolithic sites in the New World. Interestingly, Wright's 1892 volume issued little new data. It summarized much of Wright's previous research originally published in 1889, which had been received with scarcely a ripple of dissent, but this time, his publication summarized the research for a popular, rather than professional, audience. Thomas Chamberlin, head of the Glacial Division of the USGS, objected strenuously to this overstepping of bounds—geologic education of a public audience was the domain of government-funded, scientifically trained, geologists, not theologians (Hinsley 1976).

The Washington crowd issued scathing reviews. W J McGee attacked Wright's authority as an untrained amateur in glacial geology, accusing him of being ignorant of new developments in the field, particularly geomorphology, which as the study of earth's features as the product of physical, chemical, or biological processes operating on the earth's surface, is specifically applicable to glacial geology. McGee wrote that "not a syllable in his latest work, or in any other of his many publications, or in his public utterances before scientific societies, suggests that he is aware of the existence of the New Geology" (1892:317). Wright simply wasn't qualified to do the work. He "is a professor of theology in a theologic seminary, yet lays claim withal to geologic skill, which serves to render his writing the more specious" (McGee 1893:86). McGee went on, stating that Wright was "incompetent to deal with geologic phenomena" (1893:94), and worse, that the introduction "is absurdly fallacious," the chapter on glacial movements "damned by error and specious misrepresentation," statements on glacial history "crude, unjust, egotistic, and a generation behind modern science," and that the final chapters demonstrated that "nothing that is true is new, and nothing that is new is true" (1893:94–95). Concluding, "Wright is a betinseled charlatan whose potions are poison. Would that science might be well rid of such harpies" (McGee 1893:95). Chamberlin, marginally more reserved than McGee, pointed out multiple errors and stated, "many like faults, of positive error, of statements so imperfect as to amount to errors, and of confusion and inconsistency of thought, characterize the whole book" (1892:304). Focusing on the Trenton artifacts, but intimating a wider critique, Chamberlin stated that "some of the most careful and discriminating geologists in this country doubt whether these chipped stones were deposited at the time the formations with which they are now connected were laid down" and summarized that "not a single find rests on expert geological testimony" (1892:304).

However, the deluge of criticism Wright's publication faced—which escalated way out of proportion to the errors it contained—may have been precipitated at least in part because he claimed scholarly authority based on a former affiliation with the USGS. Chamberlin, in his review, noted that Wright briefly worked for the USGS, and was "explicitly advised that in case he published the work, the Survey did not wish to be made in any way responsible, and a termination of relations, then only nominal, was suggested to free himself and the Survey from embarrassment" (1892:306), but Wright went ahead and published *Man and the Glacial Period* anyway, and printed his former affiliation as "Assistant on the United States Geological Survey," leading to a battle in *The Dial* enumerating exactly how many days Wright worked for the USGS and what his duties may have been (Chamberlin 1892, 1893; Wright 1892b). McGee was less polite: "the facts are, that he was temporarily employed by one of the collaborators of the bureau largely for the purpose of testing his competence as an observer; and that the test resulted unsatisfactorily to the bureau and was brought to an end several years ago" (1892:317).

Such public scientific squabbling was embarrassing, and many called for propriety (Abbott 1892a, 1892b; Cope 1893; Haynes 1893; Holmes 1893b; Wright 1892b, 1893; Youmans 1893). Youmans, editor of the journal *Popular Science Monthly*, chided government scholars: "of all arrogant things in the world official science is perhaps the most arrogant, and of all obstructive things official science is perhaps the most obstructive" (Youmans 1893:841). But as the lines were drawn between government scientists and those outside the federal funding circuit, others offered Wright their support (Brinton 1892a; Cope 1893). Notably, however, much of this support did not extend to Abbott or the American Paleolithic. Edward Drinker Cope, a paleontologist from the University of Pennsylvania, supported Wright's work and called *Man and the Glacial Period* "the best synopsis of present knowledge of the glacial epochs and its relations to human history which has yet appeared" (1893:550). His enthusiasm for the volume, however, may have been more a result of his hatred for Othniel Charles Marsh and John Wesley Powell of the USGS, who he felt had blocked access to fossils, funding, and publication (Romer 1964), rather than a strong belief in the arguments the book presented. He accused the USGS geologists of "a vigorous attack...in a way which shows an animus on their part not strictly scientific" (Cope 1893:550). His condemnation of the attacks on Wright's book as they pertained to Abbott's Paleolithic in Trenton was unfortunately less enthusiastic. "it seems that the evidence for Plistocene [*sic*] man in America, must be further investigated with careful methods, and under more favorable circumstances than are furnished by most of the so-called glacial gravels" (Cope 1893:553). Allying with Wright against the USGS was one thing, but Cope and Abbott had a distant relationship at the University of Pennsylvania, and Cope was reluctant to enthusiastically support an American Paleolithic. Yet any enemy of the government scientists was a friend, so Cope and Abbott remained collegial while their interests aligned. "December 23, 1892: I saw Cope who told me G. F. Wright had a most excellent lecture Tuesday in Philadelphia and upheld his and my view as against Holmes and McGee" (CCA/PU Box 2, Folder 3).

Similar sentiments were expressed by Daniel Garrison Brinton, who was Professor of American Linguistics and Archaeology at the University of Pennsylvania. Brinton supported the work of Wright and praised the volume on its glacial geology, stating that "the author of this volume stands among the first in this country, and his long study of that remarkable period in the geologic history of our planet invests all he says about it with uncommon authority" and the book "supplies the most compact and satisfactory exposition of our knowledge of the subject which has yet appeared—the facts carefully stated and the opinions maturely formed" (1892a:249). His review of the Paleolithic examples from Trenton and elsewhere in North America was decidedly cool, however. "That any such relics have been found under conditions which remove all doubts as to their authenticity and age is open to considerable question" and moreover, "the Trenton gravel finds require further study before we can assign their probable age" (1892a:249). Merely a short time later, however, he strengthened his claim against Abbott and stated that "a great many of what we have heretofore called 'palaeolithic implements' display with fatal clearness the peculiar earmarks of these 'quarry rejects,' hinting, therefore that they never were real implements at all" (1892b:261). Both at the University of Pennsylvania, Brinton and Abbott were not collegial. Abbott privately named him a sneak and a liar (CCA/PU Box 2, Folder 3; August 3, 1892) even before his most severe critiques went to press.

By the end of 1893, the American Paleolithic was on shaky ground. Holmes, riding the momentum gained through his Piney Branch publication, systematically dismantled the evidence from a series of widely accepted Paleolithic sites, including Little Falls, Minnesota (1892c); Madisonville, Ohio (1893b); and Trenton, New Jersey (1893c). He argued that all conclusions alleging Paleolithic occupation "based upon the discovery of rude forms of art are premature and misleading" (1892a:297) and that in quarry localities, "it is manifestly folly to attempt to select from the mass of these objects certain individual specimens to be arbitrarily called palaeolithic" (1892a:296). The artifacts were assumed to represent Paleolithic occupation based on their morphology, but "in America the conditions are such that no specimen can be safely assigned to palaeolithic culture by its form alone" (1892b:279) and accurate provenience in relation to geologic strata was crucial.

At Little Falls, Minnesota, for example, Holmes conducted controlled, stratigraphic excavations to assess the authenticity of Paleolithic claims. Prior conclusions about an American Paleolithic at Little Falls had been based on the statements of Miss Frances Babbitt, an amateur collector who found quartz bifaces similar to those published by Abbott that also replicated Paleolithic forms from Europe. These had been heralded as Paleolithic implements (Putnam 1890:159), but Holmes's careful scientific excavations into alleged glacial strata proved otherwise. He reported, "the worked quartzes are confined to the surface loams and to the heterogeneous talus gravels of the terrace, and that the shaped pieces are nothing more than the failures left by arrow-makers who may have occupied the spot at any period from glacial times down to within fifty years ago" (Holmes 1892c:281). He chided "the explanation of the unfortunate errors fallen into by the original observers is that the archaeologist identified the works of art and the geologist the geologic formations, neither thinking it necessary to determine the vital point as to whether or not the works of art were really associated with the undisturbed gravels" (1892c:281).

In Ohio, Holmes set to work on sites of alleged Paleolithic artifacts recovered by Charles L. Metz, one of Putnam's amateur collectors for the Peabody Museum at Harvard. In Loveland, gravel pits formed by the mining of fill material for the Baltimore and Ohio Railway yielded reported artifacts, but Holmes dismissed several of these specimens as perhaps representing natural, water-tumbled stones, while one bifacially flaked stone, which exhibited strong similarities to Paleolithic artifacts from Europe, was found under circumstances of questionable provenience. Holmes stated that "it is possible that Dr. Metz could have mistaken a surface mass, descended into the pit from above, for gravel in place" (1893d:151). Other artifacts presented by Metz as Paleolithic implements included a fragment of chert recovered from a cistern in Madisonville, Ohio. Metz claimed he found the artifact in gravel beneath an eight-foot-thick stratum of silt during construction of the cistern, and later sent it to the Peabody Museum where it was displayed alongside other alleged American Paleolithic artifacts. According to Holmes, however, the artifact was "identical in every essential feature with typical rejects of the modern blade-maker....To present it as evidence of Paleolithic culture is little short of folly" (1893d:154). Other artifacts, including a single alleged Paleolithic implement from Newcomerstown, Ohio, collected by W. C. Mills, was submitted to G. F. Wright who published it in his 1892 volume *Man and the Glacial Period*, and pronounced that it "resembles in so many ways the typical implements found by Boucher de Perthes, at Abbeville" (1892a:251). Holmes rejected this artifact as well, stating that though it looked very similar to Paleolithic implements from Europe, it was found in an area of eroding talus and that "it is one in which uncertainty resulting from the lack of experience and possible, I may say probable, carelessness of the collector is augmented by the treachery of the gravels" (1893d:157). All alleged Paleolithic artifacts from Ohio were summarily dismissed by Holmes's investigations and he concluded "considering the meagre and unsafe nature of these proofs, there seems little doubt that a *glacial man* for the Ohio valley has been somewhat prematurely announced and unduly paraded" (1893d:163, emphasis original).

At Trenton, Holmes conducted a careful and lengthy investigation, as Abbott's archaeological artifacts presented the most widely-accepted example of an American Paleolithic (Holmes 1893c). Conveniently, Trenton city authorities were in the middle of construction of a sewer line during Holmes's visit to Abbott's sites, resulting in a long trench that allowed extensive examination of the Trenton gravels, and a search for in situ examples of Abbott's "paleoliths" (Holmes 1893c). Holmes assigned his field assistant, William Dinwiddie, to the project, and Dinwiddie spent over a month monitoring sewer line construction and looking for any exposure that might yield Paleolithic artifacts. None were found in situ. Instead, carefully documenting erosional surfaces and drawing meticulous stratigraphic sections, Holmes asserted that Abbott's artifacts were exclusively within mixed talus deposits that could contain artifacts from any period of occupation. Instead of a secure stratigraphic context in the Trenton gravels,

Abbott's artifacts were within secondarily deposited sediments along the river banks. Furthermore, Holmes asserted, "such a talus, if art-containing, will have a large percentage of shop and quarry-shop refuse, for the reason that the exposed gravels, and the banks and beds of rivers cutting them, furnish, as a rule, a good deal of the raw material utilized by workers in stone, and the shops in which the work was done are usually located upon the slopes and outer margins of the terraces" (1893c:27). Abbott, according to Holmes, had misread the geologic context of his finds, and furthermore, had he conducted controlled archaeological excavations, as Putnam had once encouraged him to do (Hinsley 1992), would likely never have reached these specious conclusions (Holmes 1893c).

Abbott's amateur methodology proved to be the downfall of his American Paleolithic at Trenton. Holmes reproached Abbott to desist immediately with his Paleolithic claims: "It was conclusively shown that no worked stone that can with reasonable safety be called an implement has been reported from the gravels, and that it is therefore clearly useless, not to say unscientific, to go on enlarging upon the evidence of an American Paleolithic period and multiplying theoretic details of its culture" (Holmes 1893c:15). Holmes further accused, "our gravel searchers, unacquainted with the true nature of the objects collected and discussed, and little skilled in the observation of the phenomena by means of which all questions of age must be determined, have undoubtedly made grievous mistakes and have thus misled an expectant and credulous public" (Holmes 1893c:36). In other words, the amateurs made many blunders, but now that professional, government scientists like Holmes were ready to undertake an examination of the alleged Paleolithic sites, these amateurs should stop and step aside. According to Holmes, the American Paleolithic was just about finished: "if the theory of a *glacial man* can summon to its aid no better testimony than that furnished by the examples examined in this paper, the whole scheme, so elaborately mounted and so confidently proclaimed, is in imminent danger of early collapse" (Holmes 1893c:37, emphasis original).

ABBOTT'S REBUTTAL

At first, after reviewing Holmes's *American Anthropologist* (1890) article, Abbott was annoyed but expressed minimal apprehension. He felt secure in the fact that he had addressed similar concerns in the past with little difficulty, and could do it again, and that his geologic context rested on the work of someone he believed to be an established scientist in the field, namely George Frederick Wright. But by 1892, the need to defend himself and his research could not be ignored. Partly this was due to the blistering attacks on Wright, which had escalated well beyond a critique of his single glaciation theory, and by 1893, had progressed to personal insults lobbed at his credentials and experience, but the criticisms were mounting against Abbott's Trenton finds as well (McGee 1893). This was unfortunate for Abbott, as Wright had stridently defended Abbott and the American Paleolithic in the face of negative reviews (Wright 1892a, 1892b, 1893), and the two men now found themselves allied against a cadre of professional scientists backed by the power of the USGS and the BAE.

Abbott's first rebuttal was his curator's report at the Penn Museum for 1890. His response to Holmes's work was polite, but firm. Abbott proclaimed that the Delaware Valley artifacts were not identical to the quarrying debris from Piney Branch, but that even if a resemblance did occur, the fact that Piney Branch artifacts were quarrying debris did not necessarily mean that the Delaware Valley artifacts were as well. Abbott also was quick to assert that there was no evidence in Trenton that any of the Paleolithic implements were reduced further into "arrow points, drills, and scrapers of the same material" (1890a:9). Instead of indicating a flintknapping error, the thick profile of the Delaware Valley artifacts may have been an intentional feature, and any similarity between the two sites was purely coincidental. Abbott scolded that "the inferences drawn are too sweeping, and have not necessarily the bearing upon the question of man's antiquity in America, which he practically claims" (1890a:9). According to Abbott, his American Paleolithic evidence was well-established and well-proven. The burden rested on the detractors to falsify it, and in his opinion, Holmes's work only proved that the Piney Branch site was a quarry, not that the entire American Paleolithic was wrong. Furthermore, Abbott argued two years later as the debate escalated, if Paleolithic occupation existed in Europe, why could it not exist in the New World as well? "To claim that stone implements found imbedded in American gravel deposits, that are in every feature identical with those found in European gravels, are something other than palaeolithic, and yet assent to the proposition of the existence of palaeolithic man, is simple silliness and not science" (1892b:5). To the chorus of naysayers, Abbott issued his challenge "what is needed in these overcrowded latter days is a proof that palaeolithic man is an impossibility. When this is forth-coming, and not until then, will the student of early man in America haul down his flag" (1892c:345).

Abbott decided that one way to substantiate his argument was to find more evidence in the Delaware Valley within contexts more similar to the Paleolithic in Europe. If Brixham Cave in England could prove the validity of Paleolithic occupation there (Grayson 1983, 1990:10; van Riper 1993), then perhaps a similar site existed in the United States. In order to address this, in the summer of 1890, Abbott commenced a new field project focused on the exploration of cave and rockshelter sites in the upper Delaware Valley. Just like in Europe, suggested Abbott, cave sites would hold clear, stratigraphi-cally undisturbed evidence of humans in direct association with glacial ani-mals. However, it's open to question how much time Abbott actually spent on this endeavor, since his diaries instead detailed a trip to Arizona with his son, Richard, in July, and later a trip to Indianapolis in August (CCA/PU Box 3, Folder 2; July and August 1890). And his curator's report reiterated this, stating that he did not conduct much fieldwork because "I was absent in Arizona and in Indiana, and fully occupied with museum work when at home" (1890a:12). In fact, Abbott's diaries and field notes contained no dis-cussion of a trip to rockshelter sites during the summer of 1890—there's a hiatus in his diary entries from the end of 1889 until June 16, 1890 (CCA/PU Box 3, Folder 2)—and his curator's report on the expenditures slated for fieldwork stated that "many unforeseen difficulties arose; still, the work was not wholly abandoned, although only negative results were obtained, if we consider as a negative result the fact that no examples of stone or bone im-plements were procured" (1890a:11). He spent at least some of the funds ear-marked for cave exploration to purchase collections from Florida and North Carolina instead (1890a:12). However, he requested additional funding for the following season anyway, and stated "I trust that means will be available for a continuance of this cave-hunting in the upper valley of the Delaware, for doubtless abundant evidences of man's great antiquity in this region will ultimately be brought to light" (1890a:11). He bizarrely concluded that "as to the expense involved, it is proper to remark, in this connection, that the cost is the same whether there be tangible results or not" (1890a:11).

Tangible results did not appear to be forthcoming, and the first expedi-tion was "profitable principally in experience and far less than I had hoped in additions to the museum" (Abbott 1890a:11). No alleged Pleistocene deposits were identified in cave and rockshelter sites of the upper Delaware Valley. Disappointed, Abbott returned to his old stomping grounds closer to Trenton the following summer, and conducted additional field-work focused on two islands in the Delaware River, figuring that he would have better luck corroborating claims about the American Paleolithic in more familiar geographic territory. At Burlington Island, in the Delaware River, Abbott noted "a foundation of coarse gravel intermingled with large boulders" and within it "the occurrence of rudely fashioned stone imple-ments" (1892b:3). The Paleolithic artifacts at this locality, according to Abbott, were easily distinguishable from later, Native American occupa-tion not only because of their unique morphology, identical to those from Europe, but also because, he claimed, they were exclusively made of ar-gillite (1892b). Argillite, he believed, was used prior to jasper, quartz, and other cryptocrystalline lithic materials. Even the spearpoints made of ar-gillite must pre-date those of other kinds of stone. "An argillite-using man wandered far and wide over this country long before the use of jasper and quartz became so universal" (Abbott 1892b:12). More recent Native Ameri-can sites were also found, and some did contain argillite, but the absence of other materials in the argillite-bearing strata seemed to offer additional proof of Paleolithic occupation (Abbott 1892b). Geologists and archaeolo-gists were invited to visit Trenton and search for Paleolithic artifacts them-selves, but several years earlier, Abbott was accused of salting the fields ahead of experts' visits and, with claims that no one else had ever found Paleolithic artifacts in the Trenton gravels, he was deemed untrustworthy as a guide (Meltzer 2003:82, 2015:147–148). However, Wright disputed this: "Dr. Abbott is not the only competent person who has discovered imple-ments at Trenton in undisturbed gravel" (Wright 1893:66), but Lucien Carr and Professor J. D. Whitney also "found several implements at Trenton, one of which was in place 'under such circumstances that it must have been deposited at the time the containing bed was laid down'" (quoting Carr in Wright 1893:66).

Seeking other ways to support the American Paleolithic, and trying to find an argument that would stick, Abbott also drew attention to the lack of other types of artifacts in association with the alleged Paleolithic arti-facts. He asked "are we to suppose the Indian never went to the water's edge for any other purpose? Did he not take his finished implements to the river to fish and hunt?...are we to assume that never a knife, arrow-point, bead, or pot was lost?" (1892a:271). Though Abbott was not excavating stratigraphically—his finds were often from erosional faces, river banks, or open fields—he claimed a dearth of artifacts other than those of presumed Pleistocene age, which he interpreted to indicate different chronological periods. If such artifacts were ever found in these strata, he boasted, "I am willing to leave the field as fast as my short legs will permit, and not before" (1892a:271). Holmes rose to the challenge (Holmes 1893c).

Marshalling his defense, Abbott emphasized the geologic context of the Paleolithic artifacts that were found, at least according to Abbott, in situ in the Trenton gravels, but he had relied heavily on Wright (Wright 1881, 1882, 1889, 1892a, 1892b). These gravels, Abbott insisted, were "the direct result of the melting of the glaciers, as they retired northward" (Abbott 1888a:104). But Abbott was not a geologist, and trusting Wright for the geologic assessment of the sediments along the Delaware River may have been a mistake. He had even acknowledged as late as 1888 that many differing opinions had been voiced about the geologic context. "It was not only an instance of many men of many minds, but occasionally the same individual with numerous opinions" (1888b:303), but still designated Wright as his authority. When Wright's work received such harsh criticism in the early 1890s, Abbott was left with little support for the geologic context and difficulty substantiating great antiquity without it. Furthermore, both Wright and Abbott were untrained amateurs in their respective fields, and the Washington professionals who dismantled their research quickly labeled them as dabblers, not scientists.

As concerns about the validity of Abbott's work at Trenton escalated, Frederic Ward Putnam at the Peabody Museum hired Ernest Volk, a local Trentonian, in the fall of 1889 to replicate much of Abbott's field research, ideally with more scientific rigor. Volk was also an untrained amateur, but Putnam hoped he would prove a more malleable amateur than Abbott had been. His task was "simply to ascertain if there are unquestionable evidences of man's occupation at the time contemporary with the deposits during any portion of the glacial period and its immediate close" (Putnam 1911:v). Abbott attempted to stay away, unsuccessfully, as Volk's excavations were at times directly under his window (Meltzer 2015:194, and for example: "April 17, 1899: went to west side of gully where Volk is digging for relics of Indians. There until noon and again there much of the afternoon", "April 21, 1899: went to Volk's diggings and staid until dinner was ready.

After dinner, went again after a nap", and "April 26, 1899: At Volk's diggings both before and after dinner" [CCA/PU Box 4, Folder 1]), realizing however, that any perception that he was influencing Volk would cast doubt on Volk's conclusions. Volk conducted extensive work in the neighborhood around Three Beeches, most notably in the Lalor fields of a neighboring farm, but despite Abbott's urgings to Putnam to get Volk's work into print, almost twenty years passed before anything was published. When the final report was ultimately released, it was too late to weigh in on the heated debate of the 1890s. Though Volk claimed to have established that "the conclusive evidence so eagerly demanded and with so much difficulty secured asserts the antiquity of man on this continent at least as far back as the time of these glacial deposits in the Delaware Valley" (Volk 1911:128), it made little difference for Abbott at that point.

THE LAST GASP OF THE AMERICAN PALEOLITHIC

Abbott proved to be a very thin-skinned scientist who did not handle criticism well. He viewed McGee's condemnation of Wright and the larger American Paleolithic as betrayal—McGee had formerly supported the American Paleolithic. As late as 1887, McGee visited Abbott at Trenton and viewed the stratigraphic deposits alleged to contain Paleolithic artifacts, though no "paleoliths" were found during his visit. Abbott crowed in his diary "August 21, 1887: McGee and Wilson were more than ever impressed with what they saw today and the finds were very satisfactory. They were pleased with the whole trip and McGee will report at Washington to an effect that will astonish a certain clique, if I am not greatly mistaken" (CCA/PU Box 2, Folder 2). Not long afterward, Abbott stated that geologists Nathaniel S. Shaler, Thomas Belt, Josiah D. Whitney, George Frederick Wright, Raphael Pumpelly, W J McGee, Henry Carvill Lewis, and George H. Cook, had all visited the gravels and were "practically one in their view that the gravel deposits are so far ancient as to be very significant as to whatever traces of man or other mammals they may contain" (1888b:298), and further that with regard to the artifacts in question, William B. Dawkins, Edward B. Tylor, Frederic Ward Putnam, Edward Morse, Henry W. Haynes, Thomas Wilson, and B. F. De Costa "have all been more or less successful in finding traces of palaeolithic man in this river valley, and admit without qualification, his former presence" (Abbott 1888b:298). So when some of these men later published papers questioning the Trenton artifacts and their glacial context, Abbott viewed it as a personal betrayal, though he may have greatly exaggerated the testimony of his panel of experts (for an example, see discussion in Meltzer 2015:52–53).

Even within his own institution—by the early 1890s, Abbott was working as curator at the Penn Museum—Daniel Brinton published thinly-veiled insults directed towards Abbott's work. "For two or three years past there has been in the air—I mean the air which archaeologists breathe—a low but menacing sound, threatening some dear theories and tall structures, built, if not on sand, at least on gravels offering a scarcely more secure foundation" (Brinton 1892b:260). In rebuttal, Abbott's statements grew acerbic. "palaeolithic man is not to be downed even by such an array of notables marshalled to defeat him. Salisbury's cunning argumentation. McGee's shaggy front, Holmes's imperious 'begone!' and Brinton's persuasive smile do not make him afraid. He returned to earth in his own good time and came to stay!" (Abbott 1892a:270). He even took on McGee and Holmes in verse:

> *The stones are inspected*
> *And Holmes cries 'rejected,*
> > *They're nothing but Indian chips'*
> *He glanced at the ground*
> *Truth, fancied he found,*
> > *And homeward to Washington skips.*

> *They got there by chance,*
> *He saw at a glance*
> > *And turned up his nose at the series;*
> *'They've no other history,*
> *I've solved the whole mystery,*
> > *And to argue the point only wearies.'*

> *But the gravel is old,*
> *At least, so I'm told;*
> > *"Halt, halt!" cries out W. J.,*
> *'It may be very recent,*
> *And it isn't quite decent,*
> > *For me not to have my own way.'*

So dear W. J.
There is no more to say,
    Because you will never agree,
That anything's truth
But what issues, forsooth,
    From Holmes or the brain of McGee

(Abbott 1892c:345)

McGee responded, but saved his nastiest comments for Wright. "So long as poor human nature remains as it is, the knave and the dupe we shall always have with us; and it is to be regretted that a presumably competent authority in his own specialty of theology should be willing to assume either role in another line of activity" (McGee 1892:317). Seeking the moral high ground, Wright countered that "I have no complaint to make of sharp and searching criticism, because I know that it is by such processes that our individual errors of judgement are corrected and that the real facts clearly emerge. I only hope that courtesy and candor may prevail" (1892b:380).

Holmes also jumped into the fray. He stated that he attempted to present arguments based on *evidence* and not descend into the mud-slinging, but that "the generalized statements by means of which I attempted to describe the old archaeology are not sufficiently trenchant to be effective" so he would have to be more forceful (1893b:135). He joined the offensive against Abbott by "raising the question of competency" of those who studied the American Paleolithic and suggesting some held a "pedigree that appears to be shaky" (1893b:135–136), deliberately highlighting Abbott's amateur status.

Others explicitly defended Abbott and the geological work by Wright. Henry Haynes, a fellow amateur working in Mesopotamia and the Mediterranean took Abbott's side against the geologists, largely on the belief that geologists should not speak with authority about archaeological problems, but also criticizing the way in which they were doing it, saying that "they have put forward this preposterous claim in the most offensive and contemptuous manner possible, using language in regard to those who differ from them such as no gentleman would employ, and wrapping up their conceited ignorance in a cloud of fustian, which appears to pass for philosophical writing in the atmosphere which surrounds them" (Haynes 1893:67). He argued that Abbott could easily recognize the difference between quarry debris or rejects and Paleolithic implements, stating that "no competent archaeologist would ever confound one with the other" (Haynes 1893:66).

The Washington crowd fought with personal insults towards Haynes, Abbott, and Wright, criticizing their training, field methods, and credentials. Holmes wrote in a cutting response to Haynes:

> I have carefully sought references to original observations on the glacial archaeology of this country, and find to my surprise that they are limited to two lines and a quarter of text. These lines include, also, reference to the discoveries of Professor Wright, Dr. Abbott, and two others present on the occasion. The record reads as follows: 'several implements were taken by the others, *either from the gravel, or the talus* on the river bank, in my presence, and *I found five myself.*' The italics are my own, and call attention to essential features of the finds and to the fact that Mr. Haynes's investigations are expressed in five words— quite sufficient no doubt for the presentation of the matter (Holmes 1893b:135, emphasis original).

Furthermore, according to Holmes, "his most pronounced shortcoming is, however, in the line of original research; when the three lines recording his complete achievements in the American field are cut down to five words, as quoted above, and these words reduced to their *real bearing* upon the question of glacial man in America, we have only the punctuation left!" (Holmes 1893b:135).

Abbott's anger soon boiled over and his target extended beyond the individuals arguing in print to include the scholarly journals themselves. He felt that journals were favoring the Washington critics, rather than presenting both sides of the debate and scolded the journal editors for "disgraceful articles in pretentious periodicals, written by persons wholly ignorant of the subject. It is a blot upon American letters that the editors should solicit from incompetency, however prominent politically, articles that their authors know are misleading. Unfortunately, the public cannot always discriminate" (Abbott 1892b:2). As Abbott sulked and withdrew, he soon found himself not only isolated, but also unemployed. The Penn

Museum terminated his position as curator at the end of 1893. With this insult added to professional injury, Abbott simply refused to attend scholarly meetings to defend his position. Warren K. Moorehead sent pleading letters:

> No one will be there to defend Trenton. You *must* do it. Whether you want to or not, if you are silent the argument goes against you—it is fight *now* or *die*! I know whereof I speak and write no idle words. The others have strong arguments and they are going to project them. The whole archaeological world is stirred up on this matter. Now is the opportunity for an open, honest debate" (May 17, 1893, WKM-CCA, letter on file Penn Museum Archives, General Correspondence 1892–1894, Administrative Records, folder 3).

When Abbott further refused, Moorehead scolded more strongly. "I have your letter. I am sorry you do not look at the matter as we do, of course if you do not read your side will have no champion. You cannot justly ignore your opponents, there are some good men against you. They will be heard in full at Madison. The discussion is not for momentary applause, it is to be profound, complete and withal a gentlemanly debate. I do not see how you can so lightly pass it over" but Abbott remained unmoved, leaving his adherents frustrated with his sullen behavior. "Who could better defend the Delaware P. M. than the one who made the discoveries? And if *he* does not defend him a great many foreign and American gentlemen will return home disappointed (June 1, 1893, WKM-CCA, letter on file Penn Museum Archives, General Correspondence 1892–1894, Administrative Records, folder 3).

At that point, Abbott largely relinquished the public battle over the American Paleolithic to others, though he returned to the subject almost twenty years later with statements in his three volume *Archaeologia Nova Caesarea* (1907, 1908, 1909) and his penultimate book on archaeology, *Ten Years' Diggings in Lenape Land* (1912). He never wavered in his beliefs about the antiquity of humans in the New World, however he lamented in his journal, "January 15, 1893: Wright writes about the paleolithic discussion and I am sorry that he pays so much attention to it. The facts of the case are ours and let the mud-slingers have their theories" (CCA/PU Box 2 Folder 3).

LALOR FIELDS

Ernest Volk's extensive excavations around Three Beeches, specifically in the neighboring Lalor fields, funded through support by Frederic Ward Putnam of the Peabody Museum and American Museum of Natural History, yielded intriguing data consisting of argillite and other artifacts in disputed sediments. Putnam presented Volk's research at the American Association for the Advancement of Science meetings in 1896, concluding that the artifacts' provenience supported a great antiquity of human occupation in Trenton. McGee and Brinton, who were in attendance at the meeting, disputed these claims, as they had done in the past. Given Volk's continuing excavations there, McGee decided to mount an expedition to Trenton that summer with Holmes and geologist Rollin D. Salisbury in order to disprove the alleged antiquity of the "paleoliths" once and for all—again. Meanwhile, however, Henry Mercer and Wright made their own plans to visit Volk's excavations in the company of geologists Arthur Hollick and Harrison Allen, to again assess the stratigraphic context and the age of the sediments in the hopes of finding better evidence to support a great antiquity of the argillite artifacts (Meltzer 2015:184–185).

Because the Lalor fields excavations were a short distance from his front door, Abbott joined Mercer, Wright, and Volk. "June 25, 1897: I walked to Lalor's and waited on their hilltop until noon and when about to come home, Volk came with Geo F. Wright, H. C. Mercer and Arthur Hollick, Prof of Geology at Columbia College. We dug and explored until 6pm. The finds were few but significant" (CCA/PU Box 4, Folder 1). And the next day, "June 26, 1897: soon after breakfast I went to Lalor's and got to the diggings about the time the party of yesterday reached the spot. We commenced work without delay and dug in various pits until noon when we lunched on the hillside. Commencing soon again much was done up to 4:30pm, when Mr. Hollick left for New York and a general clearing up and taking account of stock was done. Soon after, we took a circuitous route homeward visiting a gravel pit near by which was of great interest....the finds of today were even more satisfactory than those of yesterday and Mr. Hollick, Wright and Mercer were all satisfied with them as evidences of man's activity in the Valley of the Delaware at a very remote time" (CCA/PU Box 4, Folder 1). Abbott gloated, "June 27, 1897: found Dr. Harrison Allen of Philadelphia, Dr. Norton of Trenton and Volk. We had a long talk about the gravel. Volk found a paleolith as we were coming away....Dr. Allen admitted he was 'convinced'" (CCA/PU Box 4, Folder 1).

Putnam received the news that the excavations satisfied the project team that the argillite artifacts were indeed in situ in the yellow sands, which were of glacial age, and agreed to participate in a session at the American Association for the Advancement of Science meetings the following year, but Mercer wanted to publish the results right away (Meltzer 2015). Putnam discouraged him, partly because he wanted to make a splash at the meetings, but more likely, because he needed to justify the fieldwork expense to high-profile donors, and the conference was a better venue to garner attention from a bigger audience (Meltzer 2015).

Meanwhile, McGee, Holmes, and Salisbury's expedition went to Trenton to perform their own assessment. Abbott, who was well aware of the steady stream of visitors to the Lalor fields, was certain they would be convinced of the authenticity of his Paleolithic claims. He wrote to his friend, Mrs. Robins, that "It satisfied everybody that I was right and the Kickers have nothing left to Kick about, but of course from force of habit, lack of decency, and want of candor, they will kick, but who cares? I can lead in archaeology where the most of them can't so much as follow. Really, there's nothing more to tell. They came, they saw, they were conquered" (CCA-JSR/PANS; July 1, 1897).

In August of 1897, the results were presented at the American Association for the Advancement of Science meetings in Detroit, and two weeks later, a second session to discuss the American Paleolithic occurred in Toronto at the British Association for the Advancement of Science meetings, attended by quite a few participants from Detroit. Debates raged about the yellow sands—were they eolian? Fluvial? Primary or secondary deposits? And furthermore, were the artifacts found within these sands in their primary context or intrusive into deeper strata?

Yet again, opponents fell along party lines, with amateur archaeologists and geologists like Wright, Abbott, and Volk (Putnam advocated for Abbott and Volk in absentia) supporting an American Paleolithic, and government and university scholars such as Holmes, McGee, and Salisbury denouncing a great antiquity at Trenton. According to McGee, meeting attendees were swayed by the convincing arguments of Holmes and Salisbury, who claimed that the artifacts were intrusive and not contemporaneous with a glacial period. However, Wright allegedly wrote to Volk immediately afterward that "objectors to antiquity in Lalor field were squelched at Detroit meeting" (CCA/PU Box 4, Folder 1; August 5, 1897).

In Toronto, the outcome was even more catastrophic for the American Paleolithic. Sir John Evans, whose book *Ancient Stone Implements of Great Britain* (1872) Abbott used as a model for *Primitive Industry* (1881), reviewed alleged paleolithic artifacts that Putnam brought with him to the meeting and proclaimed them Neolithic, rather than Paleolithic. A review of the meeting summed up that he "declined to believe in the existence of Paleolithic implements in America comparable to those of the river-drift of England and France" (Chamberlain 1897:582). Abbott was corresponding with Evans since at least 1874 and sent him over sixty artifacts, those in the Pitt Rivers Museum at Oxford, so the declaration was a blow. However, he persisted in his belief that the American Paleolithic would ultimately succeed, particularly with the work Volk was doing at Lalor fields. But Abbott blamed Putnam for keeping Volk's exculpatory data private. Volk, he said, had made "extraordinary suggestive finds and his specimens, notes and photos remain boxed up indefinitely" arguing that it "is not only cruel to me, but unfair to the whole scientific world" (CCA to FWP, April 26, 1899, as cited in Kraft 1993:8).

A POSTSCRIPT TO ABBOTT'S AMERICAN PALEOLITHIC

Abbott's Three Beeches farm never yielded the evidence of Pleistocene occupation that Abbott had alleged more than a century and a half ago. In the 1990s, a project within the Abbott Farm National Historic Landmark recovered a Paleoindian fluted point (Bello and Pagoulatos 1995), but nothing that dated to a Pleistocene age. In fact, none of the extensive archaeological investigations conducted later by Ernest Volk, Dorothy Cross, Louis Berger and Associates, and others revealed any evidence of an American Paleolithic, despite excavations that extended well into the deeper levels of the Trenton gravels. Instead, artifacts were associated with later periods of prehistory, not a glacial or immediately post-glacial occupation as Abbott had argued more than a century before.

More than seven years after Abbott's death, archaeologists finally discovered and documented indisputable evidence of human antiquity in the New World during the Pleistocene. Unfortunately for Abbott, it didn't come from Trenton, New Jersey, but instead from a Pleistocene bison kill site near Folsom, New Mexico. The Folsom site, excavated in the mid-1920s, contained distinctive fluted points in direct association with Pleistocene bison. These spearpoints were vastly different from the alleged Paleolithic artifacts that were argued by Abbott and others to be the hallmark of Pleistocene occupation in the New World, but their discovery in situ embedded between the ribs of an ice age mammal left little room for doubt (Figgins 1935; Meltzer 2015). Pleistocene occupation of the New World was proven, but it did not look anything at all like Abbott's vision.

Soon after Folsom was discovered, other Paleoindian sites also were revealed. Sites like Blackwater Draw, New Mexico, containing Clovis points that date to approximately 13,000 years ago, was excavated in 1932 (Howard 1935, 1939), and others including Meadowcroft Rockshelter, in Pennsylvania (Adovasio et al. 1978, 1990; 1999); the Topper Site, in South Carolina (Goodyear and Steffy 2003); Cactus Hill, Virginia (McAvoy and McAvoy 1997); Manis Mastodon, in Sequim, Washington (Gustafson et al. 1979); and others place humans in the New World in the latter years of the last glaciation.

Today, there is little doubt that the earliest humans in the New World were ancestors of Native American peoples. Abbott's theory that his *Homo delawarensis*, may have arrived prior to Native Americans was easily falsified, and seemed to have gained little traction in the 19th century anyway. Now the debate revolves around when and how early humans arrived in the Americas and what that route (or routes) may have been (Anderson 1990, 1996, 2005; Bradley and Stanford 2004; Goebel et al. 2008; Goodyear 2005; Haynes 2002; Lepper and Meltzer 1991; Meltzer 1988, 2002, 2004; Pitblado 2011; Smallwood 2012; Stanford 1991; Tankersley 2004). Ongoing research, including modern techniques of analyzing genetic data, may ultimately reveal a surprisingly complex picture of human migration, settlement, and technological development.

6

The Penn Museum
of Archaeology and Anthropology

A scant three weeks before William Henry Holmes delivered his first presentation to the Anthropological Society of Washington to discuss preliminary results from excavations at Piney Branch, Charles Conrad Abbott was approached with a job offer from the nascent University of Pennsylvania Museum of Archaeology and Anthropology (now the Penn Museum), soon to open in Philadelphia. Had the timing been delayed by even a few months, Abbott may have never received the offer, but in the summer and early fall of 1889, Abbott's archaeological reputation rested on a solid foundation. He had conclusively—or so it was thought—documented a Paleolithic in the New World that rivaled that of the Old World, and, in large part for recognition of his work on the American Paleolithic at Trenton, was recently elected vice president of Section H of the American Association for the Advancement of Science. Professionally, things were going well for Abbott. Financially, he remained destitute.

Though still collecting for the Peabody Museum at Harvard with funding provided by Frederic Ward Putnam, Abbott's financial difficulties through the 1880s remained unchanged, despite archaeological fame. He continued to support his family with a meager farm income, odd jobs, and small royalty payments from his natural history publications. A job offer in Philadelphia was ideal, as it would provide financial security and keep Abbott close to the Delaware Valley sites that he knew best. At the Penn Museum, he would have the opportunity to create collections and exhibits in much the same way that his mentor, Frederic Ward Putnam, had grown the Peabody Museum at Harvard University, albeit without the endowment. Finally, Abbott felt he had gained a long sought-after acceptance into the professional scholarly community.

Abbott was lucky to have received the offer. In the late 1880s and early 1890s, the field of archaeology made significant strides towards professionalization: Harvard University would grant their first Ph.D. in archaeology in 1894, leading to new educational expectations for those seeking entry into the upper echelons of the discipline (Kehoe 1999:5); the Smithsonian Institution publicized advances in archaeological methods in their annual report, resulting in new standards for research (Trigger 1989); and newly formed professional societies proliferated and created opportunities to share research findings with other experts (Trigger 1989). Archaeology was becoming a profession. An elite cadre, primarily made up of government and academic archaeologists, perpetuated the growing rift between amateur and professional that expanded with the burgeoning debate over an American Paleolithic, and by their actions, they ensured the exclusion of those who were not members. But with employment at the University of Pennsylvania's new archaeological museum, Abbott finally achieved professional status. His success was short-lived, however. Abbott's lack of curatorial expertise, irascible personality, abysmal work ethic, and the ultimate downfall of an American Paleolithic soon led to his termination from the Museum.

THE JOB OFFER

In October 1889, Abbott received an invitation to meet with a committee of scholars and administrators to discuss plans for a new museum of archaeology at the University of Pennsylvania. He immediately contacted Putnam with concerns that such a meeting would constitute a conflict of interest, given his ongoing affiliation with the Peabody Museum at Harvard. "Now, please understand one thing at the outset. I am invited to give my view as to methods of field work &c., and I do not see how I can refuse, as there will be soon an exhaustive survey (archaeological) of vicinity of Philadelphia and they have piles of money to do it" (CCA to FWP, October 16, 1889, as cited in Hinsley 1992). Putnam did not object, and the meeting took place one week later. Abbott recorded in his diary:

October 23, 1889: Ed took me to town and at 4:58, I went to Philadelphia. At 7pm, presented myself to Macauley at the Philadelphia Club,
where I met Drs. Pepper, Leidy, Jayne, Somerville, and Brinton, and also
Cope, Bennett and Macauley the host. After an elaborate dinner (which
made me sick), the "business" of the occasion was brought up and I was
prominently mentioned in connection with the proposed Museum at
the University of Pennsylvania. There was a vast deal said by Pepper,
and I was called on to reply. I spoke very guardedly, thinking of Putnam
as I did so, and bound not to be disloyal to Peabody. Dr. Pepper and
Brinton seemed very desirous I should take a position, and I could not
but consider such a matter seriously (CCA/PU Box 2, Folder 2).

Little did Abbott realize, but while negotiations were ongoing, Putnam
was in private communication with University of Pennsylvania Provost
William Pepper to recommend Abbott for the position. He wrote to Pepper
that at the Peabody Museum, Putnam was able to support Abbott's research
into the American Paleolithic, but "now that the scientific world gives him
the full credit he so richly deserves, and he is offered an honorable position
by the University of Pennsylvania, I am filled with happiness for his sake"
(FWP to William Pepper, October 28, 1889, as cited in Hinsley 1988). Yet he
quietly cautioned Pepper about Abbott's sensitive ego, stating that he was "a
singular man, and one who has to be treated differently from common mor-
tals," but that if treated well, and with the respect he and his scholarship
deserved, Pepper would gain someone who would "work hard for your new
museum....and you will have an important man for its development" (FWP
to WP, November 8, 1889, as cited in Hinsley 1988).

Despite Putnam's reassurances of support, Abbott remained concerned
that an affiliation with the University of Pennsylvania would offend Putnam
and harm his relationship with Harvard. Upon leaving his initial meeting
with the Museum founders, Abbott returned to Three Beeches accompanied by Daniel Garrison Brinton and fortuitously discovered Putnam in his
neighborhood meeting with Ernest Volk to investigate a railroad cut for archaeological specimens. Abbott discussed the job offer in more detail with
Putnam and gained confidence that his acceptance would not burn bridges
with the Peabody. He recorded in his diary that "October 24, 1889: Volk and
Brinton in loose gravel each found a fine paleolithic implement. Then we
went to Volk's house and examined the "finds" he had previously made....

Gave evening to long talk about the matters that transpired yesterday in Philadelphia and I wrote my terms to Brinton as he requested" (CCA/PU Box 2, Folder 2).

Abbott negotiated the terms of employment over the following week and returned to Philadelphia to finalize his contract. "November 1, 1889: Went directly to Philadelphia Club and finding Macauley, had a long talk with him about Brinton's letter and found a bit of fear on my part was groundless. Then we walked up Walnut St. and called at Brinton's but finding he was out, went to Dr. Pepper's and had a talk with him. The doubts, difficulties and odds and ends of detail are all cleared away now and I am supposed to be at work in the interests of the new museum" (CCA/PU Box 2, Folder 2). Finally, two weeks later, he learned that the job was officially his. "November 13, 1889: Had a long conference with Dr. Pepper and he said the appointment was made by him, then and there, to date from Nov. 1, so I left him at last, duly authorized to say I am the Curator of the American Archaeological Museum of the University of Pennsylvania" (CCA/PU Box 2, Folder 2).

Abbott negotiated a salary of $1000 per year, a large sum considering that he was the only salaried curator of four at the start of the Museum and that he had virtually no curatorial experience (Horan 1992; Madiera 1964). His position at the Peabody Museum was largely one of field collector, though he did oversee the display and arrangement of his collections there, but that gave him little background to perform the duties of curator. He relied heavily on Putnam for advice and guidance, and modeled his annual reports directly on those from the Peabody Museum. In many ways, he approached the job as he did the position of field collector at the Peabody—collecting artifacts himself when the opportunity arose and negotiating the purchase or donation of materials collected by others. "I entered upon my duties and arranged, so far as it was practicable, the material then in my charge, cataloging and numbering each specimen. As this work did not occupy all my time...frequent excursions were made to various promising fields in the vicinity of Philadelphia, and many valuable archaeological specimens were secured" (Abbott 1890a:5). But these were not Abbott's Three Beeches fields that he knew so well. He rented a house at 219 Clinton Street in Trenton for one year after gaining the position as curator, and then beginning on November 27, 1890, lived in Bristol, Pennsylvania, where he resided with his family for the remainder of his employment in Philadelphia.

In recognition for his years of service at Harvard, Putnam pressed the Peabody Museum Board of Trustees to pass a resolution thanking Abbott and congratulating him on the new appointment "a position to which we consider him fully entitled, not only as the discoverer of Palaeolithic man in the Delaware valley, but also by his many and important contributions to American archaeology" (Robert C. Winthrop, Chairman of the Trustees of the Peabody Museum of American Archaeology and Ethnology. Boston, Nov. 21, 1889 [Putnam 1891:72]) to which Abbott commented "November 23, 1889: got the resolutions referred to by Putnam yesterday. They are very neatly worded and I am glad a copy was sent to Dr. Pepper" (CCA/PU Box 2, Folder 2).

Abbott believed that the curator position was his just reward for decades of unrecognized toil in archaeology and the solution to his problems, both financial and scholarly. Finally, he would have an academic home that rewarded his efforts in the field and provided the freedom to create an archaeological museum rivaling those at other institutions. In his diary, he recorded "November 17, 1889: it is a position where a man can be himself and not at the beck and nod of a pack of nincompoops," yet things soon deteriorated. In the margin of this entry he later recorded "Three years after! Not so sure now we can ever be rid of damned fools. Plenty of them about the museum and I have to use up time fighting them" (CCA/PU Box 2, Folder 2).

A NEW MUSEUM OF ARCHAEOLOGY

Founded in 1751 by Benjamin Franklin as the "Publick Academy of Philadelphia," the earliest iteration of the University of Pennsylvania was designed to provide higher education in both the Classics and more pragmatic skills. In 1791, Penn gained its current name and became the only non-religious university in the United States at that time. By the mid-19th century, Penn transformed itself into a world class institution and moved from Center City Philadelphia to its current location west of the Schuylkill River, adding the Law School and the School of Engineering and Applied Science in the early 1850s. During a late-19th century period of intellectual excitement, the University grew rapidly, adding the School of Dentistry, the Wharton School of Business, the Veterinary School, and the School of Fine Arts over twelve years between 1878 and 1890.

In the years following the Civil War, Philadelphia experienced a renaissance of science, art, architecture, and culture. In 1876, the Centennial Exposition introduced the American and international public to a cosmopolitan city that unfortunately still lagged behind its European counterparts in cultural and scholarly institutions. A few of the wealthy Philadelphia elite and members of the intellectual leadership aspired to rectify this deficiency by encouraging their peers to donate money and assets. The University of Pennsylvania was a privileged beneficiary of many of these donations, though occasionally through backdoor affiliated organizations (Hinsley 2003).

Taking advantage of this momentum and philanthropic largess, Provost William Pepper, who served the University between 1881 and 1894, spearheaded an initiative to bring a museum of archaeology to Penn. Pepper initially approached the Philadelphia Academy of Natural Sciences about relocating to the University as its archaeological museum, but the Academy declined, leaving Pepper frustrated and forced to develop a museum from scratch (Winegrad 1993). In 1887, additional incentive to create an archaeological museum arose. A group of men approached Pepper with the proposal to mount an archaeological expedition to Nippur, Iraq, led by Penn faculty John Punnett Peters and Hermann Volrath Hilprecht, and expedition photographer John Henry Haynes. Pepper agreed to provide a fire-proof facility to house artifacts from the expedition upon their return to the United States. The Nippur project provided the stimulus that Pepper needed to establish an academic Department of Archaeology and Paleontology, a fund-raising organization in the form of the University Archaeological Association, and a University Museum.

In 1886, Daniel Garrison Brinton was appointed Professor of Archaeology and Linguistics, becoming the first official faculty member of the new academic program. Brinton was particularly well known for his support and analysis of a purported Lenape (Delaware) Native American text called the *Walam Olum*, which, in the 19th and 20th century, was believed to represent a historical account of prehistoric events and legends of the Delaware Nation (Brinton 1885). More recent analyses, many with the assistance of Lenape speakers, have demonstrated the *Walam Olum* to be a hoax, perpetuated by its alleged discoverer Constantine Samuel Rafinesque (Newman 2010; Warren 2005). At the time of his tenure on the faculty, however, Brinton was considered a preeminent scholar of Native American language and culture.

Like many faculty in the Department of Anthropology at the University of Pennsylvania, even today, Brinton's appointment soon included affiliation with the nascent University Museum, a position that gave him influence over Abbott and contributed to their antagonistic relationship. In fact, the employees' personalities of the emerging University Museum could not have been more incompatible. Brinton, Abbott, Sara Yorke Stevenson, and Stewart Culin were at best distant and at worst openly hostile to each other, resulting in petty arguments that escalated during Abbott's employment (Hinsley 2003:6). After one such encounter, Abbott raged in his diaries "June 3, 1892: I mean to have some punishment meted out to Culin, if I do it with my own fists" (CCA/PU Box 3, Folder 2).

The earliest collections of the new Museum, including those from Nippur, were temporarily displayed in an old examination room on the top floor of College Hall and opened to the public in 1889. However, a new University Library under construction was intended to provide exhibit space for the new Museum. This building, designed by architect Frank Furness, still stands on 34th Street and serves as the Fisher Fine Arts Library, today a National Historic Landmark. It opened in 1890 with American Section artifacts prominently displayed in the gallery on the top floor of the building. With typical pessimism upon moving in, Abbott commented, "September 9, 1890: find that my office is not so cramped and ugly a hole as I had imagined it" (CCA/PU Box 3, Folder 2).

The Museum quickly became a popular attraction, though a cantankerous Abbott may have been perfectly happy to work in a museum surrounded by artifacts never visited by the public. "September 18, 1890: Visitors are daily becoming more numerous at the Museum and the place bids fair to become quite popular. Whether this is desirable or not remains to be seen. Certainly it is unavoidable, and may prove of advantage by advertising its needs" (CCA/PU Box 3, Folder 2). Given its rapid growth, plans for a dedicated building were underway by 1892, directed largely by Sara Yorke Stevenson, the curator of the Egyptian and Mediterranean Section, and a powerful voice in the Museum leadership (Pezzati 2012), on land acquired from the city of Philadelphia in 1894 at the corner of 33rd and Spruce Streets. Initially, the Museum was to be named the "Free Museum of Science and Art" but was always colloquially called the "University Museum" and the name was officially changed in 1913. Its current name, the Penn Museum was adopted in 2006 (Pezzati 2012).

This new building, which forms the original core of the modern-day Penn Museum, was designed by three architectural teams who held faculty affiliations with the University: Wilson Eyre, who led the team; Cope and Stewardson; and Frank Miles Day and Brother. The building was supposed to consist of multiphase construction consisting of a complex of interconnected buildings with three central rotundas, but only the first section was ever built as designed, completed in 1899 (Haller 1999; Pezzati 2012).

ACQUIRING AMERICAN SECTION COLLECTIONS

Unlike the Peabody Museum at Harvard University, the Penn Museum did not have an endowment to pay for salaries or daily operating expenses, let alone expeditions and collections. The University Archaeological Association, which was to raise funds for the support of the museum and its projects, gathered donations from wealthy members of the community, but a disproportionate amount of funding was donated for expeditions in the Classical world. Among the intelligentsia persisted the belief that museums should educate the public about the Classical world as the apex of human cultural development (Hinsley 1988). Wealthy donors put their money behind this principle. In 1892, for example, $920 was raised for the Egyptian and Mediterranean Fund, while merely $50 was donated for the American Fund (Hinsley 2003). Minutes of the Museum board meeting in 1892 noted that though thousands of dollars were being spent on Nippur, the University of Pennsylvania Press was threatening suit over nonpayment for the printing of Abbott's first curator's report, and funds were unavailable to pay a $15 invoice to a collector in North Carolina (Madiera 1964). Though such interest in antiquities of the Old World over the New was not atypical—Putnam had faced similar challenges at the Peabody Museum (Putnam 1877)—a lack of funding meant that Abbott needed to be frugal about artifact acquisition and field exploration.

One solution to the funding problem was to build collections through gifts of specimens. In May of 1890, the Museum sent a letter to more than 3,000 alumni of the University of Pennsylvania medical school inquiring about collections and requesting donations and information regarding archaeological resources. Donors would be recognized, but the Museum "does not enter the market as a buyer of antiquities." Instead, it was hoped that collections would be presented in the spirit of education. "An engraved acknowledgement, signed by the Provost and other officers of the University, will be promptly sent to anyone making a donation to the University and all questions about American Archaeology (other than commercial ones) will be cheerfully answered by the experts connected with the Museum" (May 1890, copy of letter on file Penn Museum Archives, American Section, Administrative Records). The letter was signed by Francis C. Macauley and Stewart Culin, but inquiries and materials were to be sent directly to Dr. Charles C. Abbott in the Department of American Archaeology. In his annual report, Abbott commented that "Valuable specimens have been already received, as well as assurances that the museum will be remembered whenever objects within its scope can be obtained" (Abbott 1890a:25). However, Abbott received at least one critical response from Atreus Wanner, a paleontologist: "I very highly value your admirable 1st report. But what a grasping, all devouring Curator you are! America, North and South, Europe, Asia, Africa—in short the whole Earth—is made to contribute to your infant collection" (AW/CCA, February 16, 1891, on file Penn Museum Archives, CCA papers, correspondence, 0044). It is unclear whether Abbott responded.

Overall, the request for artifact donations to the museum was wildly successful. Abbott crowed in his annual report that "the additions to the collections have far exceeded all expectation. The growth of the museum can best be shown by reference to the official catalogue. The initial entry was made December 2d, 1889, and the last for the museum year is 7500; recording 12,631 specimens, nearly every one of which has had painted upon it a number corresponding to one in the catalogue, and there are many specimens that have not yet been entered" (Abbott 1890a:27). The very first artifact to enter the collections was a grooved stone axe collected by Michael E. Newbold, a farmer in Burlington County, New Jersey, who sold specimens to Abbott for the museum in 1889 (Kosty 1999). Early collections also included several hundred "axes, hammers, pestles, net-sinkers, 'teshoas' or skin scrapers, mica, ceremonial objects, arrow-points, drills knives, flint flakes, scrapers, large chipped implements, pipes made of clay, and palaeolithic implements from the Trenton (N.J.) gravel" collected by Abbott in the vicinity of Three Beeches and donated to the museum (Abbott 1890a:30). Artifacts were sent from all over the United States during the first year of the museum's existence. Penn alumni and museum supporters gave artifacts from further afield, too, including "wooden implements, gourd bowl, arrow, rope, cloth, and mummy (skeleton) from Peru" as well as "Clubs from Fiji, Samoan and Santa Cruz Islands. Comb, staff, 'nulla' and spears from South Pacific Islands. Idol from Duke of York Island, and model of human head made of gum" (Abbott 1890a:30).

COLLABORATIONS WITH HENRY CHAPMAN MERCER

In part to counter the criticisms toward an American Paleolithic, but also to build collections for the Museum, Abbott proposed a field project to investigate sites throughout the Delaware Valley and eastern Pennsylvania, in collaboration with Henry Chapman Mercer (Fig. 6.1). Mercer and Abbott came from very different backgrounds, but soon became colleagues and friends. Mercer was born to a wealthy family in Doylestown, Pennsylvania, and educated at Harvard University. He later earned a law degree from the University of Pennsylvania, but never practiced law. Instead, he began informally partnering with Abbott on projects at the Penn Museum, and later accepted a formal position, ultimately replacing Abbott as Curator of the American Section.

Mercer was interested in stone tools, including alleged Paleolithic occupation of the Delaware Valley. He first garnered scholarly attention for his publication of *The Lenape Stone: Or the Indian and the Mammoth* in 1885, in which he examined a carved stone that appeared to depict a mammoth, therefore suggesting a Pleistocene provenance. Though the artifact was later demonstrated to be a forgery, Mercer devoted his 1885 publication to a scientific discussion of the stone's possible origins, citing evidence from other archaeological sites, as well as text from the *Walam Olum*—at the time believed to be a genuine document. Though also an amateur, his work on the Lenape stone (Mercer 1885) brought Mercer an early degree of respectability in the archaeological community and his partnership with Abbott further solidified his presence in the field.

On one of these field expeditions in the spring of 1891, Abbott and Mercer explored lithic quarry sites to gather the data they deemed necessary to respond to William Henry Holmes's critique of the American Paleolithic, but both also had a related interest in prehistoric caching behavior, particularly as it applied to stone tool material (Abbott 1893; Dillian and Bello 2010, 2012; Mercer 1895). If Holmes's argument about Piney Branch and other debunked Paleolithic sites was correct and what Abbott

6.1 Excavation by Abbott and Mercer, ca. 1890. Caption reads, "Ancient Neolithic Camp Site under sand stratum 8 feet thick. Right bank of Delaware at mouth of Trip Run, Northampton Co., Pa." Image no. 240578 courtesy of the Penn Museum.

was calling Paleolithic implements were really just evidence of early stages of bifacial reduction, prehistoric people must have taken these bifacially-worked quarry blanks somewhere for later use. Perhaps they stored them in caches that could later be recovered and used as needed.

Oddly, though Abbott claimed to love being in the field, his field notes were minimal and he spent more time commenting on camp activities and visitors than on the details of the archaeological research itself. For example, "May 23 1891: Up at 5:30am and after a bath, laundered some of my underwear" (CCA/PU Box 3, Folder 3). On May 25, a presumably cleaner Abbott and Mercer traveled to Ridge's Island, a large island located in the Delaware River, and today renamed Treasure Island, where according to Abbott's notes they "hunted relics with great system" (CCA/PU Box 3, Folder 3). Their surveys successfully identified prehistoric features, and he recorded, "Late in the afternoon, Mercer found a superb cache of argillite lances, one hundred and ten in number. They were buried in a space about twelve inches square and nine inches high. They were not systematically arranged. Many surface found specimens were gathered, and we came back from the Island in a great state of excitement" (CCA/PU Box 3, Folder 3). The next day, Abbott and Mercer "Went over on the island about 8am and staid until after 4pm wandering from one end to the other, but did not get much in way of archaeology but enjoyed the beautiful trees at the head of the island. There I rambled alone and was much impressed by the shallow stream that divides this island from the one above" (CCA/PU Box 3, Folder 3). Even in his published accounts of the trip, Abbott commented more on his "loafing" than on the archaeological data.

The sun was well above the Jersey hills when the river was crossed and we stood on the island. I confess to our method being too cold-blooded and business-like. It had been told that the Indians once lived here; it was left to us to prove it. Nothing would come amiss, whether bones or stone weapons. It was our purpose to explore, but with the first arrow-head found, I was surfeited; kicked over the traces and made for the woods. The other labored; I loafed. Shut in by a goodly company of ancient trees, there was opportunity to reduce loafing to a fine art....as I re-entered the open country: a conclusion that led to discussion when I saw my campmate's grand discovery...a cache of more than one hundred beautifully-chipped stone knives that, from the day when the cunning artisan hid them safely until now, had been lying in the ground. They had been closely packed in a small circular hole, so closely that but little sand had sifted between the blades. This was a discovery well worth making, and he is but a sluggish lump of laziness who cannot enthuse under such circumstances (Abbott 1899:122–123).

Because Abbott was able to "enthuse," he apparently avoided the stamp of laziness, but allegations that Mercer was the driving force behind field efforts ostensibly conducted by the Penn Museum curator would ultimately haunt Abbott's reputation and contribute to the rift that formed between Abbott and the Museum's upper administration. Mercer's writeup of the expedition to Ridge's Island was much more detailed.

Mercer claimed, in an 1895 report on the expedition, that the bifacially worked argillite blades were recovered "resting upon a flat pebble hammer seven inches below the surface, and arranged in layers on their sides" (1895:378–379). There are minor discrepancies in the written record of the total number of pieces from the cache. They are listed in the accounts of Mercer as 117 (1895:378–379), Abbott counted "more than a hundred" in print (Abbott 1899:122–123) and 110 in his field notebook (CCA/PU Box 3, Folder 3; May 25, 1891), and Culin noted 116 (1895:196). Today, there are 116 specimens from this feature curated at the Penn Museum (Cat. No. 8175, see Fig. 6.2 for typical examples). An annotation entered onto the accession card indicates that one specimen was sent as an exchange to the Phillips Academy, Andover, Massachusetts, in June 1937.

Little of the fieldwork or analysis appeared to have been done by Abbott. Mercer's report was published as a special paper in 1895 as part of *The Report of the United States Commission to the Columbian Historical Exposition at Madrid 1892–1893* (Mercer 1895). The Exposition was held in El Palacio de la Biblioteca y Museos Nacionales. Room number 5 was devoted to exhibits from the Department of Archaeology and Paleontology of the University of Pennsylvania. Mercer received a Silver Medal and Diploma for his efforts at curation (Luce 1895:12, 17). A list of the materials from the Delaware Valley indicated that 116 argillite blades were displayed and had been discovered by Mercer in a cache on an island in the Delaware River (Culin 1895:196, Item #8, Case III). Mercer's report for the exposition included sketches of specimens from Ridge's Island (1895:377, fig. 9 [2nd from left], fig. 10). In the report, Mercer speculated that the objects were

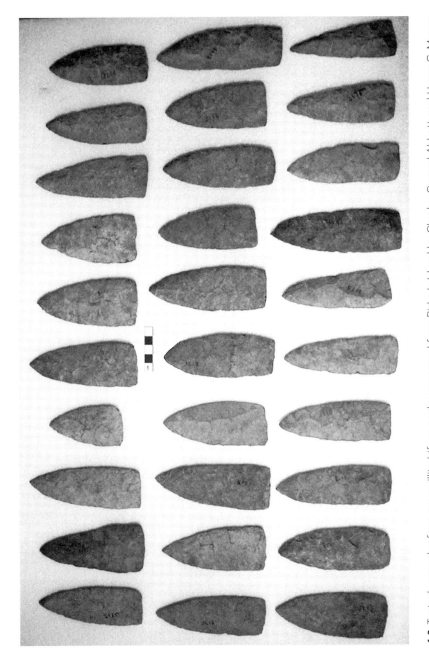

6.2 Typical examples from an argillite biface cache recovered from Ridge's Island by Charles Conrad Abbott and Henry C. Mercer (University of Pennsylvania Museum Catalog Number 8175). Photo by the authors.

"probably buried by an Indian blade worker to dig up for final shaping to order on sale or barter" and that "there was no reason for supposing that this cache...hidden without sign of ceremony or mark of mound was any-thing but the buried stock in trade of a blade chipper ready for nipping or flaking to order on sale" (Mercer 1895:378–379).

Mercer and Abbott speculated wildly about how these cached blades may have been used. Immediately following his return from the field, Mercer sent Abbott a note with a drawing of a blade embedded in a handle. He wrote "Dear Dr. Abbott, As soon as I came home I saw my *modern* Sioux war club. I bet my life I knew what our 116 *"blades"* were for. What do you say to it? Yours faithfully, H.C.M." (undated, Friday, June 1891, HCM to CCA, on file Penn Museum Archives, see Fig. 6.3). Archaeological examples of biface caches along the Delaware River are not uncommon and were probably re-lated to anadromous fish processing, rather than serving as cached material for future flintknapping or trade, or for that matter, mounted on a "war club" (Abbott 1881:195–204; Bello and Stewart 1996; Cavallo 1982, 1984; Cresson 1982; Cross 1956:68–69, 77, plates 14b, 21b, 22c; Funk 1976:64–65, 82–83; Kinsey 1975:69–71; Kraft 1986:105–108, 2001; McCann 1972:18, 20–22; Ritchie and Funk 1973:137; Volk 1911:144–145, 147, plates 63 and 121; Witthoft 1948). At the Abbott Farm site complex in the vicinity of Three Beeches almost fifty years later, Dorothy Cross excavated a cache of 127 argillite bifaces almost identical in form to the bifaces of the Ridge's Island cache during her Indian Sites Survey excavations (Cross 1956, Cache 8, Excavation 9).

Abbott and Mercer spent the latter part of the summer of 1891 explor-ing other islands in the Delaware River, seeking to provide further evidence to support Abbott's claims of Pleistocene occupation of the New World. Abbott documented "paleoliths" in contexts similar to those at Trenton but was unable to find more conclusive evidence to bolster his arguments in the face of Holmes's Piney Branch data. The artifacts were more of the same kinds of roughly bifacially worked nodules as had been found at Trenton. Though more artifacts had been found, they offered little new information, and Abbott returned to the Museum no better off than before.

PERSONALITIES CLASH

Only a month after Abbott's first day of work at the Penn Museum, Stewart Culin visited and stirred up trouble. According to Abbott's diary

6.3 Letter from Henry Chapman Mercer to Charles Conrad Abbott speculating about the use of the bifacially worked artifacts from the cache on Ridge's Island. The letter reads, "Doylestown, Friday, June 1841, Dear Dr. Abbott, As soon as I came home and saw my *modern* Sioux war club, I bet my life I knew what our 116 "*blades*" were for. What do you say to it? Yours faithfully, H. C. M., Boxes off tomorrow." University of Pennsylvania Museum Archives, American Section, CCA papers, Correspondence 0044.

"December 28, 1889: Culin came and he staid until I went in town to come home. Learned that Dr. Leidy strongly opposed my appointment as Curator. Am glad to know this as I now have learned a good deal of the secret opposition to me in Philadelphia. Culin told me a good deal" (CCA/PU Box 2, Folder 5). Joseph Leidy was a prominent vertebrate paleontologist and held an appointment as Professor of Anatomy at the University of Pennsylvania Medical School, where he likely had young Charles Conrad Abbott as a student. However, it appeared that they had a falling out a few years after Abbott's graduation, referenced in Abbott's diaries on May 7, 1885, when he bumped into Leidy at the Academy of Natural Sciences in Philadelphia one afternoon: "rambled about and finally met Dr. Leidy, whom I invited to Trenton on Tuesday next, which invitation he accepted. It is all considered a pleasant matter to have Dr. Leidy come to Trenton. The bitterness of past experiences had better die out and to more or less reunite with Philadelphians will be of value to me. It seems strange that the time should finally come when he comes here to visit me after the events of fifteen years ago" (CCA/PU Box 2, Folder 3). Abbott was not keeping a diary in 1870, when the falling-out occurred, and it is unclear what caused the rift between the two men, but Abbott clearly assumed that they had moved beyond their differences when he was appointed curator in 1889. Leidy obviously felt otherwise.

This conversation between Culin and Abbott that occurred merely weeks after Holmes's publication on Piney Branch and soon after the appointment to the Museum, bruised Abbott's already injured ego, and it colored his view of the job and the institution. He petulantly declared, "Am sorry to know it as it cools my interest in the work and if ever a chance to get out turns up, I will promptly consider it. What was in part a labor of love, what I took pride in doing, now assumes some of the aspect of mere drudgery for the sake of salary" (CCA/PU Box 2, Folder 5; December 28, 1889). By the end of 1889, Abbott perceived attacks coming from every direction.

The relationship between Stewart Culin and Abbott turned volatile very quickly. Like Abbott, Culin had no formal training in anthropology, but was self-taught, learning what he could through participation in several anthropological professional societies. His focus was on the ethnographic study of games, beginning with research in Chinese immigrant communities in Philadelphia, and ultimately including wide-reaching comparative studies of Native American, Korean, Japanese, and Hawaiian games. Culin was recognized for his innovative exhibit design, including work at the Columbian

Exposition in Chicago in 1893, where he met friend and collaborator Frank Hamilton Cushing.

Culin was appointed Secretary of the Oriental Section at the Penn Museum at its founding, and in 1892, gained the title of Director of the Museum, a promotion Abbott deeply resented. With the new appointment, Culin became only the second Museum employee, with Abbott, to draw salary. When Abbott learned that Culin would now supervise his position as curator, he recorded in his diary: "June 26, 1892: After using up the forenoon with the papers, went to Philadelphia at noon and directly to my office at Museum. Found Culin there and gave him a little information, then went to Pepper's. He told me Culin was "Director" of Museums and did not say what I was. I told him it would not work, and so find I have been ousted from my position. At least there is nothing for me to do but draw salary. Am determined now to get out if I possibly can, for I will not work under anyone" (CCA/PU Box 3, Folder 2).

Yet Culin's position at the Museum was not as omnipotent as Abbott may have interpreted. Technically, Culin supervised the American and Ethnology sections, but many of the Museum's daily activities were administered by Sara Yorke Stevenson, a close friend and confidante of Provost Pepper who served as Museum Secretary. Stevenson later ascended to become the Museum's first female President, and Curator of the Egyptian and Mediterranean Sections (Kopytoff 2006). Culin and Stevenson frequently butted heads, particularly as Provost Pepper used Stevenson as his proxy within the Museum, giving her unofficial authority over all Museum staff. However, Stevenson's own power should not be overlooked. Arguably it was Stevenson who was the driving force behind the creation of a museum at the University of Pennsylvania, and her connections with the Philadelphia elite provided the funds for facilities, collections, and salaries (Danien and King 2003).

The strong personalities of Abbott, Culin, and Stevenson, and the power struggles between the three meant each was perpetually angling for funds, equipment, recognition, and control. Petty arguments flared over minor issues. For example, a mundane request caused Abbott to send Culin a note on official Museum letterhead over the purchase of a small table, threatening "If you don't send it out soon, I'll buy one and let the council monkey with the bill. I can't wait" (CCA to SC, Sept. 1, 1891, Penn Museum Archives, Administrative Records, American Section). Abbott's solution to these arguments was to withdraw and pout. By his own account, he spent a great deal of time "loafing" and few hours in the Museum.

By spring of 1892, it was clear that Abbott's position at the Museum was precarious. As the only curator drawing salary, the cash-strapped new museum had a strong financial incentive to terminate Abbott, particularly since it was obvious that he was unproductive and unmotivated. Clues appeared in the form of delayed paychecks, evaporated research funding, and slow equipment purchases. On April 4, 1892, Abbott noted in his diary "At museum for some time and not favorably impressed by remarks made by Culin. It would appear as if my salary would not be paid, at least for some time to come" (CCA/PU Box 3, Folder 2). But unlike other Museum staff who were relatively wealthy, Abbott was unable to work without pay, though likely his ego was bruised even more than his wallet. He followed up with continued salary demands approximately two weeks after this conversation with Culin and recorded, "April 16, 1892: I spoke to Tower [Charlemagne Tower, Jr., President of the Department of Archaeology and Paleontology] and then Pepper about salary matter. The result was a row and I saw then no way but to resign and told them so. What the outcome will be, I do not know, but will very soon. My plans are now all upset and I will never give in to the present board of managers and said so. Pepper was very pleasant and I firm" (CCA/PU Box 3, Folder 2).

Abbott's frustration that spring was not confined to a single event but was a cascade of bad news. His American Paleolithic was being excoriated in the scholarly press, while his curatorship at the Museum was slipping from his grasp. Much of Abbott's ire was directed towards Culin, who Abbott believed was personally targeting him.

> May 13, 1892: To Philadelphia and at Lippincott's, then at museum and then to Dr. Pepper's. He told me my affairs were not being looked after by anyone but himself. I then saw Mr. Coates [a member of the Board of Managers], who blames Culin, and later saw Mr. Rosengarten [Vice President of the Alumni Association and later Trustee] and C. C. Harrison [Trustee of the University and member of the Board of Managers] who look upon it all as I do. Mr. Rosengarten will help me out substantially. Then came home. Did not feel like doing anything as I was so annoyed by recent occurrences and the devilish dirty business of the skunk Culin (CCA/PU Box 3, Folder 2).

Unfortunately, a large percentage of Abbott's time was occupied track-ing the schemers he believed were trying to unseat him and not in con-ducting fieldwork or building collections for the Museum. Had he ignored his antagonistic relationships with the administration and focused instead on his curatorial duties, his career path at the Museum might have been different. Instead, Abbott continued to be distracted by interpersonal con-flicts. "May 18, 1892: saw Mr. Harrison and he told me much concerning the matter of my salary. I think I am undermining the attempts of certain ill-natured dogs, who are trying to hurt the American museum" (CCA/PU Box 3, Folder 2). Abbott genuinely believed that Pepper supported him as curator, but was unaware that by 1892, Pepper was sending notes to Sara Yorke Stevenson and Henry C. Mercer indicating that Abbott's tenure in the Museum would be short-lived (Hinsley 2003; Meltzer 2003). However, after admonishing Abbott for his behavior, Pepper granted a second chance and agreed to support Abbott's salary for an additional year.

> June 1, 1892: To Philadelphia and after a bit at the museum, went to Pep-per's and had a rather satisfactory talk. The salary is now in sight and I am more than ever convinced that Culin is a sneak and cause of all the trouble. Next autumn the truth will come out. Mrs. Stevenson is another of the same stamp. Pepper says I have roused a great deal of antagonism and I will cause more very probably and the outcome I anticipate will be my leaving, but I'll have revenge first (CCA/PU Box 3, Folder 2).

Yet despite a reprieve in his financial status, Abbott apparently did not take Pepper's warnings to heart. "June 3, 1892: I have the excellent excuse (for not working) of being bored and worried by the cussed museum muddle" (CCA/PU Box 3, Folder 2). He devoted some of the summer of 1892 to fieldwork but according to his diaries, spent a long periods consci-entiously doing nothing in protest of what he felt were personal attacks. "August 3, 1892: To Philadelphia and at museum a moment and cleaned up my desk by pitching Culin's rubbish into a dark closet. Had a note from Harrison and went to his office. He had been written to by Brinton or Culin and I pronounced them both liars. He advised going on with my work, but I shall keep only on look[ing] out for something else while I am there and do nothing but most necessary work. Sorry to find Brinton is as big a sneak as Culin" (CCA/PU Box 3, Folder 2).

Abbott's bitterness grew. "September 21, 1892: Daily it dawns upon me that my life is wasted in the city and in that hated museum. The damned fools about it, I so long to kill and of course dare not, are forever in my path" (CCA/PU Box 3, Folder 2). Ultimately, Pepper and members of the Board of Trustees put Abbott on official probationary status, and attempted to elicit some quality work out of their only salaried curator. During a meeting on October 12, 1892, they outlined the problems with Abbott's performance and expectations for the future. Abbott recorded in his diary that the meeting "had as a basis, dissatisfaction as to the past, and the purpose was to exact promises from me to do differently in the future and as a whole, insulting, although this they disclaimed" (CCA/PU Box 3, Folder 2). Abbott agreed to their terms, but stated privately "It is a matter of money now, and not museum interests" (CCA/PU Box 3, Folder 2; October 12, 1892).

TERMINATION

Evidently Abbott did not take his probationary status to heart, because the day after his meeting with members of the Board of Trustees, he noted in his diary "October 13, 1892: out to the museum, but I didn't do a stroke of work" (CCA/PU Box 3, Folder 2). However, the following summer, Abbott returned to the field in the company of Henry Mercer, and continued research related to the American Paleolithic. It is unclear if his goal in the field was to disprove Holmes's conclusions stemming from Piney Branch or if he intended to simply demonstrate his industriousness as Curator, but if successful, he would perhaps be able to recapture some of the fame that he enjoyed during the late 1880s. In his curator's report to Brinton at the end of the summer of 1893, Abbott wrote, "In view of the fact that this question of palaeolithic man has been so vigorously discussed of late, I felt it demanded of me to re-open the whole question and repeat the labors of years ago." He indicated that he "was pleased to announce that I feel that this particular line of work is now concluded" and that a manuscript was ready for publication that would provide a summary of his fieldwork and results (curator's report, submitted to D. G. Brinton, Oct. 1, 1893. Penn Museum Archives, Administrative Records, American Section 0044).

The fieldwork and subsequent report may have been too little, too late, however. Two weeks after Abbott submitted his fieldwork report, he received formal notification from Brinton that his position would be terminated. Furthermore, Abbott's academic reputation was in steep decline. As William Henry Holmes and W J McGee chipped away at alleged Paleolithic sites and their geologic context, it became clear that Abbott had misinterpreted the Trenton artifacts. Though his theories still had some adherents, such as geologist George Frederick Wright, many in the scientific community abandoned Abbott by 1893. As a result, the Penn Museum had little incentive to retain him. His reputation no longer enhanced the Museum's image, and his salary was merely a drain on resources. Though he knew that he was in a precarious position, the suddenness of the termination surprised him. In his diary, he recorded "October 13, 1893: This is, I doubt not, the culmination of the trouble that has been brewing for a long time. The successful issue of the conspiracy of which Culin is the head. At times I have recorded that I felt as if I had headed it off, but this seems not the case. The management have chosen a fool and knave to succeed a man of capabilities, if Culin is to succeed me" (CCA/PU Box 3, Folder 2).

Abbott didn't go quietly. Concerns that Culin would now be filling the role of curator rankled Abbott, and he fumed that presumably Culin, Brinton, and Stevenson had won, and he had lost. On November 1, 1893, Abbott returned to the Museum and aired his grievances with Provost Pepper, noting in his diary that there occurred "a free ventilation of opinion and I excitedly said I had been swindled. Then there was a big racket and Pepper swore he would not settle with me. We were both very angry and I was frightened for fear there could be no compromise affected." Mercer stepped in to mitigate, and both men backed down. "I offered to recall what I had said and Pepper settled on terms agreed upon and I gave a receipt to effect I was satisfied, but it was forced from me and so I do not care about it but will say what I think" (CCA/PU Box 3, Folder 2).

Abbott negotiated a month's pay in severance, but his larger concern was that Culin would take over as curator. Mercer and Abbott retreated to Rathskellar, a high-end bar in the basement of the Betz building on Broad Street and, over drinks, Abbott encouraged Mercer to take the curatorship as it had been offered to him, albeit without salary. Mercer and Abbott continued to collaborate, but the experience at the Museum left Abbott with much bitterness. He noted in his diary, "November 1, 1893:...so ends my connection to the museum that has been a veritable thorn in my flesh for over two years, as these diaries duly testify....I am so glad to be free of the museum" (CCA/PU Box 3, Folder 2).

THE AFTERMATH

Abbott was not the only person to experience conflict while working at the Penn Museum during the 1890s. Following his termination, he remained in contact with many of his former colleagues, particularly Henry Mercer, with whom he had developed a friendship. In one letter, dated only March 17, Mercer wrote "I have a lot to tell you about the cataclysm in the U. of Pa. How would you like to have back your old place? I have seen a good deal of Hilprecht lately....What do you think of Sara Somersault?" (CCA/PU Box 8, Folder 6). Mercer brought Abbott news of the Museum, but others also kept him informed. In his diaries, when ruminating on these tidbits of information about his former employer, he implied that he did not care about the fate of the Museum, but there was an element of schadenfreude.

In particular, Abbott learned that Sara Yorke Stevenson and Provost Pepper colluded on plans for a new Museum facility as well as on the direction that the Museum would take in expansion. Stevenson and Pepper were highly invested in Egypt and the Mediterranean, and Stevenson served as head of that section for several years. Both maintained that expansion of the Classical collections would benefit the Museum, though this may have been tied to philanthropic donations, which tended to favor the Classical world. Abbott, Culin, and Brinton were all engaged in research elsewhere, most notably in the Americas, and argued that Stevenson and Pepper were steering the Museum in the wrong direction. Board member Charles Howard Colket resigned over the issue, stating that it would put the Museum in direct competition with other institutions in the Philadelphia area (Baker 2010:129). Colket followed up with Abbott, but Abbott recorded in his diary, "January 9, 1894: Late, in afternoon, Ria brought me a letter from Colket about Museum matters and after supper I wrote a long and detailed reply and added I wanted to hear nothing more from any one connected with it and I doubt if I ever will" (CCA/PU Box 3, Folder 5).

Brinton also resigned from his Museum position in 1894, but because his salary was paid through his academic department at the University of Pennsylvania, and not by the Museum, this was merely a rejection of his honorary affiliation. His objections stemmed from limits placed on research within the collections, and the Museum's desire to display the most popular artifacts to garner public notice, rather than those that may have served to educate, in Brinton's opinion (Baker 2010:129). However, despite stepping down from the Museum, Brinton retained his position as Professor of Archaeology and Linguistics at the University of Pennsylvania.

Stewart Culin eventually experienced his own falling-out with Stevenson and the Museum administration, though Abbott continued to hold him accountable for his own experience. Culin and Stevenson clashed over Museum policy and philosophy, and he ultimately was forced to resign in 1903. According to one newspaper account (which was later retracted), the Museum administration claimed that Culin was incompetent and that his fieldwork "had been productive of little good: that his specimens had to be deciphered and classified by others and that everything he wrote had to be revised and edited by his secretary" (as quoted in Fane 1992:18). Culin's reputational decline may have rested at least in part in his lack of professional training in the field as amateurs were slowly excluded from professional circles, and further exacerbated by his request for salary as Director. As Stevenson and Pepper tried to professionalize the Museum, having a Director without a pedigree was viewed as a disadvantage (Hinsley 2003:19), and his strong personality likely did not help interpersonal relationships.

Even as late as 1903, Abbott was resentful. In his diaries on February 2, 1903, Abbott noted that he was told that "Mrs. Stevenson admitted that the archaeological gang in Philadelphia were deceived by Culin and that I had been wrongly treated. This was ten years ago so I don't care but the rest of them are as bad as Culin" (CCA/PU Box 4, Folder 3). Unfortunately, much of the correspondence that may shed light on the discussion of Abbott and Culin was destroyed by Geraldine Bruckner, the first registrar and archivist of the Penn Museum, probably because it contained embarrassing allegations by former Board member Charles Colket directed towards members of the Museum administration (Hinsley 2003:20).

After Abbott's termination, he focused his efforts instead on his naturalist writings, for which he gained popular, and some financial, success. But, despite Abbott's intentions to leave the field of archaeology, he was still called upon to participate in topics related to ancient humans in the New World, which he often refused. George Frederick Wright, in particular, pursued Abbott and encouraged him to continue his work. In his diaries, Abbott noted: "January 9, 1894:...It seems very hard to entirely cut loose from the whole thing....He [Wright] evidently expects a monograph from me on the subject of 'gravel' man, but I do not intend to write it, unless a very great change should come over me. I am tired to death with arguing the questions involved....Got settled to my work after a while and forgetting the damned museum crowd, made good progress on the book" (CCA/PU Box 3, Folder 5).

7

Abbott the Naturalist

"It is, however, by his charming essays upon natural history—general biology, I believe is now the proper term—that Dr. Abbott has given Trenton its widest general prominence. Of some twenty-five books one may select "Upland and Meadow," published a score of years ago, followed six years after by "Travels in the Treetops," or his last summer's success, "Rambles of an Idler." They were all written in or about the old Abbott homestead, where life is always pleasant, particularly for the fortunate visitor. Nor must one forget that delightful novel of early life, "The Colonial Wooing," whose characters were read and whose scenes were laid between Trenton and Crosswicks. This is what Dr. Abbott has done."

CCA: "the above was written by Francis B. Lee for the "Trenton Times" on the occasion of the paper's 24th anniversary, Oct. 12, 1906. The issue of paper was largely historical, in a local sense."

--CCA/PU Box 14, Folder 4

After his termination from the Penn Museum, Abbott and his family left their rented home in Bristol, Pennsylvania, and returned to Three Beeches farm south of Trenton, New Jersey. Abbott recorded the event with little fanfare. "April 4, 1894: Farm-life commenced. After an absence of four years and some months, this day, we moved back to the farm" (CCA/PU Box 3, Folder 5). Returning to Three Beeches marked a homecoming to a place surrounded by nature, which Abbott loved, yet he was far less enthusiastic about returning to the drudgeries and poverty of farm labor.

Once back in Trenton, Abbott embraced his nature writing in earnest. For many years he dabbled in that arena, publishing his book *A Naturalist's Rambles About Home* in 1884, and brief nature articles (1861a, 1861b, 1868, 1870a. 1870b, 1871, 1874, 1875b, 1875c) that highlighted an early penchant for exaggeration and descriptive prose. For example, in a description of the mud-sucker (*Hylomyzon nigricans*), Abbott wrote "we once saw a large specimen in the jaws of a Water snake (*Tropidonotus sipedon*), which squealed like a young pig" (1870a:113–114). He published additional nature essays in the 1880s while also collecting artifacts for the Peabody Museum (1884a, 1884b, 1884c, 1885b, 1886, 1887, 1889), and embarked on nature writing intensively during the 1890s, particularly after the curator job at Penn ended (1890b, 1892d, 1894a, 1894b, 1895b, 1895c, 1895d, 1895e, 1896a, 1896b, 1897, 1898a, 1898c, 1899, 1900, 1906a).

In the late 19th century, nature writing was a popular genre for the well-educated, but non-scientific, amateur scholar, generally from a middle and upper socioeconomic class. The period marked a shift in thinking from one which viewed humans at the pinnacle of the animal kingdom to one that recognized humans as merely a component of a larger natural world, and particularly as these ideas applied to an understanding of the evolution of species, which was gaining a greater acceptance among well-read individuals (Mighetto 1985). From this perspective, if Darwin's theory of evolution was true, humans were no better than animals driven merely by a biological need to survive and reproduce. Science "stripped man of his illusions, setting him adrift in a void" (Mighetto 1985:34). The popularity of nature writing during this time has been argued to result from a desire to empower readers "through firsthand observation, evidence of dignity, beneficence, and morality in the natural world" (Mighetto 1985:35).

Nature writers tapped into this growing movement that culminated in a late 19th century market for popular volumes providing relatively accurate, yet much more creative, descriptions of nature. Many further encouraged the audience to get outside and experience it for themselves (Bruyninckx 2018). But despite their attractive prose, the most imaginative writers received strong criticism. Even though their works stimulated an aesthetic appreciation of the natural world, such essays should not assign imaginary characteristics to non-human species—a concern which soon grew with the increasing popularity of the genre (Bruyninckx 2018). The issue bubbled over into the scholarly and popular press in 1903, when naturalist John

Burroughs critically reviewed realistic animal fiction, which was a popular sub-genre of nature writing. Burroughs labeled it "sham natural history" (Bruyninckx 2018; Lutts 1990). Nature writing, the critics argued, should be both art *and* science (Kohler 2006).

As a result, amateur nature writers by the turn of the century were under greater pressure to present facts and accurate details in the species they described. Field experience was heralded as the best way to gain legitimacy. Prominent figures such as John Muir and Henry David Thoreau gained acceptance not only for their skill as writers, but also because their descriptions were backed up by real experience (Bruyninckx 2018; Kohler 2006; Mighetto 1985). Authors endeavored to present precise descriptions of flora and fauna, but most nature writers of the period were amateurs like Abbott, not trained scientists, and few guidelines existed to qualify a professional class. For Abbott, this was an advantage he fully acknowledged in a later unpublished autobiographical essay:

> My days of greatest activity were those when then recognized "naturalist" was nothing more than a describer of new species and was wholly indifferent as to whether the fish swam in water or walked on land was to what part the creature played in the general scheme of nature. It was years later that a specimen was recognized as having any significance except as an object for a glass jar and a not always appropriate Latin or Greek name that certainly shed no light upon the living animal, whatever it did in the gloom of official ichthyology (CCA/PANS).

Excluded from archaeology by the mid-1890s as increasing professionalization took hold and acceptance for an American Paleolithic declined, Abbott was at the time, still eminently qualified to participate in the naturalist movement, and he fully embraced the opportunity. He wrote on a wide variety of subjects, but birds were very popular and received a great deal of Abbott's literary attention. In contrast to the scientific displays and descriptions of birds that were becoming the norm in ornithological texts or in museums, nature writing celebrated bird song and behavior as examples of the joy that could be found in outdoor observation (Bruyninckx 2018). For example, in *The Birds About Us*, one of Abbott's first publications after his departure from the Penn Museum, Abbott described the chickadee as having "such winning ways that you never tire of them. Even when they have nests in the hollows of old trees, and are concerned about their young, they do not forget to be cheerful, and sing as constantly as though care was unknown" (1894a:37). He conveyed the wren's call, not by identifying sounds but instead as "always ready with a full performance. There is no tuning up, no interminable twanging of strings, or dead-and-alive tooting upon horns, but the full measure of the song proposed, and it is a welcome to spring that puts faith in the hearts of all hearers" (1894a.42). And the seasonal arrival of the Acadian flycatcher was described as "When the April sunshine has caused the leaf-buds to open, and as we look through the woods we see a pale-green shimmer, and sunlight penetrating to where in a few weeks it will be effectually shut out,—at such a time and in such a place you will see a small greenish-gray flycatcher" (1894a:117).

Because of his accessible style, *The Birds About Us* brought Abbott both critical and financial success. He intended the book for readers such as hobbyists and casual birdwatchers, who enjoyed a more poetic description of birds and their behaviors, and in this demographic, Abbott found a rapt audience and considerably less criticism than he received for his archaeological publications. Reviews generally praised the volume, though a review dated 1895 in the journal *The Auk*, published by the American Ornithologists' Union, condemned Abbott's harsh views of scientific collecting. Abbott wrote that scientists had no need to trap and euthanize mass numbers of specimens to determine variability within species or to add to museum collections. Abbott had chastised, "It is not justifiable to kill one hundred warblers in a day just to see if a particular one is among them" and that scientists would be better off to "let what we do not know go unknown until discovered by accident and let the birds live" (1894a:12). The reviewer, identified only as W. S. retorted that "if Dr. Abbott thinks that professional ornithologists are accustomed to slaughter all the birds to be found in a given area in order to determine what species occur there, he certainly has not a very close acquaintance with those whom he criticizes." And furthermore, "Had Dr. Abbott used a gun a little more and been certain of the identity of the birds of which he wrote he would have been spared the publication of many remarkable statements which appeared in some of his earlier works, and which he himself seems now to admit as errors." Overall, however, as a naturalist volume for a popular audience, the reviewer conceded that the book would "prove most attractive to the reader who possesses any appreciation for nature, while the facts recorded are in the main scientifically accurate" (W. S. 1895:68).

Also in 1894, Abbott published another nature volume entitled *Travels in a Tree-top*, which also received popular acclaim. An anonymous review in *Science* noted that:

> whether he tells us of what he finds in the top of a tremendous oak, or of what he sees from his high perch among the leaves; whether he narrates amusing stories about corn-stalk fiddles and a Quaker grandfather, or the kitchen door of his old home in boyhood times; whether he describes for us a dinner among the Indians before Columbus 'arrived,' or reminds us how the bees and buckwheat of August develop into honey and buckwheat cakes for these cool mornings—he is equally genial and charming (1894a:101).

This review was likely the only time anyone ever described Abbott as "genial and charming," but indeed, the volume tranquilly meditated on the natural world and the place of humans within it. For example, in the introduction to a chapter entitled "An Old-Fashioned Garden," Abbott wrote that "Whenever we chance, in our wanderings, to come upon some long-neglected corner of colonial times, there we will find the bloom and birds together" (1894b:134). The chapter reflected on the ways in which humans have altered the checks and balances of the natural world, by introducing non-native species, cutting trees, and eliminating natural predators. In a later chapter entitled "Drifting," he wrote of floating on the Delaware River in a small boat and snagging on a submerged log. "In the dim, misty light what a strange sea-monster this resurrected tree-trunk seemed to be! Its thick green coat of silky threads lay closely as the shining fur of the otter, a mane of eel-grass floated on the water, the gnarly growths where branches once had been glistened as huge eyes, and broken limbs were horns that threatened quick destruction" (1984b:174). The volume offered similarly embellished observations of plants, animals, and history, with easily understood discussions for the non-scientist at a time when reflective nature writings represented the height of literary fashion.

An alternate review of *Travels in a Tree-top* published in *The Saturday Review* in London, complemented "he is an enthusiastic and observant naturalist who writes in a pleasant and graceful style, and he brings up his reports of the inhabitants of a country comparatively unknown to Englishmen. We hear of beasts, birds, and fishes with most outlandish names, and of reptiles and insects of most eccentric habits" (Anonymous 1894b:329). The reviewer commented that the volume provided an instructive and entertaining view of American species for a British audience, and concluded with observations on Abbott's descriptions of freshwater turtles with the comment that these "were on a considerably reduced scale from the sea-fish that revenge themselves on gluttonous humanity by leaving legacies of gout and indigestion" (Anonymous 1894b:329).

With books such as these, Abbott found his niche and his audience. He described nature and history in ways that were understood by a generally educated class of readers, yet did not write for the scientific expert, which was acceptable in the genre. His books were within the purchasing power of the middle and upper classes, at approximately $1 to $1.50 each (about $30 to $50 today). As one anonymous reviewer wrote of *Outings at Odd Times*,

> To the nature-loving naturalist, not the perfunctory one, the reading of it will necessarily be a pleasure and an assistance; to the city dweller, with an occasional 'day off,' at any season of the year, it will prove an incentive to recreation-seeking in the best direction; to the average dweller in the country it will act as an 'eye-opener' to much that is going on about him; while to any reader of ordinary intelligence the perusal of it cannot fail to be beneficial (1890:361).

Abbott's readers could go out into their gardens and parks and on their own excursions, and similarly witness the junctures of birds, insects, plants, and humans. He wrote in friendly, conversational, and non-scientific terms, which though a weakness in his professional applications, conferred a great advantage in writing for an amateur audience.

THE INFLUENCE OF HENRY DAVID THOREAU

Henry David Thoreau's essays profoundly influenced Abbott's nature writing style. He referenced Thoreau's work extensively in his own books such as *In Nature's Realm* (1900), *Outings at Odd Times* (1890b), *Days Out of Doors* (1889), *Notes of the Night* (1896a). Later in life, in his penultimate book *Ten Years' Diggings in Lenape Land*, he summarized his perspective "to place the outdoor world on a printed page has been an aim of authorship for centuries, and not even Thoreau wholly succeeded. Nature will not suffer an interpreter to intervene" (1912:113).

Abbott was not unique; Thoreau (1817–1862) influenced many nature writers in the mid-19th century. His most popular book, *Walden; or, Life in the Woods* (1854), detailed his experiences in a cabin near Walden Pond, near Concord, Massachusetts, and advocated simple living and self-reliance in communion with nature. Abbott was a devotee and wrote in *Waste Land Wanderings* that "I once gathered a fern, a sprouted acorn, and a bluet from Thoreau's grave, without wondering, at the time, if he were then gathering greener growths on the pleasant hill-sides of another world" (1887:17). Abbott published one article specifically about Thoreau in *Lippincott's Monthly Magazine* (1895b), which was later reprinted in *Notes of the Night* (1896a), in which he described Thoreau's naturalist writing in terms that were echoed in Abbott's unpublished autobiographical essay highlighting his own efforts as a naturalist. "He was busied with the wild life about Concord when 'Science' was still occupied with the hunt for new species, and content with a mere description of form and color" and continued "Thoreau made no practice of haunting museums, objects in alcohol or stuffed with tow not appealing strongly to him; but he did care to know, and was successful in ascertaining, the habits of the animals he saw" (1896a:222). Abbott likely felt that he was supplementing the kind of writing done by Thoreau by offering more detailed descriptions of the species he observed. He wrote that "Thoreau did not add greatly to our knowledge of wild life, but he did that which is of equal merit, showed how delightful was the pursuit of such knowledge, and, in a measure, how it might be attained" (1896a:223).

Abbott may have also sensed a kindred spirit in Thoreau as an archaeologist because Thoreau also collected archaeological artifacts during his excursions, both in Concord as well as during a lengthy expedition through Maine, which formed the foundation of his book *The Maine Woods* (1864). Thoreau wrote "we strolled down to the 'Point,' formed by the junction of the two rivers, which is said to be the scene of an ancient battle between the Eastern Indians and the Mohawks, and searched there carefully for relics, though the men at the bar-room had never heard of such things; but we found only some flakes of arrow-head stone, some points of arrowheads, one small leaden bullet, and some colored beads" (1864:10) and later "I picked up some fragments of arrow-heads on the shore, and one broken stone chisel" (1864:153). Many of the artifacts were donated to the Boston Society of Natural History after Thoreau's death in 1862 and later given to the Peabody Museum at Harvard University in 1869. As Abbott was working for the Peabody Museum to build their American collections, he was likely familiar with Thoreau's collection. They consisted of "over one hundred specimens of axes, pestles, gouges, mortars, chisels, spear points, ornaments, etc. and a larger number of arrow points of very varied patterns and materials. The entire collection comprises about nine hundred pieces" (Wyman 1870:6–7). Some of Thoreau's artifacts from Maine and accompanying descriptions gleaned from *The Maine Woods* were included in an exhibit at the Peabody Museum in 2014 entitled "The Legacy of Penobscot Canoes: A View from the River."

Abbott's admiration for Thoreau led him to abscond with at least one of the artifacts from this collection, which he appears to have given to a female friend, addressed in his letters and diaries only as Mrs. Robins, with whom he had a lengthy and intimate correspondence in the mid-1890s. In an undated letter to her, he referred to the artifact in a conversation about her writing aspirations by saying "I hope when you come to write a book, you will be more logical in your arguments than in the matter of the Thoreau chisel....For my part, I think I would rather have something of Thoreau's that was associated with Concord, than the river-shores in Maine, but all this is a matter of fancy and we won't discuss it. I am only glad that you enjoy the possession of the trifle so much" (CCA-JSR/PANS; undated).

Abbott's nature writing, though not what he is most remembered for, influenced writers and thinkers into the 20th century. It has been proposed that Abbott's book *In Nature's Realm* inspired passages by Aldo Leopold in *A Sand Country Almanac* (1949; Pickering 2007). Leopold, a prominent naturalist and an early ecologist, encouraged readers to explore ecosystems and landscapes, rather than focus narrowly on individual species, but he also colorfully and expansively described the intersections of humans and the environment. Leopold offered "critiques of a society in which man lives apart or at least thinks he lives apart from the natural community surrounding him" (Pickering 2007:115). This is similar to Abbott's sentiment, as reflected in *In Nature's Realm*, in which he wrote "I am a part of nature and nature is a part of me. Tear us apart and nature is robbed and I am ruined" (1900:22). Unfortunately, many of Abbott's naturalist books are no longer in print, though are accessible online through digital libraries and databases. Pickering lamented "it is a pity that only literary archaeologists now read Abbott. His ideas have not aged into shards, and his writings reward the effort of digging them out of libraries and second-hand bookstores" (2007:120).

NATURE WRITING IN FICTION

As his commercial successes as a nature writer increased, Abbott also ventured into fiction. In 1895 he published *A Colonial Wooing* (1895c), a story populated by Quaker characters and set in colonial New Jersey. The novel was a romance involving two young people whose dialogue was presented in Quaker dialect, interspersed with the use of "thee" and "thou." In the story, Ruth, a spunky young woman, and John, a stubborn and hard-working young man, must battle family and community to gain acceptance of their relationship and ultimately to marry. An anonymous review in the *Boston Transcript* critiqued the novel with a note that "Dr. Abbott betrays his predilections for writing on natural history at every turn...His attention is too easily called from the incidents of the story by bird or beast or leaping fish to suit the veteran novel reader." Yet the reviewer conceded that "this will be no blemish to the eyes of some, it will be the most attractive feature of the book" (n.d.).

Another novel soon followed and in 1897, Abbott published *When the Century Was New*, which tells the tale of a mysterious murder that Abbott, as storyteller, claimed was revealed in documents and a skeleton exposed in the ruins of the fictional Horse-Head Inn. A dramatic discovery ensued: "the well was found half filled with rubbish several feet above the water line, and on the very top of all was a human skeleton. Not a trace of clothing was discovered. Evidently a naked body had been hidden here many years ago" (Abbott 1897:14). Nudity and death made for a dramatic setting that hooked the reader, and reviewers praised the historic detail. One reviewer wrote that a reader "will find much to please him in the bright and characteristic dialogue, the short but vivid pen-pictures of scenery and persons, and the genial philosophy of which the book is full" (Anonymous 1897:130).

Abbott also used his excavations of a historic site, which he interpreted as a Dutch trading post, on Burlington Island in the Delaware River as the setting for another dramatic work of historical fiction. In fact, he stated plans to write an opera based on the historical and archaeological findings on Burlington Island, and it was in his evolution from historical fact to operatic fiction that the details of his "Dutch house" findings transformed into something that combined several different and unconnected historical details. As early as April 19, 1893, Abbott stated in his diary entry that he "told [Owen] Wister about my plan of an opera based on Dutch House." He periodically visited Burlington Island and collected "Dutch House" artifacts through the 1890s, and was frequently accompanied on these expeditions by family and friends (CCA/PU Box 3, Folders 2 and 5).

Yet it appears that the Dutch House opera never materialized, and Abbott instead decided to turn his writings on the subject into a lengthy poem, entitled "Island Tragedy" populated by characters whose names were chosen from a Native American dictionary (CCA/PU Box 3, Folder 5; February 27, 1896). By March 7, 1896 according to his diary, the poem was completed and read before Mrs. Robins, who "expressed herself as delighted with it, using a great many emphatic expressions of approval" (CCA/PU Box 3, Folder 5).

But despite its favorable reception by one of Abbott's personal friends, the poem received little interest from publishers. It was rejected by *Century Magazine* on May 6, 1896. Abbott edited the poem and on June 4, 1896 stated that he completed a new conclusion and "wrote a new song for the children that gather within hearing of the heroine's tent. Then took a nap" (CCA/PU Box 3, Folder 5). Abbott also commissioned illustrations for the poem from Oliver Kemp, though these have not been located. After several rejections, Abbott let the idea of a long poem based on the archaeological finds on Burlington Island, drop. He stated on April 22, 1897 that he received a rejection letter that was "very severe on my text and said the Century Co. condemned the pictures." He further stated that "we determined not to accept the dictum received as final. It is an unjust decision as to the drawings... as to my ability to write a narrative poem, that is another matter, but I am going to try again, or perhaps, re-tell the story in prose, which now I do not want to do" (CCA/PU Box 3, Folder 5). However, a published, or unpublished, version of the "Island Tragedy" has never been recovered.

PROFESSIONAL ILLUSTRATIONS

Many of Abbott's naturalist and fiction writings were illustrated, some by Abbott himself, and others by professional illustrators. Reviewers praised the illustrations and the overall appearance of his books, for example in a review of *In Nature's Realm*, which contained over ninety drawings, a reviewer complemented "how fascinating are the illustrations of nature scattered through it. Anyone who hungers now and then for a quiet stroll into field and wood will find here a volume that holds him with delight" (Anonymous 1901:218). Because the books were to be collected and displayed in middle and upper-class homes, the appearance was important, as well as the content. By the mid-1890s, Abbott developed a relationship with artist Oliver Kemp, who produced the sketches for *In Nature's Realm*, and other volumes such as the ill-fated "Dutch House" opera and poem. Kemp lived in Trenton, New Jersey, and was only 24 years old when he started collaborating with Abbott on his publications. He was listed in the 1900 U.S. Census as "artist" but should not be confused with Oliver Kemp the *Saturday Evening Post* illustrator, who was approximately ten years younger and much more widely published.

Other illustrations for volumes such as *Travels in a Tree-Top* were prepared by Alice Barber Stephens, who today is best known for her illustration of the 1903 edition of Louisa May Alcott's *Little Women*. Stephens created a sketch of a young man, who does not at all resemble Abbott, lounging under a tree as the first plate entitled "April Day Dreams" for his book *The Freedom of the Fields* (1898b). Stephens also prepared a drawing of Abbott in the company of Mrs. Robins in a garden scene that formed the fronticepiece of *Travels in a Tree-Top* (Fig. 7.1). On a copy of the original plate, Abbott wrote "*Not* a very good likeness of Mrs. R. or myself" (CCA/PU Box 15, Folder 4, emphasis original).

By the mid-1890s, Abbott started experimenting with photography as a means of illustrating his books and naturalist papers, rather than relying on sketches. His "In a Village Garden" (1895d) and "The Beauty of the Lilies" (1895e) contained photographs of plants and flowers gleaned from United States Nurseries founders J. R. Pitcher and W. A. Manda's botanical publications and catalogues. In *Clear Skies and Cloudy* (1898a), Abbott used local landscape photographs and noted in the preface that "the accompanying illustrations were all taken by or for the author, and are points of view at his own home, or just over the boundary, on the lands of his neighbors" (1898a:12).

Once published, these illustrated and naturalist books relieved much of the financial pressure Abbott experienced following his termination from the Penn Museum and allowed him to hire labor for the Three Beeches

7.1 Sketch of Mrs. Robins and Charles Conrad Abbott by Alice Barber Stephens. Notation on the image in C. C. Abbott's handwriting reads, "*Not* very good likenesses of Mrs. R. or myself. Fronticepiece of a new book of mine." Charles Conrad Abbott Papers (C0290), Box 15, Folder 4; Manuscripts Division, Department of Rare Books and Special Collections, Princeton University Library.

farm. His diaries in the late 1890s highlight a period of relative calm, as Abbott worked on the farm, on his books, and visited Volk's excavations in the area around Three Beeches, tempting Abbott into resuming archaeological research.

DABBLING AGAIN IN ARCHAEOLOGY

Despite Abbott's stated intentions to completely disconnect from archaeology, he had difficulty adhering to this resolution. Approximately two weeks after moving back to Three Beeches, Abbott was in the fields collecting again. He recorded in his diary: "April 22, 1894: Soon after breakfast, while sitting at my desk, I suddenly concluded to go relic hunting as I used to do in years gone by. Tramped over the field, across the gulley and found a good many specimens" (CCA/PU Box 3, Folder 5).

During Abbott's final few months at the University of Pennsylvania, and continuing following his termination, he also was interested in a historic archaeological site on Burlington Island that he labeled as a Dutch trader's house, and he continued collecting and informal excavations there for several years. However, these collections posed a problem for Abbott: he no longer had an institutional affiliation and had no place to send the materials he obtained. In the spring of 1894, he reopened communication with Frederic Ward Putnam at the Peabody Museum, hat in hand, and apologized for his petulant behavior in the past. He wrote, "I have within a few days moved back to my farm after four years in hell—I mean Philadelphia. Since November last, when I left the University, a great many scales have dropped from my eyes and I see now with clearer vision and wish that I had known years ago what I know now" and asked that he be able to send the "Dutch house" material to Cambridge to be placed with the rest of his collections. However, Abbott requested payment for the material, as was his arrangement with Putnam during his informal employment with the Peabody Museum, but concluded with an apology, "I trust I may again consider myself an 'assistant in the field' (for I do not expect to see Cambridge for years, if ever) and that 'by gones being by gones' offering now a humble apology it may be no impropriety to sign myself, Sincerely yours, Abbott" (CCA-FWP/HPM; April 6, 1894). It is unclear how Putnam responded, but Abbott's letters to Putnam continued and over the next few months, he sent several boxes of artifacts collected from Burlington Island.

Abbott's archaeological work during the mid- to late-1890s was largely limited to surface collection on his farm, writing and sketching artifacts from his "Dutch House" site, and observing—and often participating in—excavations being conducted by Ernest Volk on Lalor fields. Volk's work was commissioned by the Peabody Museum (later he was working for the American Museum of Natural History in New York City while Putnam held a joint appointment there), and initially the project was designed to definitively answer questions about early humans in the Delaware Valley, but the excavations continued long after Holmes dismantled Abbott's theory. Instead, Volk's work demonstrated a deep occupational history of prehistoric Native American people in the area. Abbott enjoyed stopping by, though there's no concrete record of how Volk viewed Abbott's frequent interruptions. Abbott's visits, fortunately, were dictated by whim and weather. He wrote at one point, "June 3, 1896: went down to Volk's diggings, but it was too sunny there so came back and took a long nap" (CCA/PU Box 3, Folder 5). However, it appeared that Abbott supported Volk's excavations, and considered Volk an ally in his theories about the American Paleolithic, which Abbott tenaciously insisted upon throughout his lifetime. He recorded in his diary, "July 12, 1896: How sick I am of this whole subject, especially as my *particular* views are the correct ones, as Volk has in part and soon will wholly demonstrate" (CCA/PU Box 3, Folder 5).

Abbott's friendship with Henry Mercer also continued long after Abbott's termination from the Penn Museum, despite several of Mercer's publications casting doubt on the American Paleolithic (Mercer 1893, 1894, 1898). Mercer resigned from the Museum in 1897 and also turned away from archaeology, beginning a career collecting historic tools and becoming an expert in ceramic tiles. He and Abbott remained in contact over the years. In 1905, Mercer and Abbott met and talked about past experiences and Abbott noted in his diary:

> April 9, 1905: Had more of a chance to see Henry Mercer and we did a deal of talking in a brief time. The conversation generally was of the recent controversy and upheaval at the University of Pennsylvania. I was much surprised at some things he said and amused at many others. He intimated that a possibility existed of my drifting in that direction again if I was willing, which very certainly I am not. I do not believe that peace of mind is practicable in a Philadelphia atmosphere, and I

would not believe on death a good many people there with whom one would frequently come in contact (CCA/PU Box 4, Folder 4).

For both men, their experience at the Penn Museum led to a resentment that lasted for many years. "May 7, 1907: Philadelphia....passed by the Archaeological Museum which I had never seen before and did not enter, not caring to bring up a flood of recollections of years gone by but they came in a measure in spite of me and I grew a trifle warm when I saw a bronze statue to that infamous liar Pepper and thought of that foul she-fiend and moral prostitute Sara Stevenson" (CCA/PU Box 5, Folder 1).

"MRS. ROBINS"

During the latter half of the 1890s, Abbott developed a relationship with a woman referred to in his diaries and correspondence only as "Mrs. Robins," who was Mrs. Julia Stockton Robins of Haverford, Pennsylvania, a woman approximately twenty years younger than Abbott. She was married to Edward Robins, a newspaperman and author, but the flirtatious notes between her and Abbott, and his fond comments about her in his diaries, suggest that their relationship, if not physically intimate, was at least very emotionally close. They corresponded extensively throughout this period, and Mrs. Robins and her husband even visited Three Beeches. Abbott's notes to her are on file at the Philadelphia Academy of Natural Sciences and were written on an unusual green notepaper. He wrote to her, "You are certainly amusing at times. What magic lurks in this green paper. It was some paper made to print bank checks on but the color was 'off' and so it was made into these pads, which I have some left. I bought all the man had, because it was cheap, and now you put a special value on it. I shall have to keep it for your letters exclusively then" (CCA-JSR/PANS; undated).

Many of his letters to Mrs. Robins were discussions of the natural world and playful comments on everyday life. She published her own observations of birds and nature (Robins 1896), suggesting that their initial correspondence may have been based in Abbott's naturalist publications. There's no evidence of her letters to him. He wrote to her of everyday things, for example, "The meadows were beautiful and I hated to leave them for so prozy a matter as dinner, especially as we didn't have the apple-pie I anticipated" (CCA-JSR/PANS; undated). Undoubtedly the letters were part of an ongoing conversation between the two, as Abbott referenced previous events and correspondence. "I do not believe that you would have had energy enough to have read any communication, had I sent one lately, so thoroughly enervating has been the weather for a week. At all events I have had no ideas worth communicating, and even now it is with much misgiving that I venture carefully to your last letter" (CCA-JSR/PANS; dated "Saturday and today, 8th thru 12" 1895).

In some cases, Abbott's letters to Mrs. Robins were meant to amuse. For example, "On Wednesday last, I ventured to Asbury Park for the day and was entertained for awhile and finally grew very weary. I do not like an ocean bounded by a flood of Wesleyan fanaticism. I undertook to bathe but the water, even boisterous waves could scarcely penetrate the prescribed suits worn at such a time" (CCA-JSR/PANS; dated "Saturday and today, 8th thru 12" 1895). In another letter, he signed it "I feel cloudy and am going to take a walk to get rid of blues. Somewhere I will mail this...Yours truly, C(rusty) C(ranky) A(bo)" (CCA-JSR/PANS; undated).

Sometimes, however, Abbott's notes were far from nice. "O hang the bicycle riding. I never saw any woman on one that did not look out of place, and that's all there is of it. When it comes to squatty dumplings like the average girl it's not taking to my eye and for you, above average height, why I cannot imagine. But why waste ink on such rubbish of a subject. It's a matter of taste on an unimportant subject" (CCA-JSR/PANS; July 1, 1897). He further revealed an anti-feminist bent at times in saying "It's fortunate you are a woman and needn't bother with natural history, other than birds" (CCA-JSR/PANS; undated).

The correspondence peaked around 1897–1898, and Abbott frequently visited her at her home in Haverford, Pennsylvania, to read her segments of his writing and discuss natural history. By the end of 1898, however, the relationship was on the decline. Abbott wrote in his diary, "December 20, 1898: Mrs. Robins letter long and yet empty, so a hard one to answer" (CCA/PU Box 4, Folder 1). Merely a few months later, he noted, "February 18, 1899: Wrote a letter in reply to Mrs. Robins and burned it. I wish she would not write. I am awfully tired of the correspondence but do not like to say so" (CCA/PU Box 4, Folder 1). And a week after that: "February 25, 1899: Got a silly note from Mrs. Robins about not writing, but I will not undertake to write a letter when I've nothing to say, just to keep up a correspondence. It is absurd" (CCA/PU Box 4, Folder 1). That winter, Abbott's diaries recorded the closest to a confession of their relationship as can be found in his personal papers: "November 23, 1899: A letter came from Mrs. Robins, desiring a reopening of recent correspondence, which I thought had better end as there was nothing to write about and too frequently led to misunderstanding" (CCA/PU Box 4, Folder 1). There is no record of Mrs. Abbott's view of the relationship.

"NATURE FAKERS"

The beginning of the end of nature writing occurred with the "sham natural history" controversy that arose in 1903 and stemmed from John Burroughs's critical review of fiction that purported to present tales of animals' exploits that were allegedly rooted in actual, observed behavior (Bruyninckx 2018; Lutts 1990). Burroughs, a highly successful nature writer, published an article in *Atlantic Monthly* that attacked well-known authors Ernest Thompson Seton, Charles G. D. Roberts, and William J. Long. He alleged that in these authors' works "the line between fact and fiction is repeatedly crossed, and that a deliberate attempt is made to induce the reader to cross, too, and to work such a spell upon him that he shall not know that he has crossed and is in the land of make-believe" (1903:300). The worst of Burroughs's condemnation was directed at Long, who was criticized as an awkward imitator of more skilled nature writers. The works were described as "True as romance, true in their artistic effects, true in their power to entertain the young reader, they certainly are; but true as natural history they as certainly are not" (1903:300).

Long vigorously defended his writing but did so with little scientific background to substantiate the "facts" of his work; Seaton and Roberts largely retreated and thus escaped the worst of the forthcoming critical deluge (Lutts 1990). Long was an ordained minister who rejected Darwinian evolution and argued that human and animal minds reflected a will and consciousness granted from God (Long 1906). Burroughs believed that nature was independent of religion, and though observers may feel a spiritual connection to nature and the environment, accurate descriptions of plant and animal life should not project spiritual beliefs (Lutts 1990). Instead, Burroughs argued that Long's "statements are rarely convincing; rarely do they have the verisimilitude of real observations" (1903:309). Ultimately, dismayed that these texts were being used in schools and portrayed as accurate depictions of the environment, Theodore Roosevelt publicly denounced the "nature fakers" and further criticized unscrupulous publishers and school administrators (Lutts 1990).

Though Abbott was never publicly criticized as a "nature faker" or purveyor of "sham natural history," the controversy impacted his own nature writing. By drawing attention to problems of exaggerated prose and anthropomorphic descriptions of plants and animals, it created new standards of accuracy for nature writers who wished to be taken seriously among professional scientists and led to the ultimate decline of the amateur nature writer (Lutts 1990). Once again, Abbott found himself left behind by yet another rapidly professionalizing field. His last nature work entitled *The Rambles of an Idler*, was published in 1906.

8

Burlington Island and Historical Archaeology

"Buried inches deep in gradually-accumulating soil rest the ruins of an ancient house: buried fathoms deep in the mouldy pages of forgotten books are records of stirring times, before Philadelphia was, when there were Dutch on the Delaware."

--Abbott (1892d:312)

During the tumultuous years when Charles Conrad Abbott was working at the Penn Museum, he and his family resided in a rented house in Bristol, Pennsylvania, placing them much closer to Philadelphia than Three Beeches in Trenton and making for a simple commute by train. While there, Abbott used the location as a base for exploring the Delaware River shoreline for evidence of Paleolithic occupation but found little. However, his surveys successfully identified a 17th century historic archaeological site on Burlington Island, a short paddle by rowboat from Bristol. Between approximately 1891 and 1894, Abbott excavated the site of what he alleged was a 17th century Dutch fur trader's house. Though Abbott never published scholarly articles on his excavations, his work there marks one of the earliest documented instances of historical archaeology in the Delaware Valley. Brief published accounts of his research exist in newspaper editorials (Abbott 1906b) and two literary volumes entitled *Recent Rambles, or In Touch with Nature,* published by J. P. Lippincott and

Co. in 1892, and *Travels in a Tree Top*, with the same publisher in 1894. Both of these volumes contained elaborate musings on the natural world with only a tangential discussion of Burlington Island archaeology. Either because Abbott did not feel that his historical archaeology was important enough to publish in scholarly venues, or because he had soured on professional archaeology as a whole, his unpublished personal diaries and correspondence provide the most complete record of his activities on Burlington Island.

Abbott's initial explorations on Burlington Island focused not on historical archaeology, but instead were part of his ongoing efforts to document an American Paleolithic. He surveyed the shores of the island with the goal of finding roughly flaked, bifacial argillite artifacts that would help bolster his argument for ice age or pre-ice age humans in the New World. By 1891, an embattled Abbott faced a precipitous decline in scholarly standing in the face of William Henry Holmes's Piney Branch quarry data, and he struggled in vain to regain his earlier status. Though Abbott claimed to find a few "paleoliths" on the Island, he also discovered historic artifacts that piqued his interest in early Dutch settlement of the Delaware Valley. He observed, "no one day's digging was so full of meaning, or brought me so closely in touch with the past, as when I uncovered what remained of the old Dutch trader's house" (Abbott 1894b:172).

HISTORY OF BURLINGTON ISLAND

Burlington Island is located in the Delaware River, directly across from the city of Burlington, New Jersey, nearly one hundred miles upstream from the Atlantic Ocean (Fig. 8.1). It was an important political and geographic feature during colonial times that was alternately claimed by both the Dutch and the English in the 17th century. The Dutch established the earliest permanent occupation in 1624 when the Dutch ship *Nieu Nederlandt*, commanded by Cornelius Jacobsen Mey, transported a small contingent of Belgian Walloon settlers to Burlington Island. Records indicate that the settlement included a trading house for commerce with the local Lenape people and the palisaded Fort Wilhemus (Bisbee 1972:11; Weslager 1961:59). The Island has been variously called Matinakonk (Bisbee 1971:39; Dankers and Sluyter 1867), Matinicum (Soderlund 2015), Koomemakonokonk, or Tenneconck (Bisbee 1971:39).

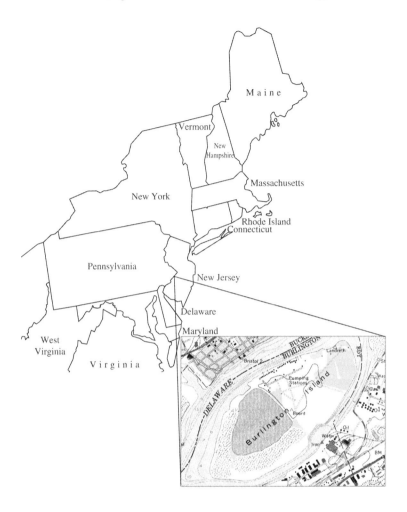

8.1 Locator map showing Burlington Island, New Jersey. USGS Topographic Quadrangle: Bristol, P.A.-N.J., 1955 (Photorevised 1981).

A government presence on Burlington Island began in 1625, when Willem van der Hulst (alternately Verhulst) established a residence there that permitted him to "from time to time as occasion may require, betake himself to the North River to regulate matters there" (Van Laer 1924:64), but Verhulst's term was brief. In 1626, he was evicted from office and sent home to Europe (Jacobs 2004:108; Dillian et al. 2013). The Dutch West India Company in New Netherland replaced him with the appointment of Peter Minuit as Director, but soon after, the population of Burlington Island was removed and consolidated to Manhattan Island as the new political center of Dutch occupation of North America (Bisbee 1972:12; Weslager 1961:68). At the time, it was deemed politically and economically advantageous to locate the Dutch stronghold in Manhattan instead and Burlington Island was temporarily uninhabited (Dillian et al. 2013).

Approximately thirty years later, in 1659, Alexander d'Hinoyossa, the Vice-Director of New Netherland (Bisbee 1972:14), reoccupied Burlington Island and "made it a pleasure ground or garden, built good houses upon it, and sowed and planted it" (Dankers and Sluyter 1867), but within five years, the English took control when Sir Robert Carr seized Burlington Island on behalf of the Duke of York. Four years after that, on December 15, 1668, the Island was granted to Peter Alricks (alternatively recorded as Alrichs or Aldridge, and possibly the same as a "Peter Kendricks" named by Abbott [1906b]), a Dutch businessman, who hired farm laborers to work the property (Dillian et al. 2013; Weslager 1967:196).

In 1671, tragedy struck Alricks's Island farm. Peter Veltscheerder and Christian Samuels, two of Alricks's Dutch servants, were attacked and killed by two Lenape men, Tashiowycan and Wyannattamo (Bisbee 1972:15; Soderlund 2015), an act that figured prominently in Abbott's interpretations of Burlington Island's archaeological record (Dillian et al. 2013). Tashiowycan and Wyannattamo were allegedly motivated by the death of Tashiowycan's sister from disease, possibly smallpox (Nelson 1886:214; Soderlund 2015), but regardless of the cause, the English authorities required punishment for the murders. Lenape leaders warned the local English representatives that though the Lenape community regretted the incident, Tashiowycan and Wyannattamo had relatives who would seek revenge if they were executed by the English for their crime (Soderlund 2015:127). Ultimately, despite the potential for exacerbating tensions between the Lenape and European settlers, English authorities insisted that Lenape leaders submit Tashiowycan and Wyannattamo, dead or alive, for justice (Reed and Miller 1944:68). Tashiowycan was killed by the English (Smith 1765:72; Soderlund 2015:129), but Wyannattamo escaped (Soderlund 2015:129). Abbott incorporated this titillating event into his fictionalized interpretations of Burlington Island's archaeological record (Dillian et al. 2013).

Burlington Island changed hands a number of times after that, but in 1674, the Treaty of Westminster finally granted New Netherland, and with it Burlington Island, to the British. Records suggest that at that time, two local farmers, Peter Jegou and Henry Jacobs farmed the property, but were not owners (Bisbee 1972:16). In 1682 Burlington Island reverted to public ownership.

HISTORICAL ARCHAEOLOGY

When Abbott conducted his archaeological investigations, Burlington Island was sparsely occupied, with agricultural enterprises the main activity. Abbott referenced chicken houses and local residents in his field records (CCA/PU Box 3, Folder 5; March 24, 1894), but appeared to have free access to the property for survey and excavation, or at least did not get caught: "let it be whispered, there is a supreme delight in digging out of bounds. Of course an archaeologist, historian, or curiosity crank looks upon himself as not amenable to common law, and in his case trespass is not trespass. I speak from experience" (Abbott 1892d:316).

Abbott wrote of his discovery, "I found a yellow brick upon the sand; and, looking farther, another, and curious old red bricks, and bits of roofing tiles, and pipe-stems; scattered everywhere odds and ends that could only have come from some old house near by" (1892d:313). The surface finds piqued his interest, and he returned to the Island many times, but his archaeological methods had not improved in the years following his initial employment with Putnam as a field assistant. He recorded, "sitting upon the damp sand, dotted with bits of the old house and pipe-stems, I burrowed into the low bank with a garden-trowel" (1892d:318). He noted that he had discovered artifacts and features in situ but did not record their provenience in either his literary or personal writing.

> A part of a wall was finally exposed, and many small, pale-yellow bricks. The larger red ones were generally perfect, but every yellow one was broken. Next came a part of the roof, still intact, three large curved tiles, and beneath them portions of what I took to be a charred beam. Handwrought iron spikes were found, all twisted out of shape, the effect of heating when the house was burned. One little fragment of glazed earthenware, being slightly curved, I fancied a bit of a beer-mug; but there was no question about the pipes. Either this old Dutchman was the most inveterate of smokers or he had on hand a stock for trading (Abbott 1892d:318–319).

His notes suggest that the amount of material excavated and surface collected from this site was relatively large. In a newspaper article, he recorded that he "gathered up more than a thousand relics of these people" (1906b). Among these, for instance, he collected over five hundred pipe stems (Abbott 1894b:168), but the collections that survive are comparatively small and merely allude to the diversity of the original assemblage.

Abbott and his son Richard "Dick" Abbott made frequent excursions to Burlington Island, and diary entries detail their almost daily visits. "April 16, 1891: Dick and I went over to Burlington Island and found a fine lot of relics" (CCA/PU Box 3, Folder 2) was a typical record in Abbott's daily diary during this time. In some cases, the excursions were in the company of guests and strangers encountered along the way. "April 21, 1891: Soon after breakfast, Dick and I went over to Burlington and started hunting on Assiscunk Creek. Met a Mr. Travis and went to his house. A most curious man. Got some information from him however. Saw signs of relics in spots" (CCA/PU Box 3, Folder 2). And further, in the company of Henry Mercer he noted, "November 21, 1891: Dick, Joe, Mercer and myself went over to Burlington Island. Mercer wanted to see the place and hunted relics until noon. I got tired but stuck and was excited over some old bricks which I think can be turned to account historically....It is altogether a most interesting matter" (CCA/PU Box 3, Folder 2). Abbott's descriptions of his fieldwork were not scientifically detailed (although he did produce a section drawing of Burlington Island; Fig. 8.2), a pattern apparent in his publications on the American Paleolithic as well, and a trait for which he received much-deserved criticism. In *Recent Rambles*, he described his excavations as "something more than mere shoveling of dirt, pitching aside with a spade sand, gravel, and clay." But his focus was clearly on the artifacts, rather than careful documentation. "It may mean more important discovery at any moment and the bringing again to light of day of long-buried treasure" (1892d:315).

By November of 1891, Abbott was convinced that the historic artifacts from Burlington Island were related to the Dutch occupation. "November 22, 1891: Soon after breakfast, Dick and I went to Burlington Island and on lower end of it found a lot of bricks, roofing tile and other matter of an old Dutch house as I take it to have been. Brought back a good lot of the spoils and busied myself all the forenoon in drying two large and perfect tiles for roofing. Early in afternoon studied these so far as one or two books

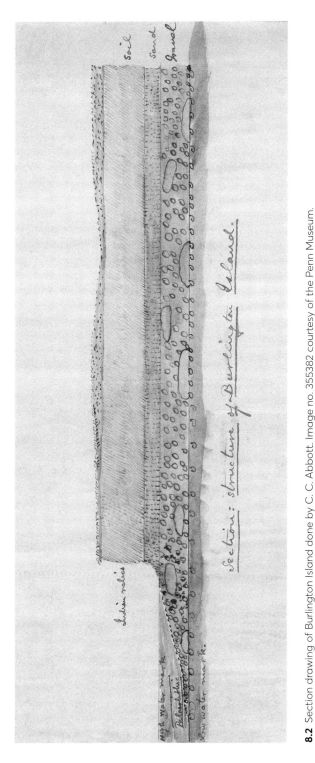

8.2 Section drawing of Burlington Island done by C. C. Abbott. Image no. 355382 courtesy of the Penn Museum.

availed anything and planned an article about the place and its early colonial traces" (CCA/PU Box 3, Folder 2). The next day, Abbott continued his research, "November 23, 1891: Busied myself mostly with looking up historical matters in reference to the bricks and tiles found yesterday on the island" (CCA/PU Box 3, Folder 2). The claim that artifacts from the site were Dutch persisted in Abbott's records throughout the early 1890s. "April 15, 1892: Over to Burlington Island and poked about the site of Old Dutch house. We found some curious bits of old blue china and glass" (CCA/PU Box 3, Folder 2).

Abbott soon began referring to the historical site on Burlington Island as a "Dutch fur-trader's house" in his correspondence (CCA-FWP/HPM Record 722, Accession 94-9; March 22, 1894). In *Recent Rambles*, he wrote "It was not enough to search for the spot whereon had stood the house, for this was soon found; but who lived here; when did he build; when and why did he leave? A hundred questions plagued me at once, and I took refuge in the book-stack" (1892d:314). Admirably for Abbott, who seemed to have little patience for methodical research, he visited numerous historical societies, libraries, and museums, in order to gather background information on the island and its history (for example, as noted in diary entries dated November 27, 1891; November 30, 1891; and December 2, 1891 [CCA/PU Box 3, Folder 2]). However, despite careful research, Abbott's aggrandized historical tale of the death of two servants working for Peter Alricks conflated multiple historical events, likely for the sake of drama, and he stated in *Recent Rambles*, "About the same time, the two men living in the island house were murdered. I was delighted, and hurried back to the island. To think of murder and a state of siege and all the wild tumult of midnight surprises having happened so near to home!" (1892b:315).

However, even during Abbott's time, it was apparent that his fantastical explanation of the Dutch House on Burlington Island deviated into fiction. For example, despite Abbott's clear attempts to find accurate historical information on the "Dutch fur-trader's house," he appears to have been a bit confused about the chronology of its occupation. He stated in *Recent Rambles* that a tract of land was purchased by Peter Jegou in 1668 (1892d:314), but in 1668 Burlington Island was granted to Peter Alricks, a Dutch businessman. Peter Jegou and Henry Jacobs did not arrive until 1674 and were not the owners of the Island but at best tenants of the Governor and perhaps merely squatters. Abbott wrote that "Peter Jegou was an extensive landholder, and to perfect his title and otherwise save his bacon from the greedy clutch of envious Quakers, took the oath of allegiance to the English government" (1906b). Though Jegou eventually purchased property, he owned Chygoes Island, which is now part of mainland Burlington City, not Burlington Island (Veit and Bello 1999).

DUTCH HOUSE FICTION

In April of 1893, Abbott stated his intention to write an opera based on the Dutch fur-trader's house at Burlington Island (CCA/PU Box 3, Folder 2; April 19, 1893), but was unsuccessful at telling the story in operatic format. Two years later, he was incrementally writing the "Dutch House" story, as he called it in his diaries (CCA/PU Box 3, Folder 5; April 30,1895 and May 1, 1895). The fictionalized account of historical events at Burlington Island soon earned the title "Island Tragedy" and was transformed into a poem (CCA/PU Box 3, Folder 5; March 7, 1896), but multiple publishers declined the manuscript. "March 12, 1896: Dr. Bird accepts 'Skies' and sends money but has no use for 'Dutch House.' I am not surprised and so less disappointed" (CCA/PU Box 3, Folder 5), and only a few weeks later "May 6, 1896: Today, I sent my 'Dutch House' poem to the Century Magazine and do not believe it will be accepted" (CCA/PU Box 3, Folder 5). After only a few days for review, "May 11, 1896: Got back my poem, declined 'because of its length' which is a polite lie of the Editor probably" (CCA/PU Box 3, Folder 5).

Yet Abbott persisted with his goal of publishing a fictionalized account of the Burlington Island site in some form. "May 28, 1896: After breakfast, smoked and read Emerson's poems and thought a good deal about the 'Dutch House' making some notes there on....After supper, came up to my desk for some time and wrote an introduction to 'Dutch House' of some fifty odd lines and planned to continue this for some lines additional" (CCA/PU Box 3, Folder 5). The next few days, in early summer of 1896, Abbott devoted his writing efforts to revisions of the Burlington Island story and enlisted Oliver Kemp's assistance with illustrations. The singlemindedness with which Abbott pursued this effort was noteworthy. "June 12, 1896: Oliver Kemp came and we discussed illustrating the 'Dutch House' for an hour. Dick brought a letter from Century Co. while he was here, saying didn't think they would take it, but send it on. This did not discourage me at all" (CCA/PU Box 3, Folder 5). Unfortunately, Abbott soon conceded that it was futile:

> June 15, 1896: Up early and before breakfast had accomplished a good deal and begin to see the end of this interminable revision of the Dutch House. I shall be glad beyond measure to be rid of it, as after all my trouble, it is a rank failure. To my desk, where I staid until dinner was ready, and at work again afterwards until moved to take a nap, which I did. Then downstairs but not much in the yard, and soon again took up my work of revision and copying and kept at it until nearly tea time and again after supper until 10:20pm, when it was done. Unless now I convert it into a long prose novel, I can do nothing more. As it is, it is a finished production, but I am very doubtful as to its favorable reception by any publisher and my plans are chaotic concerning it. I shall probably let it rest in the little black trunk until some circumstance shall arise to determine me (CCA/PU Box 3, Folder 5).

Abbott picked up his Burlington Island story at several points during the next few years, but chafed at critical review. "The born hypercritic is the nerves' worst or most effectual irritant," he wrote in his diary after a particularly negative review (CCA/PU Box 3, Folder 5; July 11, 1896). But he continued to write and revise through winter and spring of 1897, receiving a damning review that April (CCA/PU Box 3, Folder 5; April 22, 1897). In spring of 1898, he again renewed interest in the "Dutch House" story, and submitted it to Alden March of the *Philadelphia Press*, a weekly periodical, who declined to publish, and then submitted the manuscript to *Lippincott's Magazine*, which also refused. "December 1, 1898: Express office... [received] from Morris [Harrison S. Morris, Editor of *Lippincott's Magazine*] my Dutch House mss with a long criticism. This I considered during the evening and after supper, wrote a long letter to him about it and other matters" (CCA/PU Box 4, Folder 1).

Abbott edited the manuscript again over the next few days. "December 3, 1898: I will now undertake a new version of my 'Dutch House' based on Morris' criticism." And again, "December 4, 1898: Took up the 'Dutch House' and commenced in earnest to revise it, adopting suggestions made by Morris. Got interested and kept at it until nearly noon" (CCA/PU Box 4, Folder 1). But by New Year's Eve of 1898, Abbott questioned his efforts. He wrote a final diary entry that year on a dreary note. "December 31, 1898: I will make no comment on the year closed tonight. There was enough literary activity to show I was not idle, but there was no remuneration worth speaking of, and the rejection of my story by Lippincott's was a bitter disappointment although it will lead to its being a very much better written story, but will it ever be published?" (CCA/PU Box 4, Folder 1). It never was.

Despite Abbott's fanciful interpretations of the history of Burlington Island, and his assertion that his finds were associated with a "Dutch fur-trader's house," there is little explicit historical evidence for a trading post located on the Island, and his dramatic interpretation of murder and intrigue was a conflated account of multiple people and events. Fort Wilhemus, built in 1624, functioned as settlement, garrison, and likely center for interactions with the local Lenape population. However, the Burlington Island collection is from a much later period, dating from the last third of the 17th century. Nonetheless, the archaeological artifacts do clearly show a Dutch presence in the 17th century and include items that would have been traded with Native American people, such as copper, beads, and tobacco pipes. It is particularly noteworthy that the artifacts do reflect an occupation of the Island at approximately the time when Alricks's servants were murdered.

"DUTCH FUR TRADER'S HOUSE" ARTIFACT ASSEMBLAGE

Abbott's collections of archaeological artifacts are now housed at the Peabody Museum at Harvard University (Cat. Nos. 52-46-10/34016 through 52-46-10/34034). According to Abbott's diaries, the collection was submitted on April 2, 1894. He included a note to Frederic Ward Putnam in which he said:

> I...send the balance of "Dutch House," less one brick, which shall only go out of my possession to go into the museum. This one big box sent to-day completed the shipment and I earnestly hope that when received, the contents of the two boxes already sent and that of the one sent today will be placed in a case and labeled (ultimately) in accordance with the marks on the smaller objects, and the general label of Relics of a Dutch Fur-Trader's House Built in 1668 on the lower (S.E.) End of Burlington Island, Delaware River. House plundered and partly

destroyed by Indians and fur trader murdered in 1670. House reoccupied by English a few years later: when destroyed (by fire) not now
known, but previous to 1776. Discovered and ruins excavated by Dr.
Charles C. Abbott, in 1892–1894 (CCA-FWP/HPM Record 727, Accession 94-9; May 8, 1894).

Abbott's collection may not have been received with the same level of
enthusiasm as he felt it warranted. The accession records for the Peabody
Museum indicate it was not catalogued or accessioned until 1952, despite
its receipt by Putnam more than fifty years earlier (Dillian et al. 2013).

Abbott hoped to receive some financial compensation for his Dutch fur-
trader's house collection, but preferred that the artifacts go to the Peabody
Museum. His stated reason was that he felt that this historic collection
added chronological depth to his more massive collection of prehistoric
Native American artifacts, but really, he was hoping Putnam would purchase the collection as he had done with Abbott's prehistoric artifacts in
the past. He wrote to Putnam "I want to make a proper disposition of it, and
think that as it contains some Indian objects that it might fittingly be added
to the Abbott collections as the last chapter to the story, as my paleoliths are
chapter 1" (CCA-FWP/HPM Record 722, Accession 94-9; March 22, 1894).
However, it is just as likely that he had burned too many bridges in Philadelphia to find a home for the artifacts there, and his only other congenial relationship with an archaeological museum was at the Peabody. To Putnam,
however, he wrote on April 6, 1894 that "I refused an offer of $100 for the
'Dutch House' collection because my collection at Cambridge seems to be
its proper place" (CCA-FWP/HPM Record 724, Accession 94-9).

But Abbott was being a bit disingenuous. Earlier that spring, he tried
to sell the Burlington Island collection to the Penn Museum, but they were
not interested. In his diaries, he recorded, "March 12, 1894: To Philadelphia
in 9:14 train…My object in seeing Pepper, Harrison, and so on, was to try
soon to sell 'Dutch House'" and later, "March 28, 1894:…All efforts to sell
the 'Dutch House' came to naught. I will not give it away" (CCA/PU Box 3,
Folder 5). Less than two weeks later, he indeed gave it away, but not to the
Penn Museum.

Instead, the Burlington Island artifacts were remitted to the Peabody Museum, with the sole exception of a single tile housed at the Penn
Museum, which is curated and labeled as "Pan Tile, Dutch trader's house

Burlington Island" (Cat. No. 9186; Dillian et al. 2013). This tile is likely the same one that Richard Abbott found on Burlington Island, and that Abbott took for consultation with several experts in Philadelphia. "January 31, 1894: Went to see Barber, taking him a piece of heavy tile which Dick found on the Island. He says it must have come from the 'Dutch House' and is very old and from the East Indies probably. He is to work it up and let me know." And later, "February 16, 1894:...then to see Barber, who says the tile may be Dutch of three hundred years ago" (CCA/PU Box 3, Folder 5).

Abbott wrote in *Travels in a Tree-Top* of his excitement regarding the artifacts. He stated:

> I could enthuse, without being laughed at, over what to others was but meaningless rubbish, and I found much that, to me, possessed greater interest than usual, because of a mingling of late Indian and early European objects. With a handful of glass, porcelain, and amber beads were more than one hundred of copper; the former from Venice, the latter the handiwork of a Delaware Indian. With a white clay pipe, made in Holland in the 17th century, was found a rude brown clay one, made here in the river valley. Mingled with fragments of blue and white Delft plates, bowls, and platters, were sundried mud dishes made by women hereabouts during, who can say how many centuries? How completely history and prehistory here overlapped! (1894b:171).

He described them to Putnam as "The roofing tile, quaint yellow bricks, rude hardware, tile, parts of windows, hundreds (fragments and some nearly perfect) of the most ancient forms of European clay tobacco pipes, bottles (broken) with beads (Venetian) etc. etc. make together a most interesting and I think unique series of objects of the time of initial contact of Indian and white man" (CCA-FWP/HPM Record 722, Accession 94-9; March 22, 1894). In many ways, Abbott was correct. Although comprising only 196 items, it is one of only a few collections that represent early European colonization of the Delaware Valley (Dillian et al. 2013; Veit and Bello 1999).

Notable artifacts in the collection include beads, pipes, glass, and two copper tinklers, which mark a mix of European and Native American manufacture (Beauchamp 1903:19; Dillian et al. 2013; Dilliplane 1980:79; Ehrhardt 2005:119–120; Faulkner and Faulkner 1987; Kraft 1975:154; Veit and Bello 1999; Wray et al. 1990:249). Seventeen glass trade beads, including fifteen round beads with redwood bodies and compound stripes, were also recovered. Similar beads have been found on Dutch sites dating from 1630 to 1730 (Karklins 1983:111, 115; Kidd and Kidd 1970; Veit and Bello 1999). The copper and porcelain beads Abbott mentioned do not appear to be in the Peabody Museum collection, and it is unclear if they were ever submitted to Putnam. The "amber" bead was actually made of glass, which Abbott knew and noted in his diary, but apparently chose not to disclose. "February 12, 1894: A supposed amber bead from the Dutch House proves to be glass, so Beatte the lapidary told me" (CCA/PU Box 3, Folder 5).

Abbott claimed to have discovered over 500 tobacco pipes on Burlington Island (1894b:168), but only 61 fragments are present in the Peabody Museum collection today (52-46-10/34025). However, these artifacts offer some chronological data for the site or sites where they were collected. Some have heels marked "EB," most likely indicating Edward Bird, an English-born pipemaker who worked in the Netherlands between 1635 and 1665 (Dallal 1995:99; Huey 1991:76; Miller 1991:76; Veit and Bello 1999), and one marked "IS," which is possibly the mark of John Sinderling, who worked from 1668 to 1699 in Bristol England (Hurry and Keeler 1991:68–69; Veit and Bello 1999). Two stems were marked with a fleur-de-lis, probably of Dutch origin, and one was marked "VBAK" possibly for TVBAC or tobacco (Dillian et al. 2013; Veit and Bello 1999).

Prehistoric artifacts are also represented in the collection, but the bulk of the artifacts date from the last third of the 17th century. Though some, such as beads, pipes, kettles, and tinklers would have been valuable trade items for exchange, there's no clear evidence that the site was a "fur-trader's house" as Abbott alleged. Instead, some of the artifacts, particularly the pan tiles, were more likely associated with a European-style domestic structure than a simple trading post. Furthermore, Abbott's artifact collections may have come from more than one occupation site: a Contact Period Native American site and a 17th century European domestic structure. Without accurate provenience data for the artifacts, it is impossible to determine.

BURLINGTON ISLAND TODAY

During the early 20th century, not long after Abbott and his family moved back to Three Beeches farm, Burlington Island evolved into a popular resort with extensive picnic grounds, bathing beaches, and amusement rides including a roller coaster called the Greyhound. This park, despite periodic proposals for bridge access, was serviced by steamboats and continued to draw large crowds until it was destroyed by fire in 1928.

After the amusement park era, a series of commercial enterprises, most notably the Warner Company, mined and dredged portions of the lower section of the Island for gravel. Roughly 100 acres of the southern tip of Burlington Island was removed in the 1950s, creating a large lake, and other parts of the Island have been used to store dredged materials from the Delaware River. The site Abbott excavated was located close to the southeastern tip of the island, according to the limited provenience information recorded in his diaries. Based on historic map evidence, it is possible that it survived the dredging but a visit to the island in 2008 did not reveal any surface evidence of Dutch occupation (Dillian et al. 2013). Today, debate continues over the island's future. Proposals to build a golf course and hotel convention center on Burlington Island have been put forward, and recently, the U.S. Army Corps of Engineers has revealed plans to use 300 acres to dump additional dredge spoil from the Delaware River (Gray 2016).

Today, historical archaeology is a professional discipline, with codified field and laboratory practices, graduate degrees, professional societies, and peer-reviewed journals, but in the 19th century, Abbott's work in historical archaeology was unique. Only a few earlier examples exist, including excavations by the Pilgrims in the 17th century (Schuyler 1977:1), 18th century excavations on St. Croix Island in Maine (Cotter 1994:16), mid-19th century excavations of Miles Standish's house (Deetz 1996:39), and an 1853 attempt by the New Jersey Historical Society to relocate the site of Fort Nassau—another early Dutch outpost—on the river using maps, historical diaries, and landscape features (Mulford 1853). It took until discussions at the 1958 annual meeting of the American Anthropological Association for historical archaeology to gain its distinct professional status (Cotter 1993). After a decade of planning, the Society for Historical Archaeology was formally incorporated as a professional scholarly society in 1968 (Jelks 1993), approximately 75 years after Abbott's research into a "Dutch fur-trader's house" at Burlington Island on the Delaware River.

9

The Princeton Years

"September 14, 1875:…went to Princeton….A rather tiresome day as the college is so innocent of anything of interest to me. I shudder at the thought of people living in so crassly archaic and fanatic an atmosphere."

--Abbott (CCA/PU Box 2, Folder 2)

On November 27, 1900, Charles Conrad Abbott received a letter from Ernest C. Richardson, Princeton University Librarian and Corresponding Secretary of the Princeton Historical Association, asking if he would donate his personal papers and books to the Princeton University Library because "you have an interest in Princeton through marriage, and in this case you may not be indifferent to the advantage which the collection will be for the study of American History in this University" (CCA/PU Box 8, Folder 3; November 27, 1900). Richardson, not subtly, stroked Abbott's sensitive ego. More than ten years had passed since Holmes's work at Piney Branch cast doubt the American Paleolithic in Trenton, and, though Abbott had largely withdrawn from archaeological debate, his bitterness remained. He still occasionally collected artifacts, but much of his intellectual effort focused on naturalist musings, not archaeology. When Princeton University contacted him about donating papers, books, and historical materials to the library, Abbott welcomed a long overdue acknowledgment by the academic community.

Abbott's introduction to the Princeton University Library was facilitated by Francis Bazley Lee, a lawyer from Trenton and member of the Princeton Historical Society. Lee (1907) published on the genealogy and history of central New Jersey, which included a history of the Abbott family, likely bringing the two men together in research. Lee and Richardson knew each other through the Historical Society, and as Richardson disclosed to Abbott, had schemed to court Abbott for his important archaeological papers (CCA/PU correspondence from E. C. Richardson; Box 8, Folder 3; November 27, 1900).

Richardson appealed to Abbott's desire to disseminate archaeological knowledge, but also as Abbott was aging, to preserve his name for posterity. He wrote to Abbott, "I believe that every University is bound to teach American History first of all, the history of the state in which it is located, Constitutional, Political and Archaeological, thoroughly from top to bottom, and to train men into the method of research in a way which can only be done by the use of such collections" (CCA/PU Box 8, Folder 3; November 27, 1900). It did not take long for Abbott to agree to donate many of his papers, diaries, manuscripts, and notes, which ultimately saved the bulk of Abbott's unpublished writing from a fire that destroyed Three Beeches in 1914. On December 11, 1900, Lee and Abbott selected materials for donation, according to Abbott's diary, and thus established the Abbott Collection at the Princeton University Library (CCA/PU Box 4, Folder 1).

During conversations and correspondence regarding the Library archive, however, Richardson casually mentioned to Abbott that a small museum was taking form on campus. He wrote "I wish to say that we have really a very nice growing museum in what is known as the E. M. [Elizabeth Marsh] Museum, in which Professor Libbey takes especial interest and for which he has gotten a good many archaeological and ethnological specimens, not comparing, of course, with Harvard, but with some excellent specialties and growing" (CCA/PU Box 8, Folder 3; December 3, 1900). This tangential statement sparked Abbott's interest. Could he create an archaeological museum at Princeton along the same model as the Peabody Museum at Harvard University, with wealthy benefactors and the academic credentials of a prestigious university? Over the next twelve years, Abbott pursued the establishment of a museum at Princeton University, contributing approximately 1,300 specimens that he collected from the area around Three Beeches in Trenton. But the archaeological museum, as Abbott had imagined it, never materialized. Princeton's resources were focused else-where, and Abbott's pattern of petulant behavior and lax work habits con-demned the project from the outset.

PRINCETON CONNECTIONS

Princeton University was a logical academic and social fit for Abbott. His in-laws' family networks and wealth facilitated inroads into the Princ-eton academic and philanthropic community. Abbott's wife, Julia Boggs Olden was a member of the affluent and influential Olden family of Princ-eton, with long connections to the University. Her father was Job Gardiner Olden, a businessman who served for more than twenty years as the As-sistant Treasurer of what was then called the College of New Jersey, now Princeton University.

Julia's paternal uncle was Charles Smith Olden, a Republican elected as the Governor of New Jersey from 1860–1863, and who later served on the state's highest court, the New Jersey Court of Errors and Appeals, from 1868–1873. Charles S. Olden built the estate of Drumthwacket, in Princeton, which was purchased by Moses Taylor Pyne after Olden's death, and today is the official residence of the Governor of New Jersey (Drumthwacket Foundation 2016). Charles Olden was not a graduate of Princeton, but vol-unteered his time in support of the University. He served as the Treasurer from 1845–1869 and during this time, increased the school's endowment from about $40,000 to $500,000. He further served on the Board of Trust-ees, first as state Governor, and later as an elected member, a position he held until his death in 1876 (Drumthwacket Foundation 2016).

Though much of the Olden family's active involvement in the adminis-tration and leadership of Princeton University occurred prior to Abbott's as-sociation with the school, large donations of time, money, and land may have provided access and contacts. Certainly members of the University were forthcoming to Abbott with money and resources in ways that might not have otherwise been available without his wife's prestigious family network.

JUNIUS SPENCER MORGAN, JR.

In 1901, Abbott was introduced to Junius Spencer Morgan, Jr., a member of the Princeton University class of 1888, who served as Associate Librarian from 1898–1909 (Rollins 1932). Morgan was the nephew of financier John Pierpont Morgan, one of the richest men in American history, and himself a partner in the Wall Street firm Cuyler Morgan and Co. Junius Morgan moved to Princeton while still employed in New York City, as part of a growing movement of commuters from outlying suburbs. *Harper's Weekly* wrote of this suburban transformation that "the intellectuals of the dweller on Manhattan Island tend to become jaded and his liver to grow careless and indifferent, and the combination of intellectuality, repose, good roads, and sport which Princeton is able to offer seems to appeal most successfully to his imagination" (1897). Junius Morgan embraced the arts and was an avid collector of a wide range of antiquities, from manuscripts to archaeological artifacts. As a result of both his wealth and his interests, Abbott regarded him as a potential benefactor of archaeological research, and ultimately perhaps, supporter of a Princeton museum akin to George Peabody at Harvard University.

Interestingly, Morgan and George Peabody had a family business connection that Abbott was likely aware of, though it is not mentioned in his personal papers or correspondence. Morgan's grandfather, Junius Spencer Morgan, Sr., was a partner in Peabody's banking firm, George Peabody and Co. from 1854–1864, and in 1864 succeeded Peabody as the firm's President, when he changed its name to J. S. Morgan and Co. (Chernow 1991), which merged with other banking firms over the next hundred and fifty years to become J. P. Morgan Chase today. Abbott may have hoped that Junius Morgan, Jr., inspired by both his own love of collecting and the model exhibited by his grandfather's business partner, George Peabody, would endow an archaeological museum at Princeton University to rival that at Harvard.

At the time of Abbott's early communications, Morgan was still working at his investment bank in New York City, and only nominally served as Associate Librarian at Princeton. By 1910, however, he retired from Wall Street and devoted his time entirely to philanthropic ventures, most notably as a patron of the arts and as a collector of manuscripts and antiquities. His eulogy stressed that "this quittance meant no avoidance of labor, for Junius Morgan was incapable of being a drone" (Rollins 1932:2). Furthermore, Morgan appeared to be interested in the provenance and history of his collections, not just collecting for collecting's sake. He was described as "unsullied by acquisitiveness" and "because he was scholarly, he accurately knew the technique and history of the arts within whose limits he hunted; and, because public-spirited, though not in the least didactic, he garnered with a view to the instructional merit of his gatherings" (Rollins 1932:2). By all accounts, Abbott and Morgan had similar goals for the preservation and presentation of the past, though ironically, the amateur Morgan may have been more conscientious.

Abbott envisioned filling the same role that Frederic Ward Putnam had held at Harvard—supervising the acquisition and display of collections and overseeing the museum's direction and scope. In Morgan, Abbott fancied another George Peabody willing to financially support the establishment of an archaeological museum affiliated with one of America's leading universities. Morgan appeared to be amenable to the idea and wrote to Abbott in the fall of 1901 "I hope that the Abbott collection of Indian Relics at Princeton will in time surpass in interest the one at Harvard" (CCA/PU Box 8, Folder 4; November 6, 1901). Abbott thrilled at the thought.

Abbott courted Morgan heavily. By November of 1901, Morgan sent a remittance for archaeological artifacts and the two men negotiated an informal contract for future research. On November 6, 1901, Morgan wrote to Abbott that "the seven boxes shipped by you have arrived safely and are now in the University Library. I am much obliged to you for them and enclose my cheque as per agreement for $100" (CCA/PU Box 8, Folder 4). Abbott recorded in his diary: "November 20, 1901: Met Mr. Morgan by appointment and we discussed formation of an Indian relic collection, and I made an agreement with him for the coming thirteen months" (CCA/PU Box 4, Folder 2). Initially at least, Abbott pursued the opportunity with great enthusiasm and hard work.

However, Abbott felt that he needed to protect himself from a repeat of the difficulties he experienced at the Penn Museum, which he attributed to the machinations of Stevenson, Pepper, and Culin. He wrote a lengthy document to Morgan outlining the acceptable terms of his relationship with Princeton University, if they were to go forward with an archaeological museum. His biggest concern was ownership and control over the collections and content, once they were placed within a museum. Did Abbott retain control, or was he relinquishing all rights to the material once it was placed in an on-campus facility? And would his interpretations of the artifacts be honored, knowing that his view of the American Paleolithic was controversial?

Abbott wrote to Morgan that "You may say that I am trying to cross a bridge before I come to it, but the truth is, or I can swear, from sad experience, that lack of clear understanding as to where I stand, has once caused me to lose my footing and lose ground it was not possible to recover" (draft of correspondence from CCA to JSM, CCA/PU Box 8, Folder 4; November 23, 1902). He firmly stated, "I desire to put upon the collection the impress of my individuality so far as to attach to the objects such legends as I believe they should carry with them. I offer that degree of erudition attained by over thirty years of study of the subject and it is natural that it would be most repugnant to me to have others make these gatherings of mine the story that I do not believe they really do tell, and so in after years, misrepresent me" (draft of correspondence from CCA to JSM, CCA/PU Box 8, Folder 4; November 23, 1902). Though Abbott never wavered from his belief in the antiquity of humans in the Delaware Valley, he recognized that this theory had waned in popularity, and that it could taint his position at Princeton University. He wanted to ensure that at no point would he be terminated because his conclusions were not in favor, nor would his artifacts be interpreted in ways that he did not agree with. In addition, he wanted to be sure he would have some job security, including in his letter to Morgan that "it will require several years yet to form a 'Museum of American Archaeology' worthy of the University, and is it not towards this you are looking and so my position one of equal years continuance?" (draft of correspondence from CCA to JSM, CCA/PU Box 8, Folder 4; November 23, 1902).

Morgan replied on December 4, 1902 with reassurances that he was working in Abbott's best interest.

> I will take up the matter you refer to with the proper parties. I have had a talk with my partner Mr. C. C. Cuyler, who is Chairman of the Trustee Committee on Grounds and Buildings. He tells me that the thing for me to do is to write a letter to President [Woodrow] Wilson, stating what we are doing and tell him that we wish to put the objects in cases in North College on exhibition, but to consider the collection as a 'Loan Collection' for the time being. This would give us absolute control of the collection until such a time as we may decide to turn it over to the University. If this proposition, generally, meets with your approval, I will go ahead. I would not allow the matter to worry you, as I have no

doubt but that everything will be arranged to our satisfaction (CCA/PU Box 8, Folder 4).

Abbott may have had reason to be concerned. His position at Princeton University was not an official one. Though he received regular payments from Morgan for his archaeological research and collections, he was not on the University payroll while working towards a proposed "Museum of American Archaeology." As a result, his status was rather tenuous and relied on the good will of Morgan and later benefactors. Fortunately, Morgan was a powerful force within the University, and was able to obtain space and resources for Abbott's museum, at least for the duration while Abbott remained in his favor.

CREATING A PRINCETON MUSEUM

In 1902, Junius Spencer Morgan introduced Abbott to William Berryman Scott, the Blair Professor of Geology and Paleontology, who soon after became the founding Chair of the new Department of Geology. Scott helped Abbott get exhibit space for his archaeological collections in the Elizabeth Marsh Museum of Geology and Archaeology, which at the time was housed in the Faculty Room of Nassau Hall (Fig. 9.1). Abbott recorded an early meeting between the three men in which he wrote, "November 6, 1902: We had a long talk about the collections I am making and I learned of the growing interest in the subject....We discussed the subject of a display and then Scott and I went to the museum building and looked over places where room might be made for what I had to show. This will be decided soon and work in that direction will be commenced. Then we had a long talk about geological matters and the discussions of my work, long ago" (CCA/PU Box 4, Folder 2).

By early 1903, plans were underway to bring all of Abbott's current collections to Princeton, and Abbott began almost daily trips to the University. He recorded a typical visit in his diary, "January 7, 1903: Went to Princeton. At library saw Mr. Collins, assistant librarian and gave him old letters and left a pipe with him for Mr. Morgan. After a brief talk, went to Scott's department and left a fossil for him. Learning Mr. Morgan was at home but not going out I walked there and called. He was in his library and we had a long talk about archaeological efforts and then talk drifted into other channels."

9.1 Elizabeth Marsh Museum of Geology and Archaeology, Faculty Room, Nassau Hall, Princeton University. Princeton University Library Department of Rare Books and Special Collections. Seeley G. Mudd Manuscript Library, Box MP42, Item 1256.

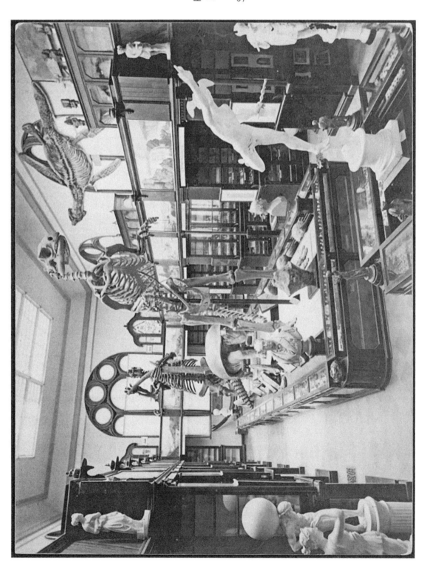

Abbott was concerned that Museum initiatives were taking a very long time but had faith that Morgan had his best interests at heart. "My main purpose in going to Princeton was to see about getting the collections already in hand in temporary cases but as yet nothing has been done in this matter. The delay will now probably be obviated very soon as I have said so much about it that Mr. Morgan will take active measures to bring about what we both wish" (CCA/PU Box 4, Folder 3; January 7, 1903).

By February, Abbott was able to set up his collections in the E. M. Marsh Museum in Nassau Hall, which housed a hodgepodge of art, archaeology, paleontology, and natural history. He recorded in his diary, "February 24, 1903: Went to Princeton. Went directly to my collections in the museum building and commenced unpacking. Then I went to lunch with Scott and resumed work and got enough stuff spread out to start cataloguing" (CCA/PU Box 4, Folder 3). But his ambivalent attitude towards the public was unchanged since his first museum employment thirteen years prior, when he questioned the desirability of a museum-going public (see Ch. 6:124). At Princeton he said, "It seemed strange and dream-like to be again in a museum and I was pleased with the idea at one moment and then doubtful of the wisdom of it all. Out door work in archaeology is beyond comparison, the most delightful of occupations, but the museum and contact with humanity—I shudder at the thought" (CCA/PU Box 4, Folder 3; February 24, 1903). Yet again, Abbott would have been perfectly content to work in a museum never visited by the public.

Abbott spent much of the spring of 1903 in this way—moving artifacts to Princeton and working on museum displays. In many of his diary entries, Abbott recorded the minutia of each day, including his arrivals and departures on campus, which indicate that he was typically at work from about 11am until about 2pm (CCA/PU Box 4, Folder 3; February through May 1903). Though he was technically not a Princeton University employee, and likely not expected to hold regular office hours on campus, one of Pepper and Stevenson's most significant criticisms of his habits during his tenure at Penn was that he never seemed to be in his office doing any work. At Princeton, this behavior persisted and was soon brought to Morgan's attention by an anonymous source (CCA/PU Box 4, Folder 3; May 20, 1903).

As a result, it did not take long for the relationship between Abbott and his benefactor to sour. By the end of April 1903, Abbott grew frustrated with his treatment at Princeton. He felt that his stipend of $100 per quarter was not regularly paid on time and should be increased, and that his collections deserved better placement within Nassau Hall. He was not being treated as he felt he deserved. In his diaries, he wrote, "April 28, 1903: More and more disgusted with the Princeton matter, but as I cannot afford to resign, must grin and bear it all. This is the exquisite torture of poverty" (CCA/PU Box 4, Folder 3).

In May of that year, Morgan was forced to confront Abbott about his behavior. According to Abbott, "May 20, 1903: Princeton....I went over to library and chanced upon Mr. Morgan who told me his associate in getting my money was dissatisfied. Immediately I was angry and there was a lively discussion and I spoke my mind freely. We went to the collection and looked it over and matters were smoothed over, but what I heard, rankled and I could not get the rubbish of the fellow out of my mind. Home late in afternoon and tried to get a nap, but could not" (CCA/PU Box 4, Folder 3). Making matters worse, Abbott's wife would not take his side. "Had much discussion with Julie about the matter in Princeton and she rather sided with my unknown critic, which was not pouring oil on troubled waters. It is all too like the experiences I had in Philadelphia and I am afraid I cannot keep my temper any better now than then, but at any cost, I will maintain what I consider my dignity and not yield therein by so much as a hair's breadth" (CCA/PU Box 4, Folder 3; May 20, 1903). Unfortunately, just as he had ten years previously, Abbott again stubbornly refused to concede or to change his behavior. In fact, he further entrenched and clearly stated that he would not spend any more than the bare minimum time working for the Museum.

A week later, during another trip to campus, Abbott encountered Morgan again, and Morgan's response seemed to only reinforce Abbott's decision to do little but collect a paycheck.

May 27, 1903: to Princeton, and yet there was a trifling repugnance remembering last Wednesday. Carried with me over 200 specimens and left in 9:20 car. Found Scott and Farr and after brief conversation went to my room and set out the objects I had brought. Then I went over to library and had a chat with Collins about books and other matters and was joined by Mr. Morgan who went with me on his own initiative to the museum and made arrangement for a table and chair for my use 'on rainy days' supposing I will come up then and catalogue &c. It was my suggestion to be so far equipped but as to anything like regular attendance that is an absurdity under present conditions. My liberty can only be had at a much higher price than the present figure. Mr. Morgan laughed at what was said a week ago and was amused that I should have been so worked up about it. Excellent knowledge as to the future (CCA/PU Box 4, Folder 3).

Despite interpersonal problems, and Abbott's bruised ego, he continued to send artifacts to Princeton for museum displays. He developed a friendly relationship with Marcus Farr, who was a vertebrate paleontologist on the faculty in the new Department of Geology at Princeton University. Farr was interested in Abbott's work at Trenton and joined him in the field on several occasions during 1903 and 1904. The two seemed fond of each other, as evidenced in a short note from Farr confirming the receipt of artifacts for the museum: "If as you state in your letter to me, these boxes contain biscuits, grape-nuts, and baking powder, petrified before acquiring their secondary and present characters, verily we may say with Solomon: 'There is nothing new under the sun,' although I have sometimes had my doubts in regard to this statement. Hoping to see you with us in the near future, I am, yours very truly, Marcus S. Farr" (CCA/PU Box 8, Folder 6; September 2, 1903).

Though Farr was welcoming, and Abbott appeared collegial with other members of the Geology Department faculty, his despondency grew as he reflected on the trajectory of his new museum career. "December 31, 1903: It is a common practice to plan for the future on this day and to make resolutions concerning many habits and the practice is a bad one. Promise nothing and you cannot be held accountable for broken promises; expect nothing and you will avoid a heap of disappointment. Even extravagant hoping is dangerous for hope too often begets confidence of favorable outcome and the good we do get loses value because of less volume than a wild fancy pictured. So endeth 1903" (CCA/PU Box 4, Folder 3).

Abbott believed that his efforts to build archaeological collections for a museum were unappreciated and that, yet again, he was not accorded the status that he deserved. His employment was contingent on Morgan's good will, and his artifacts and theories were not generating the excitement he believed was warranted. By June of 1904, he lamented in his diaries that "everything I take is received in a matter-of-course way, there is very little incentive to keep on the look out for them" (CCA/PU Box 4, Folder 3; June 3, 1904). That fall, his statements were eerily reminiscent of ten years prior, when he began to fear the end of his museum career at the University of Pennsylvania. He wrote in his diary, "October 18, 1904: Went to Princeton. Saw Farr and had a natural history talk and then went over to library and fortunately saw Morgan. He made a poor mouth over my suggestions but I kept on talking enthusiastically and think the work will continue for another year, anyhow. I do not think, however, it will go beyond that, as there is not a particle of interest taken in the subject by anyone there, and there is no chance afforded me to display the collection and through it, excite an interest" (CCA/PU Box 4, Folder 3). Almost a year later, the relationship between Abbott and Morgan was effectively over. Abbott chronicled,

> September 27, 1905: considering what I shall say to Morgan if we meet tomorrow, as I expect we shall. I will not repeat the pleasing of Oct. 19, 1904, but tell him it is a quick yes or no and no condescension on my part because of his wealth. I have not been treated by him as I should have been but will afford no other opportunity for him or anyone in Princeton to put on airs. As I feel now, the outcome of the interview tomorrow is much a matter of doubt but Morgan will have to seek my services and not I plead for consideration. That much is certain (CCA/PU Box 4, Folder 4).

MOSES TAYLOR PYNE

Just as Abbott started to fear that his Museum of American Archaeology at Princeton University was destined for failure, he met Moses Taylor Pyne. Pyne was a member of the Princeton University class of 1877 and had inherited a large sum of money from his maternal grandfather, Moses Taylor, who was the first president of the National City Bank of New York and the primary stockholder of the Delaware, Lackawanna and Western Railroad. As a young man, Pyne worked for the railroad as general counsel, but retired early to devote his time to philanthropic pursuits, of which Princeton University was a principal beneficiary (Leitch 1978). In 1893, he purchased the estate of Drumthwacket, which was built by Abbott's wife's paternal uncle, Charles Smith Olden.

At the age of only twenty-eight, Pyne was elected to the Princeton University Board of Trustees, a post engineered to bring a younger perspective

(Leitch 1978). Allegedly, University President James McCosh complained that the Board needed Pyne because it was "full of old dotards and sometimes they go to sleep" (Martin 2006). Pyne also served as Chair of the Trustees Committee on Grounds and Buildings from 1886–1897 and in that role, greatly influenced the architectural style of the modern campus, choosing designs in the Collegiate Gothic style. He personally funded the construction of two buildings, Upper and Lower Pyne, and persuaded his mother to contribute a third building to the campus. As a major donor and influential member of the Board of Trustees, he wielded considerable influence over the direction and scope of the University's growth (Leitch 1978).

After stepping down from the Committee on Grounds and Buildings, Pyne served as the Chair of the Finance Committee until 1908. In addition to overseeing expenditures, Pyne personally covered deficits in the University's budget from his own funds with the presentation of a large donation each year at Commencement. According to the Princeton Alumni Weekly, "whenever the college needed a classroom building or a row of houses or a parcel of land, after a decent interval there it was—Pyne either by himself or with a group of friends had met the subscription and named it after someone else" (quoted in Martin 2006).

Abbott and Pyne started corresponding in earnest in 1905, with Pyne soon providing Abbott with the monthly stipend he previously received from Morgan. The relationship between Morgan and Abbott had soured, leaving Pyne to write to Abbott that "I fear from what he told me last fall that he intended to stop the payments this spring. Of this sum, I was giving $25 per month and he was giving or collecting the balance. I shall be glad to continue my portion, provided you can suggest any scheme by which it would be of service" (CCA/PU Box 8, Folder 6; May 3, 1906). Abbott replied in protest and Pyne was contrite: "I am extremely sorry this trouble should have occurred and that Mr. Morgan should have left matters so unsettled when he went away." In the exchange, Abbott requested more money, but Pyne refused, and wrote "I am sorry I cannot make it larger now, but the expenses of the University which fall upon me are so extremely onerous that I have practically nothing to spare" (CCA/PU Box 8, Folder 6; May 15, 1906).

Abbott fumed. He believed that Morgan treated him unfairly, and that Pyne, as a major benefactor to the University, Chair of the Finance Committee, and an exceptionally wealthy man, was simply being stingy in withholding a larger stipend in exchange for Abbott's artifacts and expertise. The frustration continued throughout the summer of 1906, and he recorded in his diaries, "June 18, 1906: got at work at the accumulated Indian relics and packed away three big boxes of them and put them in the attic. I have got more of this work to do and I am going to pack the entire lot now down in my room and await developments. Certainly I do not propose to ship anything more to Princeton until a very different state of affairs is brought into being. I am really very tired of the whole subject. It no longer presents any attractive features as long ago the story was told and no retelling is any improvement on my original version" (CCA/PU Box 4, Folder 4).

Typically for Abbott, he peevishly withdrew from the Princeton University community when things were not going his way. This behavior was reminiscent of his time at the Penn Museum, though as usual, he blamed others for the situation. But Abbott spent only minimal hours on campus. Morgan was well aware of Abbott's slack attitude towards work on the fledgling Museum, otherwise he likely would not have recommended terminating Abbott's stipend, a decision which was clearly communicated to Pyne. But Abbott's stubbornness resurfaced, and wrote in his diaries a month later, "July 11, 1906: I went for letters and got one from Mr. Pyne which set me to thinking and I wrote a very full reply. He will have to reinterest Morgan or someone else before I do what he apparently expects of me. Time will show what is to come of it all and I wish it was all over for I am deadly tired of the whole business and hate the very name of Princeton and always did" (CCA/PU Box 4, Folder 4).

Pyne tried to appease Abbott by appealing to his ego and purse, though a snarky letter on July 10, 1906, in which Pyne stated "I see no reason why you should not have at least a table and chair in the room in which your collections are placed" (CCA/PU Box 8, Folder 6) may not have helped matters. Abbott remained sullen and despondent throughout much of that summer. "July 25, 1906: Went for letters and got one from Mr. Pyne saying he hoped something could be done by September. I somehow have my doubts about it and cannot scare up any enthusiasm. Let come what may of Mr. Pyne's efforts, it would not place me in a satisfactory position and to be merely tolerated about the building is not in accordance with my pride" (CCA/PU Box 4, Folder 4).

By August, Abbott's thoughts turned destructive. "August 2, 1906:...I do not know that it is very wise to get reinterested in the subject. It brings up a train of nasty retrospective thought and I have the will again, tingling my finger tips even to do murder. Weak fool to admit it, but who likes an honest life work to benefit others and make the worker a sufferer. If it didn't seem so very like sending pearls to be set before swine, in going to Princeton, I would care less. It will need another century to rid that seat of learning of its theological bias and really scientific or a seat of learning in toto and not as now a seat also of belitting assumption" (CCA/PU Box 4, Folder 4).

Things improved somewhat thereafter, and Abbott traveled to Princeton occasionally to construct his museum displays, but he fought with members of the Geology faculty and as before, his irascible personality destroyed relationships. He recorded one instance in his diary.

> August 8, 1906: to Princeton. Went directly to where I have my collection....I had a brief interview with Van Ingen [Professor of invertebrate paleontology and stratigraphy] and shall avoid another. He cussed and swore outrageously about my having the room I have now secured and referred to me as 'butting in' where I was not wanted. I listened but made no ill-natured reply and kept very cool, but might finally have warmed up had not Scott come in. He heard a part of it and did not rebuke Van Ingen but I hardly think he approves of such outbursts of insulting language. If he does, I would like to know it and never again would I darken the building's door. Found progress had been made in preparing the case for me and Scott said other cases would be emptied so the whole room would be at my disposal. He seemed really interested in what I was doing and if so I shall find my going there much more pleasant. Fortunately, I have no occasion to see Van Ingen on any pretext (CCA/PU Box 4, Folder 4).

Despite Abbott crossing members of the faculty and sullenly avoiding work as much as possible, Pyne maintained his financial support, albeit not at the level Abbott would have desired, and Abbott continued slow progress towards a Museum of American Archaeology. Pyne intimated in late August of 1906 that the future "might bring something to the fore" (CCA/PU Box 4, Folder 4; August 23, 1906), and followed through on this promise by increasing Abbott's stipend from $25 per month to $50 per month through at least May of 1907. He noted, however, that he was "trusting this will be satisfactory and that the work will go on more pleasantly" (CCA/PU Box 8,

Folder 6; September 18, 1906), a not subtle warning that Abbott needed to work on his collegiality if he wished to continue.

By mid-November of that year, Abbott's attitude had changed, perhaps because of Pyne's encouragement, additional funding, or instead, his lightly veiled threat if Abbott could not bring himself to behave professionally.

> November 14, 1906: to Princeton. I saw Mr. Pyne and he went with me to the room where is my collection and we talked for over an hour and he showed a great deal of interest in what I am doing and in the objects already gathered and also in what I proposed to do and relieved my mind very much by saying I could keep right on indefinitely and not to worry on that score. I even suggested what is so close to my own desires, an illustrated report on the collection and to this he gave assent if cost was not exorbitant, which it will not be. Such a publication would give me abundant opportunity to reply to the objections of so many in this country who find fault with every bit of offered evidence of antiquity. It was such a contrast to any interview I ever had with Morgan and exalted rather than depressed me. The work has now an added interest, whereas after talking with Morgan, I often felt like giving up could I have afforded to do so. Did some work there opening a box and then went into Farr's room and smoked a cigar and while so engaged started for home (CCA/PU Box 4, Folder 4).

Professionally, things were improving for Abbott as well. The first of his three volume set *Archaeologia Nova Caesarea* (1907) was published with financial support from Pyne. In it, he continued to insist on the antiquity of his discoveries along the Delaware River: "the fact remains that large rudely chipped but distinctly fashioned implements of metamorphosed slate—argillite—which are indistinguishable in pattern from European Paleolithic implements, have frequently been found in deposits of gravel, the history of which is unmistakably that of the closing activities of the glacial period" (Abbott 1907:7). In this first volume, Abbott maintained the existence of "three horizons of Paleolithic, pre-Indian, and Indian, here in New Jersey" and that these include "pre-glacial occupancy of the country" (1907:11–12).

The publication of *Archaeologia Nova Caesarea* provided Abbott with the platform to re-enter scientific debate on the antiquity of humans in the New World with the support of Pyne as a wealthy benefactor and the prestige of a Princeton University affiliation on his resume. In print, Abbott presented additional examples of his Trenton "paleoliths" and disputed Holmes's claims that these merely represented quarrying debris. Holmes, Abbott argued, would never be able to objectively examine the archaeological evidence "because of pre-conceived notions of modernity," and, according to Abbott, Holmes's statements on the debate only served to confuse the issue. Abbott claimed that "it is such 'official' announcements to an ignorant public that so seriously obstructs the progress of scientific research and of truth" (1909:28). The evidence, he said, "satisfies the reasonable archaeologist who is concerned alone with demonstrable fact" (1908:29). In other words, Abbott argued, Holmes and his compatriots held a biased agenda, but Abbott's theories were supported by real data.

Pyne may not have realized that by funding Abbott's publications, he was encouraging Abbott to re-engage his old adversaries. In many scholarly venues, the debate about the American Paleolithic had waned, with most archaeologists believing Holmes's interpretation of the Trenton artifacts, based on his evidence at Piney Branch and critique of Trenton. However, those who sided with Abbott were willing to revive the fight, and a flurry of correspondence followed between Abbott, Wright, and Winchell, with Abbott loudly claiming foul play on the part of his rivals. In a reply to one of Abbott's letters, Newton Horace Winchell, on the faculty at the University of Minnesota, wrote "I was not aware of the intrigue to which you (and others, probably) have been subjected, and of the misinterpretation to which in a matter of science a scientific man (soi-disant) can descend when he thinks he has a notion to obscure or to deny something that he has not himself discovered" (CCA/PU Box 8, Folder 6; April 30, 1907).

Abbott's response to criticism, unsurprisingly, was to regard any disagreement with his theories as a personal affront. It was fortunate that Pyne was not part of the archaeological community, since he had already warned Abbott of the importance of collegiality. Pyne remained insulated against much of the bitterness that still surrounded the American Paleolithic. For example, in April of 1907, Abbott sent a copy of *Archaeologia Nova Caesarea* to William Morris Davis, a geomorphologist on the faculty at Harvard University, with a cross personal annotation, to which Davis scolded, "Your note pasted into the beginning of the paper seems, however, to imply a wrong understanding of my position regarding your work at Trenton. You speak of my view as an 'attack' on your view....I dislike very much to think that simply because I differ with another scientific man that I therefore 'attack' him" (CCA/PU Box 8, Folder 6; April 16, 1907). On the subject of the American Paleolithic, Abbott was always on the offensive.

Abbott sent copies of the first two volumes to Junius Morgan as well, following up on a conversation the two men had at a meeting of the Princeton Historical Society. "February 12: 1908:...I had not seen Morgan for many months and he seemed very lively, good natured and companionable. Now that I am under no obligation to him in my work, I do not care what I say and we spoke very freely, at best, I did. His remark of unloading me on Mr. Pyne was not altogether a sweet morsel to swallow but as I never a quid pro quo, for dollars received I do not mind what is said especially as I want the dollars" (CCA/PU Box 5, Folder 1). For his gift of books, Abbott received as a snide reply: "I promise you to preserve them and I will probably read parts of them." However, the previous week's conversation also led Morgan to spitefully remark, "By the way, *did* I call you a 'burden' or did Mr. Pyne accuse me 'of unloading you on him' and there by suggestion I was thought to have considered you a 'burden'? I am not perfectly clear on this point which I think should be investigated and probably recorded for its great importance to the future historian of Mercer County" (CCA/PU Box 8, Folder 6; February 19, 1908).

Pyne, however, was only nominally aware of Abbott's perspective on either Morgan or the American Paleolithic. He was preoccupied with funding the University, and the construction of Guyot Hall, the new geology and biology building. He wrote encouragingly to Abbott, "am glad that you have a chance for your final word. I shall take great pleasure in reading your pamphlet when it is finished, and trust you will be able to confound all your opponents" (CCA/PU Box 8, Folder 6; February 19, 1907). In continuing to support the publication of Abbott's *Archaeologia Nova Caesarea* through 1909, Pyne implicitly and explicitly approved of his work. Abbott gladdened at the situation, claimed scholarly triumph, and with that illusion of success, felt he gained security in his position at Princeton. He recorded, "May 25, 1908: Princeton. Knocked at Farr's door and he not busy, I had a talk with him that covered fully an hour and a great many subjects. Then I went to my room, or where my collection is and met Mr. Pyne and we had a long talk of two hours, the longest I have ever had, and it too covered a good deal of ground. I think he was well satisfied with the work I am doing and will see that it is properly cared for when the new museum building is ready for occupancy" (CCA/PU Box 5, Folder 1).

THE PRINCETON COLLECTIONS

Pyne wrote to Abbott on May 21, 1907 with news: "Have you heard that the money has been provided for a museum building for geology and biology at Princeton together with the proper laboratories? We hope to begin building before the end of the summer and to have the place ready for use in a year from then. This will give you the much needed space you have wished for so long" (CCA/PU Box 8, Folder 6). Finally, Abbott's Museum of American Archaeology would have a permanent facility within the University, though not on the scale of the museum at Harvard. Regardless, Abbott thrilled at the thought of moving from his small shared space in a room in Nassau Hall to the newly built Museum.

In 1909, Princeton University completed the construction of Guyot Hall, a massive science building to house geology and biology that was named after the first professor of geology and geography, Arnold Guyot. The building was designed in consultation with University faculty "to contain a museum, and the laboratories, lecture rooms, preparation rooms etc., needed for the work of instruction and research in the natural sciences" (Van Ingen 1908:417). Most importantly, the center atrium would contain the Princeton Natural History Museum, but the architects and faculty committee were concerned that the proximity of Princeton to established natural history museums in Philadelphia and New York would mean that there would be little interest in a museum of this type at Princeton. As a result, "in order to make the museum an active factor in scientific instruction it should be placed as to be at all times easy of access by the student body, and that this object is best attained by making contact with the museum and its exhibits, in some degree at least, unavoidable by students passing to and from the laboratories on the floors above and below" (Van Ingen 1908:417). For Abbott, this meant that his artifacts, and presumably his arguments about the American Paleolithic, would be viewed by all who entered Guyot Hall. The arrangement of archaeological material within the broader natural history museum was not immediately determined, but Abbott was not concerned about the details. He was simply excited that his collections were to be placed within this new museum facility. Pyne, too, appeared pleased. "I have by no means been unaware of the splendid results you have been getting and of the growth of our collection at Princeton. Next fall we ought to be able to arrange it in such a way, in the new Museum, that it will make a better showing than it has before" (CCA/PU Box 8, Folder 6; June 16, 1909).

Despite his, albeit brief, experience as Curator at the Penn Museum, Abbott had little knowledge of how a museum should operate and modeled many of his practices after those in place thirty years earlier at the Peabody Museum at Harvard. Abbott also resorted to his former practice of purchasing artifacts and collections. However, Pyne was generally not amenable to additional expenditures for artifact purchases, when he was presumably already funding Abbott's fieldwork, so any objects that Abbott wished to acquire were bought with his personal stipend. Needless to say, this resulted in very few acquisitions. Instead, Abbott attempted to persuade collectors to donate artifacts, but had little success with that either. Most of the collections at Princeton were from Abbott's Three Beeches farm and nearby properties.

Abbott recorded the specimens in a bound journal that he designed and had printed entitled "Catalogue of the Museum of American Archaeology, Volume 1, Princeton University, Princeton, New Jersey, 1903" (Fig. 9.2) but only seven pages of the massive tome were ever used. The catalog contained 314 entries enumerating approximately 1300 specimens. Almost all were collected from Trenton near Three Beeches farm. Exceptions included a "ceremonial object" from Gloucester County, New Jersey (catalog #253); two clay tobacco pipes from Salem, New Jersey (catalog #221 and #222); pebbles, some perforated, with the note "circular and oval found together" from Riverton, New Jersey (catalog #217 and #218); and a cache of twenty-four netsinkers from Burlington Island, New Jersey (catalog #137, Fig. 9.3).

The catalogue also held Abbott's notations and marginal comments about the artifacts. For example, several "spear-head" entries (catalog #83–121) contained the following "Under title of spear-head are included those forms similar to arrow-points but evidently too large for such use and effective as weapons only when attached to long staffs. Many however may have been used as knives. The specialization of implements and weapons did not obtain among the Indians as among ourselves." These spearpoints were illustrated in *Archaeologia Nova Caesarea, Vol. II* (1908:32, fig. 3). Other artifacts from the Princeton University collections that were also illustrated in *Archaeologia Nova Caesarea* included arrow-points (catalog # 173–179;

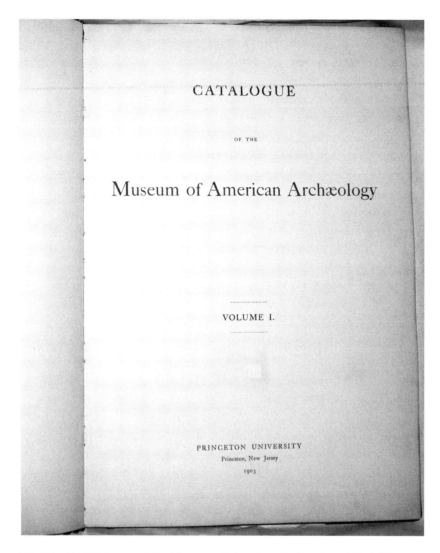

9.2 Abbott's Catalogue of the Museum of American Archaeology, Vol. 1, Princeton University, Princeton, New Jersey 1903. On file, New Jersey State Museum, Trenton. Photo by the authors.

9.3 A cache of twenty-four netsinkers from Burlington Island, New Jersey, from the Abbott Collection at Princeton University, now housed at the New Jersey State Museum, Trenton (Princeton University Museum Catalog Number 137). Photo by the authors.

Abbott 1908:21, fig. 1), and ceramic pottery sherds (catalog #299; Abbott 1909:58, figs. 7, 8).

Abbott's marginal comments on these artifacts in the catalog were also reflected in the text of *Archaeologia Nova Caesarea*. For example, Abbott illustrated a bannerstone, which is an atl-atl or spearthrower counterweight, from the collections (probably catalog #68). These types of artifacts, which have utilitarian purposes though were sometimes highly stylized, were described in the catalog merely as "ceremonial" but contained the remark "these are always perforated for a handle and are never effective as weapons. Known also as 'bannerstones.'" In the text of his Volume II, he argued that their unique appearance was evidence of a long occupation of the Delaware Valley. He stated in a rather circuitous manner "that an article of absolutely no use, but symbolic only, and so foreign to the purposes of migratory people and not long established at any one locality, would not have been made, as thousands of them were, by the Lenape, had they not been here in the valley of the Delaware for ages" (1908:68, fig. 6).

Other artifacts from the Princeton University collection included gorgets, pestles, chipped stone bifaces, celts, pipes, drills, pottery, and "rude implements" described as "distinctly of the European Paleolithic type. There is no reason to believe they did not come from the bank, and not from the surface." The notes continued with "the 'unfinished' objects or 'rejects' found on surface and common to many localities, are as a class distinguishable from the somewhat similar objects from the gravel" (catalogue #301–313).

Abbott intended these collections to be displayed so that his sequential chronology of Paleolithic, to ancestral Native American or "argillite man," to modern Native American would be reflected just like at the Peabody Museum, but found instead that many of his artifacts were not placed in visible public corridors. In part, this was because Abbott was simply not on campus. In 1910, Pyne's financial support for Abbott's work expired. He wrote to Abbott "I am writing Mr. Seaman to make the payment desired by you—$150 for the three months' work—closing the arrangement between us. I shall be glad to see the collection in Guyot Hall" (CCA/PU Box 8, Folder 6; March 29, 1910). Abbott tersely noted in his diary, "April 8, 1910: heard from Mr. Pyne. Princeton is a closed incident, but I can open it if I choose, but I do not" (CCA/PU Box 5, Folder 3).

Despite Abbott's statement in his diary that he would not continue his pursuits at Princeton, he wrote again to Pyne, who replied kindly but without promising continued financial support. "The work that you have done for the University and the collections that we have there now will certainly prove a monument to your energy and ability" (CCA/PU Box 9, Folder 6; April 25, 1910). Without a paycheck, Abbott would not go to Princeton to supervise the Museum layout. He simply trusted that his artifacts would receive prominent placement when the display cases in the main floor of Guyot Hall were filled.

In early 1912, Abbott finally visited the Museum. "February 24, 1912: I went to Princeton and to Guyot Hall, hoping to see Farr, but I failed to find him. I saw [Professor of vertebrate paleontology, William J.] Sinclair and learned that my collection had been unpacked and put in trays and so far was accessible but in a locked room and not on exhibition" (CCA/PU Box 6, Folder 1). But more worryingly for Abbott, it appeared that his agreement with Morgan regarding ownership of the collections was not going to be honored.

> Sinclair said he had been notified the collection had been put in his charge and was the property of the college. I made no remark. I took two specimens and came away. I want one of them figured, if I can arrange for so doing with Mr. Pyne. As I now understand, I must go to Sinclair for permission to see any specimens and as this is not satisfactory, I will keep clear of the place until I have had word from Mr. Pyne about the matter, and if Sinclair is to have the arranging and display of it, I will have nothing more to do with it. At present there are no cases available. I suppose my association with it is a matter of the past. To put it on exhibition and label it is not a job I care for and its value will be lessened if I have nothing to say in the matter (CCA/PU Box 6, Folder 1; February 24, 1912).

Abbott fumed, and justifiably so. In his initial correspondence with Junius Morgan in 1902, Abbott had expressed concern about access to his collections and sought reassurances that he would retain control. He had written "when the collections are arrayed in cases in a college building, do they not pass to the control of the college authorities and so, might they not be handed over at any moment without regard to any consideration to which I might have a moral claim?" and furthermore, he wrote "I do not wish to learn, after proceeding with my work of arranging the collection that I am in this situation but a crank with a fad, tolerated until a few cases are filled with specimens and then requested to step down and out" (draft of correspondence from CCA to JSM, CCA/PU Box 8, Folder 4; Nov. 23, 1902). At the time, Morgan had responded with reassurances that the University would view the artifact collection as a loan and that Abbott would retain ownership and control over the materials and the way in which they were presented (CCA/PU Box 8, Folder 4; December 4, 1902).

Abbott had been swindled, though probably not intentionally. He commented in his diary, "March 6, 1912: recent Princeton episode and letter have sickened me as to the collection here and I shall be glad to forget that I have been in any way associated with the institution, but I shall keep my real thoughts to myself and simply ignore the place, and above all else keep what I have in way of relics until I win out on some points" (CCA/PU Box 6, Folder 1). Sinclair offered a solution—not giving Abbott his collections back, which Abbott probably did not really want anyway, but providing research space, display space, and access. "March 7, 1912: Got a letter from Sinclair offering me a room in a basement that *could* be lighted. I was very much amused. Asks other silly questions. I certainly am not inclined to visit Guyot Hall, but must not offend Pyne" as Pyne supported the publication of Abbott's final volume *Ten Years' Diggings in Lenape Land, 1901–1911*. The next day, however, Abbott responded "March 8, 1912: mailed a letter to Sinclair declining his offer of a subterranean apartment for 'spreading' the collection" (CCA/PU Box 6, Folder 1).

A week later, the animosity still simmered. "March 14, 1912: Got a letter from Mr. Pyne and it had with it a statement by Sinclair. A more infernal piece of impudence I never heard of and the work of twelve years is destroyed as a part of a cunning scheme to oust me. It is successful. Not even Pyne can ever get me into the building again. I propose now to be free again and what relics I have, retain, until forced to disgorge. Of course I am sorry, but I cannot give up all self-respect even for Mr. Pyne" (CCA/PU Box 6, Folder 1).

THE END OF THE PRINCETON MUSEUM OF AMERICAN ARCHAEOLOGY

Despite Abbott's sporadic efforts over twelve years, a Museum of American Archaeology at Princeton University never formally got off the ground. Abbott's artifacts became part of the permanent collections of the

Princeton Natural History Museum. Archaeological collections from the Classical world and Mesoamerica were sent to the Princeton University Art Museum, but Abbott's artifacts were placed in storage.

On October 15, 1979, Dr. Donald Baird, who served as the Curator of the Princeton Natural History Museum from 1973–1988, transferred the entirety of Abbott's archaeological collections and his Museum ledger to the New Jersey State Museum in Trenton. Under Baird's leadership, the Natural History Museum's collections and mission focused on paleontological and geological specimens, and not on archaeology. Though Baird's research expertise was in vertebrate paleontology, and he supported archaeology, he concluded that Abbott's archaeological specimens were better suited to the New Jersey State Museum, not Princeton. There was no longer a place for Abbott's collections at Princeton.

Today, Abbott's artifacts remain in the New Jersey State Museum in Trenton, where they are curated with other collections from around the region. At Princeton, the Natural History Museum in Guyot Hall closed in 2002, and the atrium display space was converted into offices for the Princeton Environmental Institute. The only remnants of the Museum today consist of a few side cabinets containing gems and minerals, and an *Allosaurus* dinosaur that is 25 feet long and 12 feet high and deemed too large to move (Anonymous 2009).

10

Abbott's Autumn Years

Despite frustrations with William J. Sinclair about the display of collections, Charles Conrad Abbott's split from Princeton University in spring of 1910 was more or less cordial, at least in his relationship with Moses Taylor Pyne. The two men remained in touch and corresponded at least through 1917, and Pyne continued to financially support some of Abbott's ventures. In 1912, he contributed towards the publication costs of Abbott's final volume, and it seems he made arrangements for Abbott to receive small disbursements over the years. Only a few weeks before Abbott's death, Abbott received a letter from W. J. Seaman as Pyne's representative, noting a check enclosed for "$50 for the quarterly payment now due on account of the pension" (CCA/PU Box 14, Folder 1; July 1, 1919).

Abbott's enthusiasm for archaeology persisted into his later years, though declining health made fieldwork problematic. Even thirty years after the collapse of the American Paleolithic, he insisted in private and in print that his interpretation of the Trenton "paleoliths" was correct and that he had found a Paleolithic identical to that of Europe. Abbott's archaeological interactions at the end of his life were devoted to substantiating these claims through supporting other, younger archaeologists who adhered to his opinions. He noted in his diary that "January 1, 1913: I found a core of argillite in the sand that interested me exceedingly and I began a train of thought which expanded to a volume and I wondered how Mr. Pyne would take the suggestion of another brochure, illustrated, on local archaeology," but he conceded his age and deteriorating health made such endeavors difficult. "I guess the fever will pass off very promptly and I escape the seriousness of such an undertaking. The subject is exhausted but the fire of my interest in it flares up now and then" (CCA/PU Box 6, Folder 2). His authorship on the American Paleolithic in his later years consisted of newspaper articles and editorial columns, rather than scholarly publications.

TEN YEARS' DIGGINGS IN LENAPE LAND, 1901–1911

Abbott's last book was published in 1912, entitled *Ten Years' Diggings in Lenape Land, 1901–1911*. The volume typified of much of Abbott's writing throughout his career, which often merged naturalist musings with scientific interpretations, and contained colorful reflections on the landscape, nature, and archaeology. For example, in the preface, Abbott wrote "when we enter the archaeological field, like going from darkness into light, from a prison into freedom, from error into truth. Time here is a stranger in a strange land. It can make no demands but we may laugh at them. An archaeologist is a free man. He has facts only as his companions, and his sole duty is to record their relationship" (1912:3).

Abbott revisited the American Paleolithic debate in the volume, with only moderately veiled barbs hurled at William Henry Holmes and W J McGee. He wrote, "The archaeological student, presumably, when engaged upon his subject, reads to be instructed; but, so far as the valley of the Delaware is concerned, he must read the vituperative critics of antiquity only to be amused. If taken seriously, he will be led completely astray" (1912:12), and further that Holmes, McGee, and others wrote articles that were "totally disregarding the truth, but determining to be sensational and secure the attention of the uninstructed crowd, only the 'yellow journal' methods have been used" (1912:12).

Like many of his earlier works, Abbott's penultimate volume was very light on the presentation of scientific data, and relied heavily on assertions of others, often in the form of verbal comments quoted in the text or personal correspondence, not published data. He cited visits to the Trenton gravels by Thomas Belt "a competent observer" (1912:131); and Edward S. Morse, who "was convinced of the occurrence of these disputed Paleolithic implements *in* the gravel" (1912:132, emphasis original); and Henry W. Haynes, George Frederick Wright, and William Boyd Dawkins who "expressed himself as 'convinced' that I had discovered traces of Paleolithic man in America" (1912:132). However, a footnote in the volume conceded that "It is necessary here to state, in justice to Prof. Dawkins, that he has recently, in a review of Wright's 'Ice Age in North America,' declared that there is no evidence of glacial man in America. As an instance of paleontological contortion, this is more amusing than important" (1912:132).

According to Abbott, all visitors to Trenton arrived wary, but ultimately Abbott convinced them of the veracity of his conclusions that an American Paleolithic persisted along the Delaware River. Abbott stated that scholars were "professedly skeptical, to a man, and some intentionally blind to the most obvious facts. The result was ever the same. They came, they saw, and the gravel conquered" (1912:132). Abbott concluded, despite presenting evidence consisting only of personal affirmations by site visitors, that "it does not seem that the above leaves anything more to be said. The ebullitions of ignorance in various symposia of which I have heard, but which I have never joined, are painful reminders of the fact that most is said where least is known" (1912:136). Abbott's refusal to participate in scientific symposia was a significant problem in the 1890s, not a virtue as he presented it here, when he was unable, or unwilling, to defend the American Paleolithic in scholarly debate.

With this final book, Abbott felt he had done all he could to win the Paleolithic argument, and he hoped that if Volk ever published the results of his excavations in Trenton area, that he would be vindicated. Abbott perhaps realized, however, that it was a battle he no longer had the stamina to fight. In his diary he noted, "February 7, 1913: I found, to my great surprise, that Volk was here. He told me of what he had been doing in the last twelve months in way of examining exposures of gravel, mostly above Trenton, or beyond the reach of tide water. He reported finding a great many argillite artifacts in this gravel under such circumstances that no doubt could arise as to their antiquity, and I was astonished at many of the details that he gave me as to the gravel on the high ground out West State Street and of what he had found in the 'river' gravel or that which is still under water." Abbott believed this would be the final piece of evidence needed for his American Paleolithic. He continued that "his whole story was as fascinating as a novel and of course very gratifying to me. This is the first time he has been communicative in any way as to what he has been doing, and is an additional evidence of my views being correct when I announced the discovery of Paleolithic man. It made me quite excited and I could think of nothing else after he had gone. After supper, I wrote about his visit to Winchell and Putnam and urged letter to soon announce the purport of his work about here, for I suppose the final report will be sometime in forthcoming. I am very happy over it all" (CCA/PU Box 6, Folder 2). Unfortunately, Volk's only substantial publication on the subject was *The Archaeology of the Delaware Valley* (1911), and whatever he found in 1913 did not make it into print.

The pain of Holmes's Piney Branch Quarry research and the ensuing battle over the American Paleolithic never truly receded for Abbott. In 1913, he wrote to Winchell, "Holmes and Salisbury were not *honest* in their treatment of the Delaware Valley. I who was savagely wounded by them have best cause to know. The wound has never healed. The poison of their misrepresentation still rankles and time has no remedy in her pharmacopeia to restore health and obliterate the scar" (CCA-NHW/HPM; June 30, 1913).

ARTIFACT COLLECTING

Even during the heyday of his career, Abbott's field methods were unprofessional (Hinsley 1988:60). One of the resounding criticisms of his American Paleolithic was that his fieldwork was not scientifically rigorous. Much of Abbott's evidence was based not on detailed stratigraphic sections, careful provenience, or scientific recording, as was meticulously presented by William Henry Holmes for Piney Branch, but instead Abbott relied on morphological similarities between artifacts and on unpublished affirmations by other scholars who visited the Trenton sites. In the thirty years after Abbott's first foray into the American Paleolithic, archaeological science had gained standardized methodologies for excavation and documentation, which further extended into museum and curatorial practices as well. Abbott's methods of collection, which largely entailed surface collection with minimal documentation, or purchasing artifacts, were out of date. The discipline had left Abbott far behind, but he did not accept it. "It is so different from mere collection and that over-worked in situ business" (CCA/PU Box 6, Folder 2; March 19, 1913).

Abbott realized that times had changed, but believed it was the result of a decline in active fieldwork on the part of professional archaeologists. He wrote in *Ten Years' Diggings* that "the two claimants to archaeological accuracy are those who dig, and those who, rather than face this labor, 'dig out.' One represents work; the other, words" (1912:152). Abbott had little respect for the latter. In his diary, he later wrote, "April 6, 1913: The truth is, real archaeology is now not in favor among the museum-ites, who like less burdensome tasks....If I was physically able to be in the field more, my interest in life would be as intense as ever" (CCA/PU Box 6, Folder 2).

Abbott also renewed correspondence with Frederic Ward Putnam at the Peabody Museum, though it required Abbott to swallow his pride and apologize for past bad behavior. "August 14, 1911: I found a letter from Putnam, in reply to one I wrote on 3rd inst. I wrote of letting disputes drop and of Volk's report. He accepts my suggestions on the ground of my being the repentant sinner and he the forgiving saint, which is not the view I take of it by a long shot, and yet will not say so as I do not care to have further invitation and like him agree to let bygones be bygones. I wrote a long and very friendly reply and now it is a closed incident" (CCA/PU Box 5, Folder 4).

In the last ten years of his life, Abbott collected artifacts from his own property, when he felt well enough, and obtained collections through his existing networks with interested members of the community. He searched for those that were unique or complete specimens, just like he had early in his career when collecting for the Peabody. His collections were chiefly unprovenienced and lacking in more mundane, less exhibit-worthy artifacts such as lithic debitage or pottery sherds, which are valuable sources of data.

In one interesting example, in 1911, Abbott obtained what he referred to in his diaries initially as a "terra cotta head" or later as the "American Sphinx" in press, which may have been a deliberate move to capitalize on the early 20th century popularity of Egyptian-style artistic objects (Sigler 1990). He wrote "found on an Indian village site, associated with many objects of rare excellence of manufacture, it stood so separate and apart from all else, was so un-Indian and truly artistic, that it called for study from other than the archaeological point of view" (1912:29). The artifact was allegedly found on the Assiscunk Creek near Burlington, New Jersey, which flows into the Delaware River from New Jersey at Burlington Island (Fig. 10.1).

Abbott was quite excited about his "American Sphinx." In June, he took the artifact to the Art Department at Princeton University, possibly hoping for a positive reception by artists and art historians, particularly of an artifact with more aesthetic appeal than his stone tools that apparently did not merit display. He recorded in his diary that "I had been at new Art School Building and shown the head to the Director, Mr. Fredericks. He was

10.1 The artifact that Abbott named the "American Sphinx" in his notes and correspondence. The Peabody Museum Catalog notes that this specimen is a cast of the original (Peabody Museum Catalog Number 11-24-10/81220). Photo by the authors.

astounded or, as he put it 'paralyzed.' His enthusiasm not a surprise to me."
And later in the day "saw Mr. Pyne across the street. I was not long in join-
ing him, although he was with a lady at the time. We went into Art School
and I showed him the head. He was greatly surprised and pleased. Others
came in and we had a lively bit of conversation over it. It was a very pleasant
surprise to me and it made a decidedly good impression on Mr. Pyne. We
talked freely of the future and he spoke encouragingly of it" (CCA/PU Box
5, Folder 4; June 7, 1911).

Many of the archaeologists who viewed Abbott's "sphinx" insisted that
it was Mesoamerican in origin. The artifact was a small, ceramic human
head that exhibited clearly rendered earspools. Abbott disagreed with that
interpretation, however, stating that it was "unquestionably the handiwork
of an unusually gifted Lenape man" (1912:29). He sought the advice of Evarts
Tracy, a renowned architect and graduate of the Ecole des Beaux Arts in
Paris to interpret the artifact. It is unclear why Tracy was consulted, however, since he had no formal connection to archaeology and did not appear
to be an expert on Native American artifacts. However, Abbott re-printed
a lengthy letter from Tracy in *Ten Years' Diggings in Lenape Land* that described the artifact's workmanship, and further expounded on Tracy's theories about its origins and influence. In the letter, Tracy allegedly stated
that the human features depicted resembled an "Oriental inspiration" and
that "the Indians travelled far north of this region until they met and held
traffic with the Eskimos, who undoubtedly were of Asiatic origin and in
communication with Asia by way of Bering Straits." He further postulated,
"Why is it not possible and likely that this sculptor had made this northern journey and met an Asiatic wanderer who came down with his northern friends to the meeting place? If so, with the wonderful Indian memory,
what more likely than that on his return he described among his adventures
the man with the strange face and, artist that he was, graphically illustrated
that description with the clay" (Abbott 1912:32–33).

Tracy's theory on the inspiration for the design of the "sphinx" fit perfectly with Abbott's ideas about the origins of Native American people. In
fact, it fit so well that it raises a concern that Tracy may have been parroting
Abbott's own interpretation, or the letter may have been fabricated entirely
by Abbott. Abbott alleged that New Jersey's earliest occupants, and their
cousins in Europe during the Paleolithic, were biologically and culturally
related to the modern Eskimo (1878:253). The Eskimo were a useful model

for the American Paleolithic because they were adapted to a glacial environment, so Abbott overjoyed at Tracy's willingness to state that perhaps the "sphinx" was made by a Native American artist who had connections with Eskimo people.

Abbott conspicuously disregarded other interpretations by individuals with a greater scholarly authority on Native American prehistory, such as Frederic Ward Putnam of Harvard University and Edward Morse of the Peabody Academy of Science. "October 18, 1911:...got a long letter from Putnam which I answered. He was much interested in photo of Sphinx I sent him and made many wild guesses based on the picture but having no details of its history" (CCA/PU Box 5, Folder 4). After further correspondence, Putnam replied. Abbott noted the letter in his diary: "December 26, 1911: letter from Putnam and he is way off about the 'sphinx' insisting it was made in Central America. Funny and he wants the original to study. I wrote I would do my own studying" (CCA/PU Box 5, Folder 4). Others concurred with a Mesoamerican origin. "April 19, 1912: soon in Philadelphia and went directly to Hall of Philosophical society. Saw Edward Morse and showed him photo of 'Sphinx' and he swore it came from Mexico. Lively discussion and both insistent. Of course, he is wrong" (CCA/PU Box 6, Folder 1).

Two years after he obtained the "sphinx", Abbott was disappointed that few other scholars concurred with Tracy's interpretation. Abbott wrote "Mr. Tracy gives an impression of its origin in greater detail, which may well be put upon permanent record, as there seems to be no flaw in his argument" (1912:31). However, he had trouble finding a museum to house the artifact that would appreciate Abbott's and Tracy's interpretation. He wrote, "April 16, 1913: To Princeton. I met Prof. Marquand at his office and lecture room and handed over the 'sphinx' much against my will, as I do not think it ought to be anywhere but with my collection at Cambridge, but this was impossible to effect" (CCA/PU Box 6, Folder 2).

The Abbott Collection at the Peabody Museum at Harvard University contains what appears to be a cast of the sphinx, according to notes in the catalog (Cat. No. 11-24-10/81220, catalog reads "cast fragment of terra cotta head"), and Abbott did mention making a cast of the piece and giving that to Princeton about a year before presenting the original to Marquand: "March 6, 1912:...The "Sphinx" I have hidden, and a cast will do for them [Princeton]" (CCA/PU Box 6, Folder 1). But despite Abbott's statement that he presented the original artifact to Marquand on April 16, 1913, neither the

10.2 A decorated clay smoking pipe found by Charles Conrad Abbott's wife, Julia Boggs Abbott on Three Beeches (Peabody Museum Catalog Number 13-57-10/88891.1). Photo by the authors.

original artifact, nor a cast, is stored the Princeton University Art Museum collections today. It also does not appear to be in the collections of the New Jersey State Museum, which houses most of the artifacts from Abbott's Princeton collections. If it remained with Marquand's personal effects, it may have been discarded or donated elsewhere. Marquand served as Director of the Museum until his retirement in 1922, and donated a number of items to the Museum, but the original 'sphinx' is not among them (personal communication, Dr. Bryan Just, Curator and Lecturer in the Art of the Ancient Americas, Princeton Art Museum, July 6, 2016).

Another example of Abbott's continued artifact collecting comes in the form of a decorated clay smoking pipe found by his wife, Julia Boggs Abbott, during one of their strolls through Three Beeches (Fig. 10.2). Abbott submitted the artifact to the Peabody Museum at Harvard University in 1913, but no additional details exist regarding its provenience (Cat. No. 13-57/10.88891.1). The pipe was well made of finely textured clay and tempered with fine sand. It was decorated and highly burnished with an undecorated rim and stem. On the pipe bowl, the maker inscribed two 25 mm wide panels that begin below the rim and continue to the junction of the stem. The decorative elements are composed of finely incised lines and punctates. One panel faces the smoker, while the other is on the opposite face. Interestingly, Abbott appeared to attach little significance to the pipe, and simply wanted it added to the rest of the material that came from his farm at Trenton.

To be fair, Abbott was in his 70s and already ailing. The kidney and bladder infections that would ultimately cause his death already manifested themselves through incontinence, pain, and fatigue. Abbott's diaries, beginning around 1912, document a decline in physical activity and an annoyance with his body's degeneration. "April 10, 1914: Realizing I cannot prance about like a colt or skip like a lamb, I resign in favor of youth and fall back on contemplation" (CCA/PU Box 6, Folder 3). Infirmity did not, however, diminish Abbott's pigheaded insistence of the veracity of an American Paleolithic. "May 30, 1913: I staid home and nursed a diarrhea and got rid of it. When warm enough, I sat under Arthur's beech and meditated and finally reached conclusion that I would not bother any more about the archaeological problems....I am right, however many the objections raised" (CCA/PU Box 6, Folder 2).

ALANSON BUCK SKINNER AND MAX SCHRABISCH

In 1912, Abbott developed a friendship with archaeologists Alanson Buck Skinner and Max Schrabisch. Archaeologists in the mid-Atlantic region today recognize Skinner and Schrabisch for documenting and mapping hundreds of archaeological sites in New Jersey for the state Geological Survey (Skinner and Schrabisch 1913). Many of these sites are no longer extant so their manuscripts provide a valuable historical record. Skinner and Schrabisch asked Abbott about site locations in the area around Three Beeches and were interested in his work on the American Paleolithic. Both Skinner and Schrabisch spent time at Three Beeches reviewing sites and talking with Abbott throughout 1912–1915. Abbott and Ernest Volk were cited extensively in sections of their 1913 volume that addressed archaeological resources within the Delaware Valley.

Alanson Buck Skinner was born in Buffalo, New York, in 1886. His father, Frederick Woodward Skinner, was an avocational naturalist and professionally, a civil engineer who traveled extensively abroad. When Alanson was young, his family moved to Staten Island, New York, and his father became active in the prestigious Staten Island Institute of Arts and Sciences. As a teenager, Alanson met William T. Davis, likely through his father's naturalist connections as Davis was one of the co-founders of the Staten Island Institute. Young Alanson joined Davis on some of his outings on then rural Staten Island to observe plants and animals, particularly turtles. Skinner developed a life-long fascination with turtles and later in life signed letters to colleagues and friends as "Mr. Turtle" adorned with cartoon turtle drawings.

While still in high school, Skinner participated in two research projects: one was an archaeological excavation of a prehistoric shell mound near Shinnecock Hills on Long Island, and the other an ethnographic expedition to Cattaraugus, in western New York, led by Mark R. Harrington, a student of Franz Boas and curator at the American Museum of Natural History (AMNH). Skinner was subsequently hired as an assistant anthropologist at the AMNH and studied at Columbia University under Boas, later working for the Museum of the American Indian, Heye Foundation. His research spanned both archaeology and ethnography, working among many different Native American Nations throughout the United States and Canada (Menyuk 2012).

Max Schrabisch was a German immigrant who settled in Paterson, New Jersey, as a young adult. He was a polyglot, fluent in five languages including Latin and Greek, and also a skilled pianist who enjoyed playing music for friends, such as during visits to Three Beeches. Abbott recorded in his diary, "May 2, 1913:...After dinner, I had a good nap and was in good shape when a man appeared in the lane, who proved to be Max Schrabisch of Paterson....Had a lot of fun with Schrabisch and he played piano for us before he left" (CCA/PU Box 6, Folder 2). Schrabisch surveyed and recorded archaeological sites throughout New Jersey and Pennsylvania in the early 1900s (Schrabisch 1909, 1915, 1917, 1930) and is most well-known for his work on rockshelter sites in northern New Jersey.

Skinner and Schrabisch visited Three Beeches often during 1912 to consult with Abbott, and occasionally with Volk, about site locations in the Trenton area. Abbott clearly enjoyed these visits, recording one such day in his diaries as "July 16, 1912: At 8:30am, Mr. Skinner came and we soon started out for a walk. We went to gully and sat down, discussing local natural history and then up on fields and over to creek and returned." Unfortunately, the day later took a turn for the worse, "When we started out in opposite direction and by the 'trail,' Skinner was taken with cholera morbus, so we came back and he went to Dick's room and after a bit of cramp, vomiting and so on, fell asleep and not down stairs until sometime after diner, when he reappeared in good shape and entertained us all by Indian stories that were well narrated. Then we got out maps of New Jersey and I indicated where I knew had been Indian villages and sites of single camps or shell heaps" (CCA/PU Box 6, Folder 1).

Abbott also introduced Skinner to Henry C. Mercer, who by 1912, was working on his Fonthill estate, a house designed by Mercer and built of reinforced concrete, and at his Moravian Pottery and Tile Works in Doylestown, Bucks County, Pennsylvania. During one visit to Fonthill, Abbott recorded the meeting as "July 23, 1912:...Skinner told Indian stories which Mercer greatly enjoyed and there was a lively discussion as to the authenticity of the Lenape stone. Skinner gave Mercer a number of reasons why it was not genuine but in so gentle a way that Mercer did not get excited over it, but later as we were coming home told me a good many reasons why it could not be what it purported. I was very glad to get this expression of opinion as it coincided with what I have always thought ever since I heard of it" (CCA/PU Box 6, Folder 1).

Though Abbott clearly enjoyed Skinner's company, he had more in common with Max Schrabisch, who like Abbott, was self-taught in archaeology. Alliances replicated the dichotomy apparent twenty years earlier between Abbott and other non-academic archaeologists versus those backed by government agencies and academic institutions. Schrabisch, like Abbott, was similarly criticized for lax scientific methods in his fieldwork and reporting. Schrabisch may have also aligned more closely with Abbott on the issue of Paleolithic occupation of the Delaware Valley and sought evidence through his investigations of rockshelter sites in the region (Veit 2002:69). At times, the relationships became clear in Abbott's diary entries. He wrote, "July 27, 1912:...Max had a tale of woe about Skinner and my sympathies are with him rather than Skinner in some ways. He has not been fairly treated as his work among rock shelters is of a great deal more interest than what Skinner can do in locating Indian village sites." Yet Abbott was weary of the fight and continued, "I do not propose to get mixed up in it in any way....I can well afford to sit back and laugh for I am ahead of them all in this matter and neither, I predict, will throw additional light on the subject. It will be cumulative knowledge only and of course confirmatory of my views" (CCA/PU Box 6, Folder 1).

Despite acknowledging Abbott's authority in the region, Skinner and Schrabisch were noncommittal on the issue of humanity's antiquity They wrote in their published volume that "there has been much controversy about the question....The rub comes on the relative age of the finds, and here we find the archaeologist and the geologist are at odds. The former often claims great geological antiquity for his finds, the latter denies it. Assuming that each is thoroughly competent in his own science, the writer is forced to take the middle ground" (1913:18). And further, "as for the still older 'paleoliths,' that such exist in the Delaware Valley seems to be demonstrated by Volk, although some archaeologists are not satisfied that the remains are of human origin" (1913:19). Abbott would have liked a more conclusive confirmation of his theories but attributed at least some of Skinner and Schrabisch's hesitation to the influence of others, as well as a heavy editorial hand. Abbott recorded in his diary that "November 2, 1912: Max Schrabisch of Paterson came and showed me a copy of his rock shelter report. I saw that his manuscript had been tampered with by the state geologist and called his attention to it. He was surprised and said he would see that the excluded paragraph was reinserted. It referred to my work in the Delaware Valley" (CCA/PU Box 6, Folder 1). Alternatively, Abbott proposed that Skinner and Schrabisch may have simply been jealous of the work conducted by Abbott and Volk. "September 9, 1912: Skinner came, not unexpectedly on my part and we made the old north porch ring with a round of archaeological chatter and I was amused at some things he said. What Volk and I did years ago still worries them because they did not get ahead of us. Also I heard of Schrabisch who was not treated altogether square. I listened and laugh" (CCA/PU Box 6, Folder 1).

Max Schrabisch encouraged Abbott's ideas about early occupation of the Delaware Valley and vicinity, and he too wished to find sites similar to the Paleolithic of Europe in rockshelter sites of the mid-Atlantic United States (Veit 2002:69). Interestingly, Skinner and Schrabisch's final volume when published merely contained the comment "Mr. Max Schrabisch, of Paterson, who has explored and excavated more of these than any other person, has made the interesting discovery that the earliest occupants had crude tools and no pottery....This, to a certain extent, connects the earlier 'cave dwellers' with the non-pottery-making argillite users of the Delaware Valley" (1913:14). There was no definitive statement of the presence of an American Paleolithic in connection to rockshelter sites, something Abbott learned later upon publication. He blamed New Jersey State Geologist, Henry Barnard Kummel for the omission, partly due to lingering resentment – Kummel was one of the geologists who participated in the ill-fated 1897 Lalor fields excavations and who concluded that Abbott's paleoliths were not in situ in glacial sediments. "May 2, 1913:...He [Schrabisch] told me about his report in Geological Survey and how Kummel had mangled it. I was not at all surprised and am curious to see the book, although I know what the authors have in it. Kummel is an ass, and I do not suppose anyone takes him seriously" (CCA/PU Box 6, Folder 2).

Even after Skinner and Schrabisch finished their 1913 volume documenting archaeological site locations in New Jersey, Skinner continued a relationship with Abbott and conducted archaeological excavations on the Three Beeches property during the summer and fall of 1914. Perhaps in order to woo Abbott enough to let him dig at Three Beeches, Skinner told Abbott "about the opposition to my views and now how archaeologists are coming around to the views that I set forth so many years ago....He said that the influence of the Holmes crowd at Washington was very much on the decline, and this I was glad to learn" (CCA/PU Box 6, Folder 3; February 16, 1914).

Abbott was excited that archaeologists, backed by the financial resources and scholarly legitimacy of the AMNH in New York, would again be working at Three Beeches, and felt that this would further substantiate his theories about the American Paleolithic. He visited the excavations often and recorded the proceedings in his personal diary: "May 19, 1914: it was shortly after dinner that Skinner and an assistant came to dig a trench from cripple to lane, just beyond the lane. I went with them until they got fairly under way. I went to the 'digging' and learned they had found an argillite (basalt?) point a foot deep in compact yellow sand overtopped by a thick layer of dauber colored sand and never disturbed. It was a very important and convincing find" (CCA/PU Box 6, Folder 3). The next day, "the digger struck a great accumulation of firecracked stones and one at a considerable depth. Later, an argillite or basalt chip, in situ in yellow sands, the undermost layer being worked" (CCA/PU Box 6, Folder 3; May 20, 1914).

The excavations also garnered the attention of other local scholars including Henry Kummel and Assistant State Geologist M. W. Twitchell. "May 27, 1914: I was amused to find Kummel and Twitchell out here and glad to learn that in their presence, artifacts came from the low lying sand. Kummel told the most outrageous lie I ever heard and posed as an advocate of antiquity....Skinner made a splendid find of a perfect basalt point in deep yellow sands" (CCA/PU Box 6, Folder 3). The artifacts and their context, as documented by careful archaeological excavation, seemed to uphold Abbott's ideas about their antiquity, at least in Abbott's mind. He noted in his diary that "May 29, 1914: The archaeologists were out early and the trenches yielded a good many nice specimens....The marine shells told the story and so the traces of man were of Pleistocene time and not recent in any sense" (CCA/PU Box 6, Folder 3).

Excavations by the AMNH team continued in the fall, and Abbott enthused that they were affirming his earlier results. "October 8, 1914:...The party of last May are coming again next week and make a very exhaustive survey and digging of locality so that the question of man's antiquity will be settled forever. Of course, I know that what I have done and Volk has done really settles it but it is well to have the whole affair gone over by others and the same conclusions reached" (CCA/PU Box 6, Folder 3). However, unlike Abbott's earlier surface collecting from the locality, Skinner and his team were carefully excavating and screening for a more complete artifact assemblage. "October 12, 1914:...I could not resist looking at the work of others and so commenced an outdoor day by going to where Skinner, Hoover, and hired men are pitting the knoll by trolley through a sieve....We are now to have a really exhaustive examination of the locality and I hope such demonstration of archaeological significance as well forever shut up those who pretend to be unconvinced" (CCA/PU Box 6, Folder 3). Two days later Abbott noted, "I went down to the place where NY party are digging and was there a great deal of the time. I was interested in watching them as they are doing what I long have asked to see done, running a piece of ground through a sieve and getting the whole of its archaeological story" (CCA/PU Box 6, Folder 3; October 14, 1914). Such a statement rings false, as Abbott was never known for rigorous field methodologies, but with Skinner's detailed excavations, Abbott felt that his research on the subject had been reaffirmed. He wrote, "October 21, 1914:...The archaeology of the matter of this region's geologic history I cleared up years ago and

Volk re-cleared it and now these trenches tell the same story" (CCA/PU Box 6, Folder 3).

Unfortunately for Abbott, Skinner did not widely publish his research at Three Beeches, so while Abbott claimed the work was "re-cleared," that conclusion never made it to scholarly press, and it is questionable that Skinner concurred. In 1915, Skinner presented a very brief discussion of Abbott's "argillite man" but avoided comment on the American Paleolithic (Skinner 1917). Skinner left AMNH in 1916 for the Museum of the American Indian, but in 1918, Leslie Spier, an anthropologist at the AMNH who participated in the excavations at Three Beeches published a summary of Skinner's work in the *Anthropological Papers of the American Museum of Natural History*.

Spier also emphasized the "argillite culture" rather than the American Paleolithic in his publication (1918). According to Abbott, the Paleolithic in New Jersey slowly died out to be replaced by a second wave of occupation, presumably Native American, which continued to use argillite stone tool material yet manufactured highly standardized spear points and other implements. Abbott referred to this intermediate occupation as the "argillite culture" or "argillite man" in his personal and professional writings (1881, 1883a, 1890c). Extensive collecting by Abbott, and later excavations by Ernest Volk on the Lalor fields to the north of Three Beeches, revealed extensive argillite assemblages in the subsoil of the bluff (Volk 1911). The yellow sands within which the "argillite culture" was found were distinct from the lower glacial gravels and the more organic soils above, or so it was argued (Volk 1911).

Spier confirmed the positioning and composition of the "argillite culture" as initially presented by Abbott and Volk (1911) and stated that "the culture is simple, especially in contrast with that of the historic Delaware; the remains including only large stone blades and arrow-heads, the pitless hammerstone, the rubbing-stone, and fire-fractured pebbles" (1918:222), but indicated that it did not appear to be an archaeological horizon that could be replicated elsewhere, instead "it remains an isolated find" (1918:222). However, Abbott was much more concerned with confirmation of his American Paleolithic, which was considerably more controversial. Spier dismissed that research and stated, "The literature is voluminous and in part irrelevant. The ideas presented concerning the 'argillite culture' are obscured by the evidence adduced for a still earlier 'Paleolithic' culture" (1918:175), but continued that "Much of the irrelevance of subsequent discussion must be laid to the lack of clearness and precision in Abbott's presentation" and that "Holmes is properly critical of the proofs for the existence of a Paleolithic culture and a culture of the glacial epoch" (1918:176). But Holmes and Volk also received critique from Spier for failing to recognize the "argillite culture" within the yellow sand stratum near Trenton (1918:177–178).

It is unclear whether Abbott ever read Skinner's or Spier's reports. By 1917, when the first of the two was published, his health was in precipitous decline, and he rarely recorded entries in his personal diary. If he had read them, he would have been disappointed that his lifelong work on the alleged American Paleolithic was not the focus of either publication, even though both gave credence to his identification of a non-ceramic, predominantly argillite assemblage in a yellow sand stratum situated above the Trenton gravels. Today, these sites would likely be assigned a Middle Woodland chronology, based on the artifact types that were recovered (Hunter and Tvaryanas 2009).

No additional work was conducted at Three Beeches by Skinner following the series of excavations into the "argillite culture." Skinner turned his attention more specifically to ethnographic research among Native American Nations of the United States and Canada during his later employment with the Museum of the American Indian. While conducting ethnographic fieldwork, he met close friend and collaborator Amos Enos Oneroad (Mah-pi-yasna, or "Jingling Cloud") who was from a traditional Sisseston-Wahpeton Sioux family from Dry Wood Lake, South Dakota. Oneroad attended the Columbia University Divinity School in New York and met Skinner through the Museum. Oneroad started working directly for Skinner as an informant and delivered lectures in New York City dressed in full Sioux regalia.

On August 18th, 1925, Alanson Skinner and Amos Oneroad were on a collecting and research trip near the town of Tokio, North Dakota, when their car skidded on a wet road and overturned into a ditch. Oneroad was at the wheel. Skinner was killed immediately. Oneroad survived, but he was profoundly affected by the death of his friend. In a letter to George G. Heye of the Museum of the American Indian, Heye Foundation, Oneroad wrote, "Surely it has been a hard and a most trying moments [*sic*] of my existence from the after effects, why was I spared? My health has been on the decline since but I am doing the best I can by trying to have a little bit of sunshine in my heart and I don't know as I will ever find another friend like him" (November 7, 1925, AEO to GGH, presented in Menyuk 2012).

ERNEST VOLK

Ernest Volk's work at Three Beeches and the surrounding farms also evolved to focus more specifically on the "argillite culture" in the yellow sand stratum. Though Volk was initially charged by Putnam to evaluate Abbott's alleged Paleolithic finds, he was soon researching the argillite culture that was presumed to be intermediate between a Paleolithic occupation and more recent Native American inhabitants. At first, Volk was working exclusively for the Peabody Museum, but by the mid-1890s, his work was supported through Putnam's affiliation with the AMNH, in New York City. Artifacts from Volk's excavations are divided between the two institutions.

The "yellow sands" described by Abbott and Volk were determined to be wind-blown sediments and are primarily found along the bluff top around Three Beeches and neighboring farms. Excavations led by Volk at Lalor fields, and visited by those on both sides of the Paleolithic debate in 1896, yielded artifacts that consisted exclusively of lithic material, both chipped and ground stone tools. No ceramic artifacts were definitively associated with the horizon. Instead, most of the analyses presented in published reports focused on these stone artifacts and their provenience. Henry Mercer, Ernest Volk, and Henry Kummel all published on the argillite culture from the Lalor fields at Trenton (Kummel 1898; Mercer 1898; Volk 1911).

Volk excavated and monitored disturbed sediments caused by road and railway construction. His report, "The Archaeology of the Delaware Valley" in the *Papers of the Peabody Museum of American Archaeology and Ethnology*, outlined an extensive focus on the bluff top to the west of Three Beeches, particularly on farmland owned by the Lalor and Wright families (Fig. 10.3). Collections at the Peabody Museum and the American Museum of Natural History include thousands of artifacts from Lalor fields as well as photographs taken in the field documenting stratigraphic profiles and artifacts in situ. The majority of the artifacts collected by Volk consisted of stone flakes, scrapers, projectile points, knives, and other tools, primarily made of argillite. Volk remained dependably consistent with Abbott's view of a three stage occupation, moving from Paleolithic, to "argillite man", to modern Native American in his interpretation of the excavated material. However, the artifacts suggest a much wider chronological range with greater diversity than could be expressed through Abbott's three-part system.

For example, in 1895 while Ernest Volk was working in the northern ("upper") section of what was referred to by Abbott as the Meadows, he found a decorated pipe fragment (AMNH Accession No. 20/11956) a short distance from Achpoachquisings Creek (today called Watson's Creek), bordering the area designated "Excavation 14" by Dorothy Cross (1956). The pipe was excavated from what Volk called an "older, medium-sized pit" (Pit 6, Trench 9, Volk 1911). Volk recorded that the pipe fragment was large and was decorated with "curious and interesting markings" (1911:80) and supplied a very small photograph but made no further mention of the specimen or other associated artifacts, because it was not part of the argument about the Paleolithic or argillite culture. Cross's later excavations in the vicinity revealed features that date to the Late Woodland period (Cross 1956).

10.3 Ernest Volk's sketch map of excavation locations in the Lalor Fields (Volk 1911:25–27). Redrawn by Ardeth Anderson, Penn Museum.

Despite Volk's biased interpretations of the Trenton sequence, his provenience data significantly improved on Abbott's prior work. However, he, like Abbott, was largely self-educated, and his scientific rigor questioned by later scholars. Dorothy Cross, for example, alleged that Volk only documented and collected argillite artifacts from the "yellow drift" and discarded all other material as intrusive, such as pottery, or lithic artifacts of jasper, chert, and chalcedony (Cross 1956:8). Spier concurred and stated that Volk's methods were "seemingly dictated in part by a desire to rule out all finds which might possibly be intrusive from the surface soil" though he conceded that "Volk's contributions are invaluable, for he showed that the artifacts are numerous, occur over a wide area, and are of a type distinct from the Delaware remains, but he neglected to make the fullest use of his data" (1918:178). Cross's excavations at Three Beeches in the 1930s used a more rigorous methodology and recorded a wide range of artifact types, materials, and chronologies spanning early prehistory through historic, Euro-American occupation (1956).

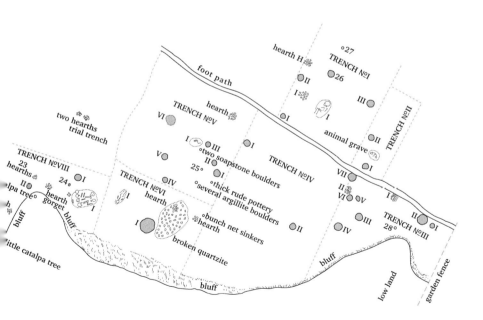

THE FIRE AT THREE BEECHES

Abbott's later years were filled with writing and full-time residence at Three Beeches until it was destroyed by fire on November 13, 1914 (*Daily State Gazette*; 14 November 1914). He recorded the event in his diary:

> November 13, 1914: While helping Julie clear up, after dinner, we noticed a fire on the meadows and before 2pm it had reached the hillside and in less than half an hour, the Three Beeches were swept by fire out of existence. I will not attempt any description of that fearful afternoon save to remark that enough was saved to be a perpetual reminder of the past. My library gone save a few books. Late in afternoon, Julie and I went to Trenton and later, came to Bristol where we staid at Joe's and although I tried to be cheerful it was agonizing to think if being without a real home after forty years of house keeping (CCA/PU Box 6, Folder 3).

Newspapers estimated the loss at about $18,000–$20,000 (between $425,000–$475,000 today) (*Daily State Gazette* 14 November 1914). The fire was allegedly caused by a spark from an engine on the Pennsylvania railroad, along the Amboy division tracks (*Daily State Gazette* 14 November 1914), though has been alternately reported as deliberately set by hunters (Hunter and Tvaryanas 2009). It was fanned by high winds and swept quickly through the dry grass in the wetland meadows below Three Beeches. According to a local newspaper account, "there was no water about the premises... the nearest hydrant was the one on the White Horse road. More than 1800 feet of hose had to be laid" (*Daily State Gazette* 14 November 1914). Abbott's farm was the only house destroyed by the fire (Fig. 10.4).

Immediately following the destruction of his home, Abbott and his family temporarily moved to the Beatty boarding house located at 910 Radcliffe St., Bristol, Pennsylvania, not far from where they lived during Abbott's employment in Philadelphia. Abbott was despondent about the move, the destruction of his collections and personal papers, and the loss of the family farm house. On New Year's Eve of 1914, he wrote, "So ended 1914, and if it had not been for the disaster of November....[it] would have been one to remember, but as it is too much bitter was mingled with the sweet and the sudden transplantation from the Three Beeches to Bristol leaves precious

10.4 All that remained of the Three Beeches farmhouse following a massive fire on November 13, 1914. Charles Conrad Abbott Papers (C0290), Box 15, Folder 2; Manuscripts Division, Department of Rare Books and Special Collections, Princeton University Library.

little of the old self remaining. My present self reminds me of those shells of cicadas we see in summer, sticking to the side of a tree" (CCA/PU Box 6, Folder 3).

He later wrote in a series of unpublished reflective essays that "the one redeeming feature of the loss of possessions is to be even happier after deprivation occurs than when one was in possession. Not for a moment do I suppose that any person was so admirably constituted that such could happen, but life means setting up an ideal and seeing how near we can come to it" and that "Forty minutes robbed me of possessions I spent as many years in bringing together, and the new condition of deprivation came without warning. I spent forty years in the full enjoyment of having, and now what of the opposite when 'I have' becomes 'I had'?" (CCA/PU Box 1, Folder 6, labeled "Thoughts without Thinking: Essays of a Materialist, by Charles Conrad Abbott." It is undated, but an earlier page in this volume says "Much of the material here used in a revised form, was originally printed in the Newark (N.J.) Evening News [IV] and is reproduced in accordance with an agreement with the Editor, made at the time of the original appearance. C.C.A., Bristol, Pa., Dec. 19, 1916").

In many ways, Abbott attempted to make the best of the situation, focusing on the freedom that can be achieved by owning very little, but the loss of his books and papers was a significant blow. "I am at least free from the care incident to possession....I had become dependent upon a multitude of inanimate objects; shelves of books, bundles of scribblings, objects of virtue and more of no virtue and so an abiding place so filled that any room was more desired than my company, provided these gatherings of mine gave the subject their attention." He posited, "Is it not therefore nearer akin to happiness to rejoice in my freedom rather than mourn over my loss (?)" [parenthetical question mark in original] but concluded "what if all those choice possessions were swept away by the devouring flames, the earth is still intact and—herein lies my happiness—so am I" (CCA/PU Box 1, Folder 6).

On January 26, 1915, the Three Beeches farm was sold and Abbott never visited the property again. In his diary he wrote, "deeds were actually delivered and money paid, and now 'Three Beeches' passes into history. It is strange to think I have no hold on a spot I made famous" (CCA/PU Box 6, Folder 4; January 26, 1915). Abbott later wrote, "it is no easy task to calmly sketch the cares of the family from 1874–1914 as occupants of Three Beeches—40 years of clouds and sunshine and ending in a catastrophe little short of death to all of us. The whining idiot that said that some great good might come of it only embittered me the more. Such is and always will be my attitude towards what has been. No argument can alter it, no platitudes change my purpose. Nature marked me for a victim, after all those years when I thought I was a favored child of hers" (CCA/PANS).

AN "OFFICIOUS BLADDER" AND OTHER AILMENTS

Despite Abbott's efforts to find a silver lining, the loss of Three Beeches catapulted him into a deep depression that characterized the autumn years of his life. He ceased regularly writing in his diary, and those entries that were recorded often highlight his resentment and anger. By 1915, Abbott was also experiencing significant problems with his health, including incontinence and infections that bothered him greatly and further reduced his ability to concentrate or get out into the field. "April 18, 1915: I gave up diary records today as there was too little of record and I was otherwise not in the mood....It was this illness that made me give up the diary and everything else" and at the bottom of the same page, he wrote "September 22, 1915: Was mistaken here as I have not power of expression as my efforts at writing fail because of weakness....The break in this diary from date at top of page [April 18] to Sept. 9 covers a period that was largely marked by ill health and no incident of any importance" (CCA/PU Box 6, Folder 4).

His incontinence became a constant source of anger that was reflected in sporadic diary entries. "August 10, 1912: I was not in very good shape. My bladder was somewhat officious and wanted to be voiding itself wholly without regard to my convenience and worst of it all, I had to submit" (CCA/PU Box 6, Folder 1). And more typically, "March 1, 1916: There was nothing going on except the activity of my bladder, so cuss words continually bubbled over" (CCA/PU Box 6, Folder 4). Of course, Abbott's comments were without any hint of conceit, "June 22, 1913: I could not go anywhere on account of urinal activity, but I bore the affliction with becoming grace" (CCA/PU Box 6, Folder 2).

During the last year of his life, Abbott wrote very little. In 1918, he penned in his diary that "I was requested to resume my diary, and I do so under protest. Recording an aimless existence is not exhilarating. A week of it is an example of monotony. I cannot make something out of nothing and material for record is as scarce as possible. Frank has been coming in at about 11am and we have a cigar and at noon he goes. After dinner, I take a long nap and then wait for the Bulletin and read it. In evening, I read a book of some sort and then to bed. Now this entry will apply to the past three months and is likely to be a fair statement as to days to come" (CCA/PU Box 6, Folder 6; September 12, 1918). October 10, 1918 was his last diary entry "I was promised a copy of Bolch's book today, according to his letter of 11th Sept. But it did not come nor have I had a word from him for a month. I am so used to such disappointments that this one did not make any impression. I had a longer nap than usual, this afternoon. Frank came in just as I came down stairs" (CCA/PU Box 6, Folder 6).

In his final letter to his son, Richard, Abbott wrote "I have lost hold on time and am asleep much of my time, as I fall asleep over everything I try to read...I am bad, no word from anybody" (CCA/PU Box 13, Folder 6; July 13, 1919). Abbott died two weeks later of Bright's Disease, which is the historical term for chronic nephritis, a severe kidney infection that can lead to kidney failure. His incontinence, fatigue, drowsiness, and frequent fevers may have been early symptoms of the disease, for which no treatment was available in the early 20th century. He was 76 years old.

MEMORIAL

Abbott was buried in the historic Riverview Cemetery, located on Centre Street in Trenton, New Jersey, not far from the old Three Beeches farm. It was an early Quaker cemetery, established in 1685, and later expanded in 1858 into a park-like property, designed by Calvert Vaux, a landscape architect most well known for collaborating with Frederick Law Olmstead on the design of Central Park and Brooklyn's Prospect Park in New York (Riverview Cemetery Corporation 2010). His grave marker is a glacial boulder with a bronze plaque that reads, "In this neighborhood Dr. Abbott discovered the existence of Paleolithic man in America" (Fig. 10.5).

Obituaries published in leading journals highlighted Abbott's work on the American Paleolithic, and some authors such as George Frederick Wright used the occasion to strike a final blow in the debate, describing visits to sites near Three Beeches as "perfectly convincing evidence of the accuracy of his [Ernest Volk's] observations, and confirmatory of the testimony of Dr. Abbott concerning the prevalence of argillite in the undisturbed glacial strata, establishing a sharp distinction between the occupation

10.5 The grave marker of Charles Conrad Abbott and Julia Boggs Olden Abbott. It is made of a glacial boulder with a bronze plaque that reads "In this neighborhood Dr. Abbott discovered the existence of Paleolithic man in America." Photo by the authors.

of Paleolithic man and that of the aboriginal Indians" (Wright 1919:453). However, the journal *American Anthropologist*, which had staunchly supported Holmes and was widely understood to be the voice of the Bureau of American Ethnology and the Smithsonian Institution archaeologists, merely published the announcement, "Charles Conrad Abbott, the author of 'Primitive Industries' died July 27th. A notice of Dr. Abbott's work and writings will appear in a later issue" (Anonymous 1919:345). The obituary, when published a few months later, recounted Abbott's work as "His first

archaeological discoveries seem to have been finds of crude argillite implements on his homestead at Trenton. These were followed up by other discoveries, until in 1883, he developed the conception of three superimposed
cultures in the soil of his estate" (Wissler 1920:70). It included no mention
of the American Paleolithic.

11

Abbott's Legacy

DOROTHY CROSS AND THE INDIAN SITE SURVEY

After investigations into the "argillite culture" by Skinner, Spier, and Volk had concluded, there was no formal archaeological work conducted at Three Beeches or the surrounding area for approximately twenty years. However, local collectors were well aware of the archaeological potential of the property, and frequently visited the former Three Beeches farm to gather artifacts from the surface and shallow pits, particularly once there was no one living on the property to restrict access. Construction areas were also popular hunting zones for amateur antiquarians as the urban sprawl from the city of Trenton soon overtook the area. Unrestricted looting garnered concern among New Jersey's professional archaeologists and beginning in 1936, Dr. Dorothy Cross was tasked with documenting the archaeological resources at Three Beeches and surrounding farms in order to record a rapidly disappearing cultural resource.

Dorothy Cross Jensen (1906–1972) received her B.A. and Ph.D. from the University of Pennsylvania and worked for the New Jersey State Museum, ultimately serving as State Archaeologist, and later as an instructor of anthropology and archaeology at Hunter College, City University of New York. Professionally, she published under her maiden name but used her married surname when teaching. She conducted fieldwork and museum studies in the United States and abroad, serving as a valuable contributor to the University of Pennsylvania and American Schools of Oriental Research Expedition to Iraq in 1931–1932. Her publications on pottery and cuneiform tablets from the second millennium B.C. kingdom of Arrapha continue to be cited in contemporary archaeological research of the region (Conant 1974).

Cross ceased work in Iraq prior to the outbreak of World War II and returned to the United States to focus her research on sites in New Jersey, specifically the Delaware Valley. Between 1936 and 1941, Dr. Cross, who was at the time affiliated with the New Jersey State Museum, conducted extensive excavations at Three Beeches and surrounding farms, in an area that ultimately became known simply as the Abbott Farm. The project was funded in part through the Works Progress Administration and was one of the largest ever conducted in the state, employing hundreds of workers for excavations, mapping, and documentation (Hunter and Tvaryanas 2009).

Cross's early research in the Delaware Valley coincided with the formation of the Archaeological Society of New Jersey (formerly the New Jersey State Museum Advisory Committee for Indian Research) and a push for systematic excavations at the Abbott Farm. One of the stated goals of the Archaeological Society of New Jersey (ASNJ) was to support scientific research and to reduce looting activity within the state. Because the area around Abbott's Three Beeches property had been a well-known target for collectors for many years, the ASNJ wanted to initiate rigorous and controlled excavations before many of the sites were damaged or destroyed. As early as 1930, plans and fundraising were underway for survey and excavation at Three Beeches, but insufficient funds delayed the project for six years (Boissevain 1956).

In 1936, Dr. Albert O. Hayes, the Chairman of the Research Committee of the ASNJ, applied for a grant from the Works Progress Administration to fund excavations at the Abbott Farm. The grant was awarded for a project to be called the Indian Sites Survey, which was administered by the New Jersey State Museum, Department of Education, with the ASNJ acting in an advisory capacity (Cross 1956). Cross was appointed as the Supervisor of the project until September of 1938, when she was succeeded by Allan H. Smith, who a few months later was replaced by Nathaniel Knowles. All artifacts, notes, sketches, and photographs were processed, curated, and archived at the New Jersey State Museum, where they remain today (Boissevain 1956). With the Indian Sites Survey's numerous field workers, Cross personally trained many of New Jersey's next generation of professional archaeologists, using modern, scientific techniques of excavation and documentation that she had learned at the University of Pennsylvania and while working on high-profile and well-funded projects in Iraq. Her work differed dramatically from previous collections made by Abbott and Volk in her careful, technical excavation and recording, and her publications on New Jersey prehistory remain valuable references for archaeologists working in the state today (Cross 1952, 1956, 1965).

Cross's excavations were massive. She tested approximately twenty locations, mostly along the top of the bluff at Three Beeches, the Isaac Watson property, and surrounding farms. Approximately 170,000 square feet were excavated, totaling 25,000 cubic yards of sediment (Fig. 11.1; Hunter and Tvaryanas 2009:5–15). Cross recovered and documented artifact caches; hundreds of pits and hearths; and pottery, stone tools, bone and antler artifacts, and other prehistoric materials numbering in the thousands.

The Indian Site Survey project revealed that the bulk of the prehistoric occupation of the Abbott farm was confined to an area within about 900 feet of the top of the bluff and parallel to the edge overlooking the wetlands along the Delaware River, with a small area of archaeological interest between the base of the bluff and Watson's Creek. The sediments on the bluff top consisted of a plowzone approximately 6–8 inches in depth containing organic-rich sediments, overlying a sandy stratum approximately five feet thick, though the depth in some areas extended to as much as 18.5 feet. This stratum was referred to by Cross and earlier authors such as Abbott, Volk, Skinner, and Spier as the "yellow sand" (1956:14) and contained the majority of archaeological deposits and features. Below this was the Trenton gravel, which Cross described as "a mixture of an outwash deposit of the Wisconsin glaciation and older material" (1956:16) that averaged 12–18 feet thick.

Cross was as meticulous a researcher as she was an excavator, and understood that Abbott's claims of an American Paleolithic focused on the Trenton gravel. As a result, she paid careful attention to artifact provenience and stratigraphic context. Cross noted that no artifacts were found within the Trenton gravel, except in Excavation 9, where the levels were heavily mixed throughout the entire sediment column (1956:16). In some places, Cross recorded that the boundary between the yellow sand and the Trenton gravel was very diffuse, making it difficult to discriminate where one ended and the other began. Cross also identified several buried A horizons, which represented old occupation surfaces, in the stratigraphic sequence of Excavation 14 that also contained pit features and numerous artifacts

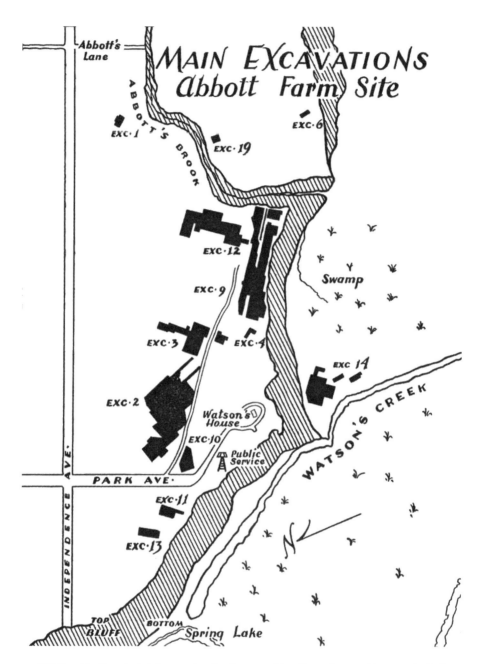

11.1 Dorothy Cross's sketch map showing the overall locations of excavations conducted with the Indian Site Survey from 1936–1941 (Cross 1956:13).

(1956:20–21). In her summary, Cross also highlighted Volk's excavations at the Lalor fields that exposed the alleged "argillite culture" that became a more significant focus of work at the Abbott Farm in the 20th century.

Cross's report, published in 1956, provided a thorough review of the work of Charles Conrad Abbott and other archaeologists and geologists at Three Beeches and the surrounding area, fairly presenting both Abbott's argument about the American Paleolithic and the counter-arguments raised by Holmes and others. However, Cross concluded that based on the Indian Site Survey excavations in the Trenton gravels, "no signs of human occupation were found in the 'Trenton gravels' except when these were close to the surface and not compact. None of the material contained therein can be considered contemporaneous with the original deposition of the gravel." Cross then clarified that "although the diggings in the compact gravel were not extensive, they covered enough space to expect to find something if man lived here during glacial or early post-glacial times" (1956:23). She noted that approximately 15,000 cubic feet of gravel sediment was excavated, but only about one third of that was compact, seemingly undisturbed, gravel.

The work of the Indian Site Survey at the Abbott Farm remains important because of the significant development that has taken place over the past hundred years as Trenton's confines extended south of the city. Many of the archaeological resources of the Abbott Farm are no longer extant or are under residential and commercial development. Cross's research, and later work by Louis Berger and Associates for compliance with Section 106 of the National Historic Preservation Act, provides the best documentation of these archaeological resources.

LOUIS BERGER AND ASSOCIATES AND THE NATIONAL HISTORIC PRESERVATION ACT

Later archaeological investigations at the Abbott Farm were conducted for compliance with federal legislation protecting cultural resources. In 1975, planning began for a massive highway interchange south of Trenton in the immediate vicinity of Abbott's Three Beeches farm and the Abbott Farm archaeological complex as identified by Cross. This undertaking required archaeological survey and excavation for compliance with Section 106 of the National Historic Preservation Act (Public Law 89-665; 54 U.S.C. 300101 et seq. [1966]) and the National Environmental Policy Act (42 U.S.C.

§4321 et seq. [1969]). The archaeological program was triggered by the Federal Highway Administration and the New Jersey Department of Transportation's support for the interchange at the intersection of highway routes I-195 and I-295 with New Jersey routes 29 and 129. The cultural resources investigation for this project was performed by Louis Berger and Associates, Inc., an engineering and environmental consulting firm headquartered in Morristown, New Jersey. Among other requirements, the National Historic Preservation Act and the National Environmental Policy Act dictate that undertakings funded or permitted by the federal government must take into account their effects on cultural resources, including archaeological sites.

Initial archaeological survey of the property was conducted by Janet Pollak, as a subcontractor for Louis Berger and Associates, Inc., who produced a technical report documenting extensive prehistoric Native American archaeological resources (Pollak 1977). By 1980, Louis Berger and Associates, Inc., took over the cultural resources investigation, working in the project area through 1989. Ten different prehistoric Native American archaeological sites were excavated as part of what became known as the Trenton Complex archaeological project. These sites were determined to be eligible for the National Register of Historic Places under criterion D, for their potential to provide data about the prehistoric past and ultimately were subsumed within the boundaries of the Abbott Farm National Historic Landmark.

Though the sheer volume of sediment excavated by the Louis Berger and Associates cultural resources team was smaller than that excavated by either Volk or Cross, the investigations were conducted with modern scientific methods and a high level of rigor. Technological innovations in quantitative and qualitative analyses yielded new data relating to paleoenvironments, geomorphology, dating, and geochemistry. In 1996, Louis Berger and Associates published a fifteen volume technical report that enumerated their results. They discovered that the Abbott Farm contained prehistoric occupation spanning the Archaic through Late Woodland period, but the most intensive use of these sites concentrated during the Middle to Late Woodland (Cavallo 1987; Dumont and McLearen 1986; Foss 1986; McLearen and Fokken 1986; Perazio 1986; Stewart 1986a, 1986b, 1987, 1998; Wall and Stewart 1996; Wall et al. 1996a, 1996b, 1996c).

The program of survey, excavation, and analysis conducted by the Louis Berger and Associates cultural resources team resulted not only in these extensive technical reports completed for compliance with the National Historic Preservation Act and the National Environmental Policy Act, but since their publication, archaeologists have used data from the excavations for a number of professional, scholarly publications and other analyses (Lattanzi 2007; Parris and Williams 1986; Schindler 2008; Schutt 2007; Stewart 1989, 1990, 1993, 1994a, 1994b, 1995, 2007).

In recognition of the potential for the property to contain significant archaeological resources related to the prehistoric and historic past, the Abbott Farm district, containing Abbott's Three Beeches farm and surrounding properties along the high bluffs overlooking the Delaware River and Crosswicks Creek is listed on the National Register of Historic Places and designated as a National Historic Landmark (Williams et al. 1976). Today, a historic marker on the property reads "Abbott Farm: Charles Conrad Abbott, M.D., 1843–1919. Noted author discovered significant archaeological artifacts here on his farm" (Fig. 11.2).

11.2 The Abbott Farm National Historic Landmark was designated on December 8, 1976. The historic marker on the property reads, "Abbott Farm: Charles Conrad Abbott, M.D., 1843–1919. Noted author discovered significant archaeological artifacts here on his farm."

THE ARCHAEOLOGY OF THREE BEECHES

In the fall of 1963, Andrew Stanzeski and Robert Cunningham began archaeological excavations at the site of the Three Beeches farmhouse, which burned to the ground on Friday, November 13, 1914. The goal of the investigation was to identify the foundations of the house and recover artifacts associated with Charles Conrad Abbott's occupation. This study uniquely conducted archaeology of an archaeologist, in which artifacts found within the project area were not necessarily primary deposits of prehistoric occupation, but instead more likely represented Abbott's archaeological collections during the 19th and early 20th century.

The house was located after brush was cleared from the property, which also revealed a well and other outbuildings. Once the foundation of the house was identified, it was partitioned into quadrants and excavated. Artifacts recovered included objects associated with 19th and early 20th century occupation as well as remains of Abbott's artifact collections. Stanzeski and Cunningham recovered prehistoric, Native American artifacts that included a broken bannerstone, six axes, one celt, projectile points, drills, scrapers, lithic debitage, and other materials that all displayed evidence of thermal fracture and burning. A human proximal femur fragment was also recovered, which was likely part of Abbott's collections, as there is no evidence that anyone died in the fire. The east corner of the house contained a broken set of china, six nut picks, and a nutcracker, perhaps suggesting the location of the house's dining room. The western corner, excavated the following spring, contained 32 coins, probably from Abbott's coin collection, as well as items of jewelry including two gold watches; a silver watch with maker's mark of A. W. W. Co., Waltham, Mass.; a gold-plated watch chain; an 18 karat gold wedding band; a locket; and five cuff-links. Abbott's personal library was probably situated towards the western side of the house, as excavations in that provenience revealed burned books, some of which were still identifiable. Titles included *The Stone Age in North America*, by Warren K. Moorehead; *The Walam Olum,* by Constantine Rafinesque; *The Lenape and Their Legends*, by Daniel G. Brinton; *Frankenstein,* by Mary Wollstonecraft Shelley; and *Archaeology of the Delaware Valley*, by Ernest Volk (Stanzeski 1974:31).

In the report of the excavations at Three Beeches, Stanzeski pointed out that there was a notable dearth of artifacts, given Abbott's active collecting in the area. The small number of prehistoric objects found during excavations were insignificant compared to the vast body of material Abbott had possessed during his decades of active fieldwork. However, many of Abbott's collections by 1914 were either housed at the Peabody Museum at Harvard University or at Princeton University. It is also fortunate that by 1914, Abbott had already begun donating personal papers to the Princeton University Library, as it is likely that valuable correspondence, unpublished manuscripts, and field notes were burned in the fire that destroyed Three Beeches farm.

In 2007, a visit to the Three Beeches farmhouse by the authors of this volume revealed surface evidence of the house foundation as well as artifacts associated not only with Abbott's occupation in the late 19th and early 20th century, but also with Stanzeski and Cunningham's excavation in the 1960s. A rusted shovel and hardware screen fragment were recovered during an informal surface survey of the site that were most likely associated with Stanzeski and Cunningham's investigation. However, looters' pits and evidence of archaeological pothunting that clearly post-dated the 1960s was also observed and, though found within the boundaries of the excavation area in the farmhouse foundation, it is possible the shovel and screens could have been remnants of more recent, illegal, non-scientific artifact collecting on the property as well.

THE ARCHIVE OF CHARLES CONRAD ABBOTT

Charles Conrad Abbott was a prolific writer in print and in private. In addition to the extensive correspondence that he maintained with friends and colleagues, he kept a daily diary from the time that he moved to Three Beeches in 1874 until his death in 1919, leaving an immense body of literature that details the minutia of his day to day life. These diaries, now housed in the Manuscripts and Special Collections division of Firestone Library at Princeton University, provide a unique insight into Abbott as a family man and as a scholar. His enthusiasm for the field is intertwined in these diaries with his frankly cantankerous personality. A few days in June and July of 1891 offer a typical glimpse of Abbott's chronicles:

June 10, 1891: (Clear, hot, cherries ripe) To Philadelphia and after work at office, at Culin's office and then came home in 1:50 train. Nose cold a nuisance and unfitted me for decent progress on my essay, but did accomplish the consumption of a quart of cherries. Took a hot bath. Later made a desperate attempt to work and finished and mailed 'Windy Bush' to 'Christian Union.'

June 14, 1891: (Clear, hot) In doors all the forenoon and did nothing but read the papers. The afternoon as lazily spent and the evening given to chatter, cigars, and moonlight.

Sunday, July 26, 1891: (Clear, cool) In doors all the forenoon disgusted with contents in part of a letter Julie writes to Maria. It is exasperating to be told to 'write' when one has no ideas. As if Ms could be turned out by the sweat of one's brow. I never undertook writing for money, but I fizzled at it. I have very seldom written when in the mood and failed! I wish this could be put in a good many pipes and meditatively smoked. Gave the afternoon almost wholly to literary work and completed part one of my 'Wildwood Beach' notes (CCA/PU Box 3, Folder 2).

The diaries were never intended for a wider contemporaneous audience, but Abbott did note in places that he was recording for posterity. On one journal, for example, the cover reads "T.F.M.O.L. It's nobody's business what the letters stand for." In the corner of the same cover, it reads "Seriously considered T.F.M.O.L. and it is a mistake to think of further effort in any line, April 24, 1912" (CCA/PU Box 6, Folder 1). In others, the covers are decorated with Abbott's doodles (Fig. 11.3), notations, and poems:

I would that I might rightly think,
Face shining fact and never wink
From fountain source of knowledge drink
    And aye keep steady;

From no chop-logic's onset shrink,
    But up and ready.

(CCA/PU Box 16, Folder 2; September 10, 1905)

Abbott was not shy about recording callous comments on friends, family, and colleagues. In one repeated theme, Abbott decried the lack of

11.3 Charles Conrad Abbott's doodle on the inside cover of one of his journals. Charles Conrad Abbott Papers (C0290), Box 16, Folder 6; Manuscripts Division, Department of Rare Books and Special Collections, Princeton University Library.

sophistication of his Three Beeches neighbors, many of whom were his relatives. He wrote:

> what is knowledge after all, but the sum total of trifles in themselves? A brick is useless as such, but one hundred thousand will make you a house worth having. Then again, how much better it is to stumble across a fact than palaver over a theory.

> Four links in the chain, then, instead of three and why not a fifth?

> "Halt!" demanded my neighbors, "This cannot go on forever."

> "True," I replied, "but I see a foot-hold for one more step," and I took it.

> My neighbors shook their wise heads. They laughed at my credulity. They called names and talked much of brazen impudence in attempting to foist nonsense upon them. What they did and may still be doing, I do not know—nor care (CCA/PU Box 1, Folder 4).

Elsewhere, Abbott boasted of his intellectual differences from his neighbors in verse:

What others saw in nature,
       I saw not;

What others have remembered,
       I forgot.

What others fondly cherished,
       I forsook;

Where others gazed delighted,
       Did not look.

What I have seen in nature,
       They saw not;

What I shall long remember,
       They forgot.

That which I value highly,
       They disdained;

Where I all day would linger,
       Ne'er remained.

My neighbors have their fancies, be it so.
Provided I am free, to come and go.

(CCA/PU Box 16, Folder 6)

Yet, perhaps exhibiting a small amount of self-reflection, Abbott wrote in a journal entitled "Old Fashioned Essays" that "I thought to write an essay on Fools and straightaway found myself heading the procession" but then "turning, as a last resort, to my neighbors, I asked to have pointed at to me, whom they considered as a typical fool. I put the question cautiously and the replies were unsuspiciously given, and in the twinkling of an eye, I was confronted with an embarrassment of riches. It was evident that all men think all men foolish but themselves" (CCA/PU Box 1, Folder 4).

In addition to amusing anecdotes and acerbic comments about others, Abbott's diaries provide useful genealogical information about his extended family and circle of friends. For example, on his 25th wedding anniversary, Charles and his wife Julia hosted a party to celebrate. Abbott recorded the attendees and their relationship to the couple:

> February 15, 1892: Julie tonight criticized my list of people present (at anniversary party on Feb. 13). It is easy to determine by looking in family record. Man and wife are placed together in some cases, parent and child in others, which is which, the reader can guess, or hunt up as an amusement. *This is written for the benefit of people in 1992*:

> Second thought. Explanation of list:
> 1. Chas H. Olden of Princeton, NJ, my wife's brother
> 2. Almira Gulick Olden, his wife
> 3. Wm G. Olden, son of above
> 4. Lucy West Olden, wife of William
> 5. Chas S Olden, son of Chas H.
> 6. Walter Olden, son of Chas H.
> 7. Cordelia Bruyere, daughter of James Stebbins and first cousin of my wife
> 8. Helen Garretson Boggs, widow of Robt M. Boggs, the brother of my wife's mother
> 9. Jane Manwaring McCaslin: daughter of Julia L. Manwaring, the sister of my wife's mother
> 10. Louisa Manwaring, sister of Jane M. McCaslin
> 11. George Abbott, son of Geo Abbott brother of my father
> 12. Edith Abbott daughter of Jas Gardner Abbott brother of my father
> 13. Sarah DeCou, widow, sister of Edith Abbott
> 14. Gardner DeCou, children of Sarah DeCou
> 15. Helen DeCou, children of Sarah DeCou
> 16. Sheldon M. Custer, of Philadelphia, husband of Helen
> 17. Helen Custer, daughter of Ephraim O. Abbott, brother of my father
> 18. Helen Moyer, daughter of Lucy Moyer a sister of my mother
> 19. Lizzie Hegeman, sister of Helen Moyer and wife of Jno Hegeman of

Passaic New Jersey

20. Percy Moyer, brother of Helen Moyer
21. Margaret Robertson Moyer, wife of Percy
22. William Hewitt, son of Anna C. Hewett, sister of my mother
23. Louisa Hewitt, sister of William
24. Robert Beatty, husband of Mary
25. Mary G. Beatty, a sister of my wife
26. Catherine L. Peters, a sister of my wife
27. Jennie Fine, now engaged to my nephew Francis L. Abbott (they were married June 15th following)
28. Mary G. Abbott, my sister
29. Francis Abbott, my brother
30. Jos. De B. Abbott, son of Francis
31. Francis L. Abbott, son of Francis
32. Charles L. Abbott, son of Francis
33. Talcott Backus, son of only able teacher in school I ever had. The brother in law of Percy Moyer

(CCA/PU Box 3, Folder 2, emphasis original)

Interestingly, it appears that beginning in 1876, Abbott decided to transcribe all his notes and daily entries from previous months into a more formal volume. He crossed out items in the former and rewrote these into longer prose in the latter. An examination of these records revealed that he elaborated quite extensively on the earlier journals. For example, an original diary entry was recorded: "January 25, 1875: In, writing all day. Johnnie up town. Sophie came in other girl's place" (CCA/PU Box 2, Folder 1), but the revised diary reads:

January 25, 1875: Another indoor day, but my manuscript piles up and I grow more and more interested in it. I had no inclination to go out of doors and take a real outing, as I ought to have done. The world seems nothing but a big fish, to me, and I know, to my sorrow, it is full of "suckers." Some of them sucked all my substance out of me, but here is a remedy against crying over spilt milk: have something to do. Johnnie did the errands and there was no startling correspondence to set tongues wagging (CCA/PU Box 2, Folder 2).

In another, the original reads "February 19, 1875: Warmer. Snow-squall. Walked up to Trenton, after hanging 'the bridge.' Home by dinner time. Read in afternoon. Cards and Mss in the evening" (CCA/PU Box 2, Folder 1), but the revised is:

> February 19, 1875: A warm day for time of year and to be contradictory, there was a snow-squall. I ignored the weather and walked to town, after hanging up my picture on the sitting room wall. It shows too plainly it will only be a passing whim and come down again. It is a farce. I read a good deal during the afternoon and so the time passed pleasantly. After supper, Uncle John wanted again to play cards. It is rather tiresome, but better than disappointing him. Later, I took to writing and got something done, but any ambition in the direction of authorship is unwise. I came here to be a farmer and find it distasteful (CCA/PU Box 2, Folder 2).

Later diaries may also have been altered, but the original text is no longer present for comparison. Abbott may have disposed of draft versions of the diaries, or they may have burned in the fire of 1914. Many of his logs retained obscure references to earlier dates that did not mention relevant events, and others were intentionally obfuscated by Abbott himself, as he hinted on New Year's Eve, 1906: "Much about minor matters might be said but there is no use in crying over spilt milk. If anyone sees these pages, one hundred years from now, let him or her guess to what I refer by scanty intimations thereof in the pages that precede this" (CCA/PU Box 4, Folder 4).

In addition to the diaries, archives at the Peabody Museum, Princeton University, the Smithsonian Institution, the American Museum of Natural History, the Bucks County Historical Society, the Penn Museum, the Philadelphia Academy of Natural Sciences, and other institutions in the United States and Europe contain copies of letters Abbott wrote to friends and colleagues. Abbott's correspondence included sketches, elaborate signatures, and other amusing glimpses into his personality. For example, in many of his letters, Abbott signed his name with ornate curlicues, loops, and flourishes (Fig. 11.4). Other correspondence and diary doodles contained pointing fingers to highlight text (Fig. 11.5). Still others, particularly to Putnam, were illustrated with artifacts referenced in the letters (Fig. 11.6). For Abbott, writing was both informative and creative.

CHARLES CONRAD ABBOTT'S LEGACY

Despite his inability to prove the existence of an American Paleolithic, Charles Conrad Abbott made valuable contributions to the archaeological record of the Delaware Valley, and is often heralded as the father of New

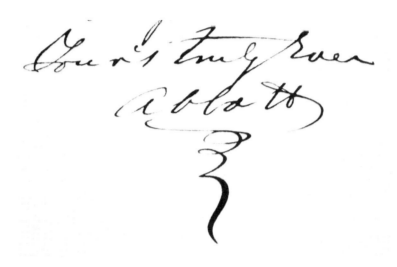

11.4 An example of Charles Conrad Abbott's signature with elaborate flourish (Letter to Frederic Ward Putnam from Charles Conrad Abbott, on file Peabody Museum, Harvard University, UAV 677.38).

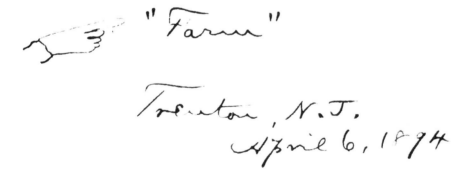

11.5 An example of Charles Conrad Abbott's drawing of a pointing finger to highlight his return address as "The Farm" (Letter to Frederic Ward Putnam from Charles Conrad Abbott, on file Peabody Museum, Harvard University, UAV 677.38, Box 13, Record 724).

I have just recieved from W. Wallace Tooker of Sag Harbor, Long Island from a shell-heap, a very remarkable (I think,) bone fish-hook; also a copper tube &c. &c. I want very much to have a cut of the fish-hook. If possible, let me know without a moment's delay.

Abbott

What are you so mad about? Why won't you tell me if the piece of metal I sent is copper, brass or silver. You're treating me very badly!!!

11.6 An artifact drawing embedded in a letter from Charles Conrad Abbott to Frederic Ward Putnam (Peabody Museum, Harvard University, UAV 677.38, Accession 2582, October 28, 1880).

Jersey archaeology (Kraft 1993). His field methods were deplorable by modern standards, but in the 1870s, when he first started working for the Peabody Museum at Harvard University, they were more typical of the time and amateur scholarship was more widely accepted. Problems arose when Abbott was unable, or unwilling, to revise his techniques as the field of archaeology changed to a more professional, scientific method of recording and collecting.

In 1952, the Peabody Museum at Harvard University deaccessioned at least 200 of the artifacts in the Abbott Collection, primarily large, bulky items such as groundstone pestles, axes, and mortars in order to make room for other items in their storage facilities. This practice is not unusual, and the Peabody Museum carefully documented and photographed the artifacts slated for removal (Negative Nos. N27943, N27944, N27945). However, Abbott would have been devastated that his artifact collections not only languished in storage facilities, but also that they were deaccessioned to make room for other materials.

In some ways, it is unfortunate that Abbott's archaeological reputation was inseparable from his theories about the existence of a Paleolithic occupation of New Jersey and Pennsylvania and, more regrettably, from his contentious and acrimonious reactions to scientific disagreement. As a field assistant for the Peabody Museum, he collected over 25,000 prehistoric artifacts that form the centerpiece of the mid-Atlantic collections. At the Penn Museum, despite Abbott's poor performance and lamentable work habits, he served as the founding Curator of the American Section.

Though Abbott's research focus was centered on Native American prehistory, he was one of the first in New Jersey to investigate a historic archaeological site at Burlington Island on a site he interpreted as a Dutch fur trader's house (Dillian et al. 2013). Furthermore, Abbott was a published naturalist and penned hundreds of articles and books describing the flora and fauna of the Delaware Valley. Despite his stated goals of creating an accurate scientific record of the natural world, he often diverged into fanciful, effusive prose. Yet Abbott considered himself a scholar of nature, and deeply resented what he felt was a lack of recognition for his contributions to the field of natural history, as well as archaeology.

Abbott was polarizing, irascible, petulant, and brash, but he was also a prolific writer, colorful character, and innovative thinker. His theories about an American Paleolithic were wrong, but his error was not in proposing and

testing new hypotheses—all scientists do this, and many hypotheses are falsified in the process of testing—instead, Abbott's error rested in his lamentable scientific methods and his inability to accept alternative hypotheses as
new data came to the fore. Today, archaeologists remember Abbott largely
for these faults, but when placed within the temporal and scholarly context
of the late 19th century, his influences become clarified. Until his final days,
Abbott hoped to someday be vindicated as the discoverer of the American
Paleolithic. He persisted, late in life "of course, my doxy is the true one, but
any one will do if you really believe it, and do not forget that all may turn
out heterodoxy in the light of added knowledge." ("Old Fashioned Essays,"
CCA/PU, Box 1, Folder 4; November 5, 1917).

Acknowledgments

We first gained our introductions to Charles Conrad Abbott many years ago. For Carolyn Dillian, that occurred while employed as a Collections Management Assistant at the Penn Museum as a student in the early 1990s; and for Charles Bello, that first introduction transpired while working as a field archaeologist in Pennsylvania and New Jersey in the early 1980s. But in both of our careers, we have found ourselves repeatedly encountering Abbott's legacy in museum research, fieldwork, and archival records. When we became colleagues and collaborators in 2001, we started researching and publishing together on the archaeology of the mid-Atlantic region and began seeing Abbott's influence everywhere—in museum collections, in Archaeological Society of New Jersey events and publications, in the maps and records of Skinner and Schrabisch, and in the sites that we excavated throughout the region. We decided to assemble a larger volume on Abbott that highlighted more than just Abbott's efforts to discover an American Paleolithic—a topic that has been published and meticulously researched by David Meltzer, in particular. Instead, our book, though it visits the Paleolithic War, tells the wider story of Abbott's life and career from his earliest days collecting on Three Beeches, to the final years of his life in Bristol, Pennsylvania, and his legacy as an archaeologist. Abbott was flawed, and his work on the American Paleolithic was decidedly so, but his career spanned important milestones in the evolution of archaeology as a discipline. We hope that this volume will provide a candid glimpse into the life of "New Jersey's Pioneer Archaeologist" (Kraft 1993).

This project took a long time to come to fruition and there were a number of individuals who helped us along the way. Page Selinsky, Editor at Penn

Museum Publications, masterfully transformed this manuscript into a book we're very proud of. A significant thank you is due to Rich Veit for being an important partner in portions of this research, particularly the Burlington Island museum, field, and archival work. Some of the Burlington Island data has been previously published as coauthored work by Dillian, Bello, Veit, and McHugh (2013); Veit and Bello (1999); and relies heavily on Veit (2000, 2002). Thank you to Sean McHugh for field assistance, drafting, and maps research. We also particularly appreciate the assistance shown us by William Wierzbowski, Keeper of Collections, and Lucy Fowler Williams, Associate Curator and Sabloff Keeper of Collections of the American Section Collections at the Penn Museum; Alex Pezzati, Douglas Haller, and Charles Kline, Penn Museum Archives. We spent several weeks in the collections at the Peabody Museum of Archaeology and Ethnology at Harvard University, and owe a great deal of thanks to Genevieve Fisher, Senior Registrar; Susan Haskell, Curatorial Associate; Gloria Polizzotti Greis; Brian Sullivan; Susan Bruce; David Schafer; and Scott Templin. Thank you to Greg Lattanzi for providing access to collections at the New Jersey State Museum. Our interpretations benefited from discussions with Meta Janowitz, Diane Dallal, Paul Huey, Marshall Becker, Bill Schindler, R. Michael Stewart, Jack Cresson, Richard Plank, Kristian Eshelman, Fran Wilcox, Catharine Bull, Patricia Whitacre, Kim Rosamilia, Fred Prescott, and Paul Schopp. We would also like to thank the Treasure Island Boy Scout Reservation, Cradle of Liberty Council for site access; the Bucks County Historical Society; the Mercer Museum Spruance Library; and the entire staff of the Manuscripts and Special Collections Division at the Princeton University Library. This research was supported by grants from the Archaeological Society of New Jersey; the New Jersey Historical Commission Minigrant Program (Grant #07HIS-T316AMI); Princeton University Committee on Research in the Humanities and Social Sciences (Grant #209-2310); the Friends of the Princeton University Library, Library Research Grant; a Coastal Carolina University Professional Enhancement Grant; and a Coastal Carolina University scholarly reassignment for spring semester 2016. We would also like to thank our spouses, Jared and Sebbie, for putting up with many research trips, piles of papers, and hours on the computer. Tars, Uma, Vesper, Wendy, Xenia, and Tansy offered helpful supervision. We thank our anonymous peer-reviewers for helpful comments that greatly improved the volume. Any errors remain ours and ours alone.

References

Abbott, Charles Conrad. 1861a. Notes on the Habits of *Aphredoderus sayanus*. *Proceedings of the Academy of Natural Sciences of Philadelphia* 13:95–96.

———. 1861b. On *Squalus Americanus*, Mitchell, Referring it to the Genus *Odontaspis*, Agassiz. *Proceedings of the Academy of Natural Sciences of Philadelphia* 13:399–401.

———. 1868. Appendix E: Catalogue of the Vertebrate Animals of New Jersey. In *Geology of New Jersey*, by George H. Cook, pp. 751–830. Board of Managers.

———. 1870a. Notes on Fresh-Water Fishes of New Jersey. *The American Naturalist* 4(2):99–117.

———. 1870b. Notes on Certain Inland Birds of New Jersey. *The American Naturalist* 4(9):536–550.

———. 1871. Further Notes on New Jersey Fishes. *The American Naturalist* 4(12):717–720.

———. 1872. The Stone Age in New Jersey. *The American Naturalist* 6(3):144–160.

———. 1873. Relics of a Homestead of the Stone Age. *The American Naturalist* 7(5):271–278.

———. 1874. Notes on the Cyprinoids of Central New Jersey. *The American Naturalist* 8(6):326–338.

———. 1875a. On the Occurrence in New Jersey of Supposed Flint Scalping-Knives. *Nature* 12:368–369.

———. 1875b. A Short Study of Birds' Nests. *Popular Science Monthly* 6:481–486.

———. 1875c. The Migration of Inland Birds. *Popular Science Monthly* 7:183–194.

———. 1876a. Indications of the Antiquity of the Indians of North America, Derived from a Study of their Relics. *The American Naturalist* 10(2):65–72.

———. 1876b. The Occurrence and Manufacture of Flint Skin-Scrapers from New Jersey, U.S.A. *Nature* 13:270–271.

———. 1877a. *Stone Age in New Jersey*. Government Printing Office, Washington, D.C.

———. 1877b. Report on the Discovery of Supposed Palaeolithic Implements from the Glacial Drift, in the Valley of the Delaware River near Trenton, New Jersey. In *Tenth Annual Report of the Trustees of the Peabody Museum of American Archaeology and Ethnology*, Vol. 2, No. 1, pp. 30–43.

———. 1878. Second Report on the Paleolithic Implements from the Glacial Drift in the Valley of the Delaware River near Trenton, New Jersey. In *Eleventh Annual Report of the Trustees of the Peabody Museum of American Archaeology and Ethnology*, Vol. 2, No. 2, pp. 225–257.

———. 1880. Flint Chips. In *Twelfth Annual Report of the Trustees of the Peabody Museum of American Archaeology and Ethnology*, Vol. 2, No. 3. pp. 506–520.

———. 1881. *Primitive Industry: or Illustrations of the Handiwork, in Stone, Bone and Clay, of the Native Races of the Northern Atlantic Seaboard of America*. George A. Bates, Salem, Massachusetts.

———. 1883a. Traces of a Pre-Indian People. *Popular Science Monthly* 22:315–322.

———. 1883b. An Historical Sketch of the Discoveries of Palaeolithic Implements in the Valley of the Delaware River. *Proceedings of the Boston Society of Natural History* 21:124–132.

———. 1883c. Paleolithic Man in Ohio. *Science* 1(13):359.

———. 1883d. Evidences of Glacial Man. *Science* 2(34):437–438.

———. 1884a. *A Naturalist's Rambles About Home*. D. Appleton and Company, New York.

———. 1884b. Are the Chimneys of Burrowing Crayfish Designed? *The American Naturalist* 18(11):1157–1158.

———. 1884c. Hibernating Mammals. *Science* 3(70):673.

———. 1885a. Use of Copper by the Delaware Indians. *The American Naturalist* 19(8):774–777.

———. 1885b. How the Burrowing Crayfish Works. *Inland Monthly* 1:31–32.

———. 1886. *Upland and Meadow: A Poaetquissings Chronicle*. Harper and Brothers, New York.

———. 1887. *Waste-Land Wanderings*. Harper and Brothers, New York.

———. 1888a. Evidences of the Antiquity of Man in Eastern North America. *Science* 12(291):103–105.

———. 1888b. Evidences of the Antiquity of Man in Eastern North America. *Proceedings of the American Association for the Advancement of Science* 37:293–315.

———. 1889. *Days Out of Doors*. D. Appleton and Company, New York.

———. 1890a. Report of the Curator of the Museum of American Archaeology. Vol. 1,

No. 1. University of Pennsylvania Press, Philadelphia.

———. 1890b. *Outings at Odd Times*. D. Appleton and Company, New York.

———. 1890c. The Descendants of Palaeolithic Man in America. *Popular Science Monthly* 36:145–153.

———. 1892a. Palaeolithic Man in North America. *Science* 20(510):270–271.

———. 1892b. Recent Archaeological Explorations in the Valley of the Delaware. *University of Pennsylvania Publications, Series in Philology, Literature, and Archaeology* 2(1):1–30.

———. 1892c. Paleolithic Man: A Last Word. *Science* 20(515):344–345.

———. 1892d. *Recent Rambles or In Touch with Nature*. J. B. Lippincott Co., Philadelphia, Pennsylvania.

———. 1893. The So-Called "Cache Implements." *Science* 21(526):122–123.

———. 1894a. *The Birds About Us*. J. B. Lippincott Co., Philadelphia, Pennsylvania.

———. 1894b. *Travels in a Tree-top*. J. B. Lippincott Co., Philadelphia, Pennsylvania.

———. 1895a. Timothy Abbott Conrad. *Popular Science Monthly* 47:257–263.

———. 1895b. Thoreau. *Lippincott's Monthly Magazine* 55:852–855.

———. 1895c. *A Colonial Wooing*. J. B. Lippincott Co., Philadelphia, Pennsylvania.

———. 1895d. In a Village Garden. *The Monthly Illustrator* 5(16):187–192.

———. 1895e. The Beauty of Lilies. *The Monthly Illustrator* 3(10):209–213.

———. 1896a. *Notes of the Night, and Other Outdoor Sketches*. The Century Co., New York.

———. 1896b. *Bird-Land Echoes*. J. B. Lippincott Co., Philadelphia, Pennsylvania.

———. 1897. *When the Century Was New, A Novel*. J. B. Lippincott Co., Philadelphia, Pennsylvania.

———. 1898a. *Clear Skies and Cloudy*. J. B. Lippincott, Co., Philadelphia, Pennsylvania.

———. 1898b. *The Freedom of the Fields*. J. B. Lippincott Co., Philadelphia, Pennsylvania.

———. 1898c. *The Hermit of Nottingham*. J. B. Lippincott Co., Philadelphia, Pennsylvania.

———. 1899. *Recent Rambles or In Touch with Nature*. J. B. Lippincott Co., Philadelphia, Pennsylvania.

———. 1900. *In Nature's Realm*. Albert Brandt, Trenton, New Jersey.

———. 1906a. *The Rambles of an Idler*. George W. Jacobs and Company, Philadelphia, Pennsylvania.

———. 1906b. The Swedes and Dutch on the Delaware. *Sunday Advertiser*. Trenton, New Jersey. March 18, 1906.

———. 1907. *Archaeologia Nova Caesarea, Part I*. MacCrellish and Quigley, Trenton,

New Jersey.

. 1908. *Archaeologia Nova Caesarea, Part II*. MacCrellish and Quigley, Trenton, New Jersey.

. 1909. *Archaeologia Nova Caesarea, Part III*. MacCrellish and Quigley, Trenton, New Jersey.

. 1912. *Ten Years' Diggings in Lenâpè Land 1901–1911*. MacCrellish and Quigley, Trenton, New Jersey.

Adovasio, James M., Joel D. Gunn, John Donahue, and Robert Stuckenrath. 1978. Meadowcroft Rockshelter, 1977: An Overview. *American Antiquity* 43(4):632–651.

Adovasio, James M., John Donahue, and Robert Stuckenrath. 1990. The Meadowcroft Rockshelter Radiocarbon Chronology 1975–1990. *American Antiquity* 55(2):348–354.

Adovasio, James M., David Pedler, John Donahue, and Robert Stuckenrath. 1999. No Vestige of a Beginning nor Prospect for an End: Two Decades of Debate on Meadowcroft Rockshelter. In *Ice Age People of North America: Environments, Origins, and Adaptations*, edited by Robson Bonnichsen and Karen L. Turnmire, pp. 416–431. Center for the Study of the First Americans, Oregon State University, Corvallis.

Agassiz, Louis. 1840. *Études sur les Glaciers*. Jent et Gassmann, Neuchatel, Switzerland.

Aiello, Lucy. 1968. A Fire in the Meadow. *CIBA Journal* 48:30–36.

Albright, Shirley S., and Lorraine E. Williams. 1980. Differentiation of Fine-grained Sedimentary and Metamorphic Rocks Utilized by Prehistoric Populations of the Mid-Atlantic Region. Paper presented at the Society of American Archaeology Annual Meeting, Philadelphia, Pennsylvania.

The American Naturalist. 1867. Introductory. *The American Naturalist* 1(1):1–4.

Anderson, David G. 1990. Paleoindian Colonization of Eastern North America: A View from the Southeastern United States. In *Early Paleoindian Economies of Eastern North America*, edited by Kenneth Tankersley and Barry Isaac, pp. 163–216. Research in Economic Anthropology Supplement 5.

. 1996. Models of Paleoindian and Early Archaic Settlement in the Lower Southeast. In *The Paleoindian and Early Archaic Southeast*, edited by David G. Anderson and Kenneth E. Sassaman, pp. 29–57. University of Alabama Press, Tuscaloosa.

. 2005. Pleistocene Human Occupation of the Southeastern United States: Research Directions for the Early 21st Century. In *Paleoamerican Origins: Beyond Clovis*, edited by Robson Bonnichsen, Bradley T. Lepper, Dennis Stanford, and Michael R. Waters, pp. 29–42. Texas A&M University Press, College Station.

Andrefsky, William. 1998. *Lithics: Macroscopic Approaches to Analysis*. Cambridge University Press, Cambridge.

Anleu, Sharyn L. Roach. 1992. The Professionalisation of Social Work? A Case Study of Three Organisational Settings. *Sociology* 26(1):23–43.

Anonymous. 1886. The Abbott Collection at the Peabody Museum. *Science* 7(152):4–5.

———. 1890. Review of "Outings at Odd Times." *Science* 16(412):361.

———. 1894a. Review of "Travels in a Tree-top." *Science* 23(577):101.

———. 1894b. Review of "Travels in a Tree-top." *The Saturday Review of Politics, Literature, Science, and Art* 78:329.

———. 1897. Review of "When the Century Was New." *Current Literature* 22:130.

———. 1901. Review of "In Nature's Realm." *The Dial* 30(355):218.

———. 1919. Anthropological Notes. *American Anthropologist* 21(3):343–346.

———. 2009. Guyot Hall at One Hundred. *The Smilodon* 50(1):1–2.

———. n.d. Review of "A Colonial Wooing." *Boston Transcript*.

Babbitt, Frances. 1890. Points Concerning the Little Falls Quartzes. *Proceedings of the American Association for the Advancement of Science* 1889:333–339.

Baker, Lee D. 2010. *Anthropology and the Racial Politics of Culture*. Duke University Press, Durham, North Carolina.

Barber, Lynn. 1980. *The Heyday of Natural History, 1820–1870*. Jonathan Cape, London.

Beauchamp, William M. 1903. *Metallic Ornaments of the New York Indians*. New York State Museum Bulletin 73, Albany, New York.

Bello, Charles A., and Peter Pagoulatos. 1995. Recent Research into Paleo-Indian Lithic Selection on the New Jersey Coastal Plain. *Bulletin of the Archaeological Society of New Jersey* 50:80–83.

Bello, Charles A., and R. Michael Stewart. 1996. A Middle Woodland Effigy from Cheesequake, Middlesex County, New Jersey. *Bulletin of the Archaeological Society of New Jersey* 51:13–16.

Bisbee, Henry. 1971. *Sign Posts: Place Names in History of Burlington County, New Jersey*. Alexia Press, Inc., Willingboro, New Jersey.

———. 1972. *Burlington Island: The Best and Largest on the South River, 1624–1972*. Heidelburg Press, Inc., Burlington, New Jersey.

Boissevain, Ethel. 1956. The First Twenty-Five Years of the Archaeological Society of New Jersey. *Bulletin of the Archaeological Society of New Jersey* 12:1–7.

Bonanno, James P. 2009. Boucher de Perthes, Jacques (1788–1868). In *Encyclopedia of Time: Science, Philosophy, Theology and Culture*, edited by H. James Birx, pp. 108. SAGE, Thousand Oaks, California.

Boucher de Perthes, Jacques. 1847. *Antiquités Celtiques et Antédiluviennes. Mémoire sur l'Industrie Primitive et les Arts à Leur Origine* (Vol. 1). Treuttel and Wurtz, Paris.

———. 1857. *Antiquités Celtiques et Antédiluviennes. Mémoire sur l'Industrie Primitive et les Arts à Leur Origine* (Vol. 2). Treuttel and Wurtz, Paris.

Bourque, Bruce J. 2002. Maine Shell Midden Archaeology (1860–1910) and the Influence of Adolphe von Morlot. In *New Perspectives on the Origins of Americanist Archaeology*, edited by David L. Browman and Stephen Williams, pp. 148–163. University of Alabama Press, Tuscaloosa.

Bowler, Peter J. 1988. *The Non-Darwinian Revolution: Reinterpreting a Historical Myth*. Johns Hopkins University Press, Baltimore, Maryland.

Bradley, Bruce and Dennis Stanford. 2004. The North Atlantic Ice-Edge Corridor: A Possible Palaeolithic Route to the New World. *World Archaeology* 36(4):459–478.

Brinton, Daniel G. 1885. *The Lenâpé and Their Legends: With the Complete Text and Symbols of the Walam Olum*. Brinton's Library of Aboriginal American Literature, Number V., D. G. Brinton, Philadelphia, Pennsylvania.

———. 1892a. Review: Man and the Glacial Period. *Science* 20(508):249.

———. 1892b. On Quarry Rejects. *Science* 20(509):260–261.

Browman, David L. 2002a. The Peabody Museum, Frederic W. Putnam, and the Rise of U.S. Anthropology, 1866–1903. *American Anthropologist* 104(2):508–519.

———. 2002b. Frederic Ward Putnam: Contributions to the Development of Archaeological Institutions and Encouragement of Women Practitioners. In *New Perspectives on the Origins of Americanist Archaeology*, edited by David L. Browman and Stephen Williams, pp. 209–241. University of Alabama Press, Tuscaloosa.

Browman, David L., and Stephen Williams. 2013. *Anthropology at Harvard: A Biographical History, 1790–1940*. Peabody Museum Press, Cambridge, Massachusetts.

Bruyninckx, Joeri. 2018. *Listening in the Field: Recording and the Science of Birdsong*. MIT Press, Cambridge, Massachusetts.

Buckland, William. 1823. *Reliquiae Diluvianae; or Observations on the Organic Remains Contained in Caves, Fissures, and Diluvial Gravel, and on Other Geological Phenomena, Attending the Action of an Universal Deluge*. John Murray, London.

Buckland, William. 1836. *Geology and Mineralogy Considered with Reference to Natural Theology*. W. Pickering, London.

Burroughs, John. 1903. Real and Sham Natural History. *The Atlantic Monthly* 91(545):298–309.

Caldwell, Joseph R. 1958. *Trend and Tradition in the Prehistory of the Eastern United States*. Illinois State Museum, Springfield, Illinois.

Callahan, Errett. 1979. The Basics of Biface Knapping in the Eastern Fluted Point Tradition: A Manual for Flintknappers and Lithic Analysts. *Archaeology of Eastern North America* 7:1–180.

Carr, Lucien. 1876. Additions to the Museum 1875. In *Ninth Annual Report of the*

Trustees of the Peabody Museum of American Archaeology and Ethnology, pp. 16–20. Harvard University, Cambridge, Massachusetts.

———. 1877. Additions to the Museum 1876. In *Tenth Annual Report of the Trustees of the Peabody Museum of American Archaeology and Ethnology,* pp. 13–26. Harvard University, Cambridge, Massachusetts.

———. 1880. Additions to the Museum 1879. In *Thirteenth Annual Report of the Trustees of the Peabody Museum of American Archaeology and Ethnology,* pp. 732–744. Harvard University, Cambridge, Massachusetts.

———. 1881. Additions to the Museum 1880. In *Fourteenth Annual Report of the Trustees of the Peabody Museum of American Archaeology and Ethnology,* Vol. 3, No. 1, pp. 29–38. Harvard University, Cambridge, Massachusetts.

———. 1883. Paleolithic Implements at Trenton, N.J. *Proceedings of the Boston Society of Natural History* 21:145–147.

Cavallo, John A. 1982. Fish, Fires, and Foresight: A Model of Middle Woodland Economic Adaptations in the Abbott Farm Historic District. Paper presented at the Eastern States Archaeological Federation Annual Meeting, Norfolk, Virginia.

———. 1984. Fish, Fires, and Foresight: Middle Woodland Adaptations in the Abbott Farm National Landmark. *North American Archaeologist* 5(2):111–137.

———. 1987. Area B Site (28-Me-1B) Data Recovery. Trenton Complex Archaeology Report 8. The Cultural Resource Group, Louis Berger and Associates, Inc., East Orange, New Jersey. Prepared for the Federal Highway Administration and New Jersey Department of Transportation, Bureau of Environmental Analysis, Trenton, New Jersey.

Chamberlain, Alexander F. 1897. Anthropology at the Toronto Meeting of the British Association. *Science* 6(146):575–583.

Chamberlin, Thomas C. 1892. Communications: Geology and Archaeology Mistaught. *The Dial* 13:303–306.

———. 1893. Communications: Professor Wright and the Geological Survey. *The Dial* 14:7–9.

Chapman, Jefferson. 1973. The Icehouse Bottom Site 40MR23. Department of Anthropology, University of Tennessee, Knoxville.

Chapman, William Ryan. 1988. Arranging Ethnology, A. H. L. F. Pitt Rivers and the Typological Tradition. In *Objects and Others: Essays on Museums and Material Culture,* edited by George W. Stocking, pp. 15–48. History of Anthropology Volume 3. University of Wisconsin Press, Madison.

Chernow, Ron. 1991 *The House of Morgan: An American Banking Dynasty and the Rise of Modern Finance.* Grove Press, New York.

Conant, Francis P. 1974. Dorothy Cross Jensen, 1906–1972. *American Anthropologist* 76(1):80–82.

Conrad, Timothy A. 1839. Notes on American Geology. *American Journal of Science* 35:237–251.

Conybeare, William D. 1830. On Mr. Lyell's 'Principles of Geology.' *Philosophical Magazine and Annals* 8:215–219.

Cope, Edward Drinker. 1893. Review: Man in the Glacial Period. *The American Naturalist* 27(318):550–553.

Cotter, John L. 1993. Historical Archaeology Before 1967. *Historical Archaeology* 27(1):4–9.

———. 1994. Beginnings. In *Pioneers in Historical Archaeology: Breaking New Ground*, edited by Stanley South, pp. 15–27, Plenum Press, New York.

Cresson, Hilborne T. 1890a. Remarks on a Chipped Implement, Found in Modified Drift, on the East Fork of the White River, Jackson County, Indiana. *Proceedings of the Boston Society of Natural History* 24:150–152.

———. 1890b. Early Man in the Delaware Valley. *Proceedings of the Boston Society of Natural History* 24:141–150.

Cresson, John H. 1982. Middle Woodland Fox Creek Lithic Technology. Unpublished manuscript in possession of the author.

Cross, Dorothy. 1952. The Indians of New Jersey. *New Jersey Historical Society Proceedings* 70(1):1–16.

———. 1956. *Archaeology of New Jersey, Vol. 2: The Abbott Farm*. The Archaeological Society of New Jersey and the New Jersey State Museum, Trenton, New Jersey.

———. 1965. *New Jersey's Indians*. New Jersey State Museum, Report 1. Trenton, New Jersey.

Culin, Stewart. 1895. Archaeological Objects Exhibited by the Department of Archaeology and Paleontology, University of Pennsylvania. In *Report of the United States Commission to the Columbian Historical Exposition at Madrid 1892–1893*, Volume 31, No. 100, Valley of the Delaware (Case III), pp. 194–202. The Executive Documents of the House of Representatives for the Third Session of the Fifty-third Congress 1894–1895, U.S. Government Printing Office, Washington, D.C.

Cuvier, Georges. 1813. *Essay on the Theory of the Earth*. William Blackwood, Edinburgh, Scotland.

Daily State Gazette. 1914. Home and Valuable Works of Dr. Abbott Destroyed by Blaze. *Daily State Gazette*, Trenton, New Jersey. November 14, 1914.

Dall, William Healey. 1877. Tribes of the Extreme Northwest. *Bureau of American Ethnology, Contributions to North American Ethnology*, Vol. 1, pp. 1–121. Washington, D.C.

———. 1893. Introduction. In *Republication of Conrad's Fossils of the Medial Tertiary of the United States*, edited by William Healey Dall, pp. v–xviii. Wagner Free Institute of Science, Philadelphia, Pennsylvania.

Dallal, Diane. 1995. "The People May Be Illiterate But they Are Not Blind," A Study of the Iconography of 17th Century Dutch Clay Tobacco Pipes Recovered from New York City's Archaeological Sites. Unpublished M.A. thesis, Department of Anthropology, New York University.

Dana, J. D. 1863. *Manual of Geology*. Theodore Bliss, Philadelphia, Pennsylvania.

Daniel, Glyn Edmund. 1981. *A Short History of Archaeology*. Thames and Hudson, London.

Daniels, George H. 1967. The Process of Professionalization in American Science: The Emergent Period, 1820–1860. *Isis* 58(2):150–166.

Danien, Elin C. and Eleanor M. King. 2003. Unsung Visionary: Sara Yorke Stevenson and the Development of Archaeology in Philadelphia. In *Philadelphia and the Development of Americanist Archaeology*, edited by Don D. Fowler and David R. Wilcox, pp. 36–47. University of Alabama Press, Tuscaloosa.

Dankers, Jaspar and Peter Sluyter. 1867. *Journal of a Voyage to New York and a Tour of Several of the American Colonies in 1679–80*. Translated by Henry C. Murphy. Memoirs of the Long Island Historical Society, Vol. 1. Brooklyn, New York.

Deetz, James. 1996. *In Small Things Forgotten: An Archaeology of Early American Life*. Doubleday, New York.

Dexter, Ralph W. 1965. The "Salem Secession" of Agassiz Zoologists. *Essex Institute Historical Collections* 101(1):27–39.

Dillian, Carolyn D., and Charles A. Bello. 2010. Museum Archaeology and 19th Century Collections: An Argillite Biface Cache from Ridge's Island, Hunterdon County, New Jersey. *Archaeology of Eastern North America* 38:39–52.

———. 2012. The Bridge Valley Cache: Evidence of Argillite Biface Caching from Bucks County, Pennsylvania. *Archaeology of Eastern North America* 40:59–70.

Dillian, Carolyn, Charles Bello, and M. Steven Shackley. 2010. Long Distance Exchange of Obsidian in the mid-Atlantic United States. In *Trade and Exchange: Archaeological Studies from Prehistory and History*, edited by Carolyn Dillian and Carolyn White, pp. 17–35. Springer, New York.

Dillian, Carolyn, Charles Bello, Richard Veit, and Sean McHugh. 2013. Charles Conrad Abbott's Archaeological Investigations at a 17th Century Dutch Fur Trader's House on Burlington Island, New Jersey. In *Historical Archaeology of the Delaware Valley*, edited by Richard Veit and David Orr, pp. 49–73. University of Tennessee Press, Knoxville.

Dilliplane, Timothy L. 1980. European Trade Kettles, In *Burr's Hill, A 17th Century Wampanoag Burial Ground in Warren, Rhode Island*, edited by Susan G. Givson, pp. 79–84. Haffenreffer Museum of Anthropology, Brown University.

Drumthwacket Foundation. 2016. Drumthwacket Timeline. Drumthwacket Foundation. Electronic resource http://www.drumthwacket.org/timeline accessed December 31, 2016.

Dumont, John V., and Dougas McLearen. 1986. Bordentown Waterworks Site (28-Me-37) Data Recovery. Trenton Complex Archaeology Report 8. The Cultural Resource Group, Louis Berger and Associates, Inc., East Orange, New Jersey. Prepared for the Federal Highway Administration and New Jersey Department of Transportation, Bureau of Environmental Analysis, Trenton, New Jersey.

Ehrhardt, Kathleen L. 2005. *European Metals in Native Hands: Rethinking Technological Change, 1640–1683*. University of Alabama Press, Tuscaloosa.

Evans, John. 1872. *The Ancient Stone Implements, Weapons, and Ornaments, of Great Britain*. Longmans, Green, Reader and Dyer, London.

Fagan, Brian M. 2005. *A Brief History of Archaeology: Classical Times to the Twenty-First Century*. Pearson Prentice Hall, New Jersey.

Fane, Diana. 1992. The Language of Things: Stewart Culin as Collector. In *Objects of Myth and Memory: American Indian Art at the Brooklyn Museum*, edited by Diana Fane, Ira Jacknis, and Lise M. Breen, pp. 13–27. University of Washington Press, Seattle.

Faulkner, Alaric, and Gretchen Faulkner. 1987. *The French at Pentagoet, 1635–1674: An Archaeological Portrait of the Acadian Frontier*. Special Publications of the New Brunswick Museum and Occasional Publications in Maine Archaeology, Maine Historic Preservation Commission.

Figgins, Jesse D. 1935. New World Man. *Proceedings of the Colorado Museum of Natural History* 14:1–9.

Foss, Robert V. 1986. Carney Rose Site (28-Me-106) Data Recovery. Trenton Complex Archaeology Report 5. The Cultural Resource Group, Louis Berger and Associates, Inc., East Orange, New Jersey. Prepared for the Federal Highway Administration and New Jersey Department of Transportation, Bureau of Environmental Analysis, Trenton, New Jersey.

Funk, Robert E. 1976. *Recent Contributions to Hudson Valley Prehistory*. New York State Museum and Science Service Memoir 22, Albany.

Gill, Theodore. 1897. Edward Drinker Cope, Naturalist: A Chapter in the History of Science. *The American Naturalist* 31(370):831–863.

Goebel, Ted, Michael R. Waters, and Dennis H. O'Rourke. 2008. The Late Pleistocene

Dispersal of Modem Humans in the Americas. *Science* 319:1497–1502.

Goodyear, Albert C., III. 2005. Evidence for Pre-Clovis Sites in the Eastern United States. In *Paleoamerican Origins: Beyond Clovis*, edited by Robson Bonnichsen, Bradley T. Lepper, Dennis Stanford, and Michael R. Waters, pp. 103–112. Center for the Study of the First Americans, Texas A&M University.

Goodyear, Albert C., III, and Kenn Steffy. 2003. Evidence of a Clovis Occupation at the Topper Site, 38AL23, Allendale County, South Carolina. *Current Research in the Pleistocene* 20:23–25.

Gould, Stephen Jay. 1980. *The Panda's Thumb: More Reflections in Natural History*. W. W. Norton and Company, New York.

Gray, Asa. 1875. Report of the Curator. In Eighth Annual Report of the Trustees of the Peabody Museum of American Archaeology and Ethnology, Presented to the President and Fellows of Harvard College, April 1875, pp. 7–52. Salem Press, Salem, Massachusetts.

Gray, Matt. 2016. Plan to Dump Dredge Spoils on Burlington Island Worries Locals, Report Says. NJ.com. Electronic resource http://www.nj.com/burlington/index.ssf/2016/10/burlington_city_officials_concerned_over_dredging.html. Accessed December 31, 2016.

Grayson, Donald K. 1983. *The Establishment of Human Antiquity*. Academic Press, New York.

———. 1990. The Provision of Time Depth for Paleoanthropology. In *Establishment of a Geologic Framework for Paleoanthropology*, edited by Léo F. Laporte, pp. 1–14. Geological Society of America Special Paper 242. Boulder, Colorado.

Green, S. William. 1948. Lawrence Scientific School Marked Era in U.S. Intellectual History. *The Harvard Crimson*, February 21, 1948.

Gustafson, Carl E., Delbert W. Gilbow, and Richard D. Daugherty. 1979. The Manis Mastodon Site: Early Man on the Olympic Peninsula. *Canadian Journal of Archaeology* 3:157–164.

Hageman, John Frelinghuysen. 1879. *History of Princeton and its Institutions, Vol. 1*, 2nd Edition. J. B. Lippincott Co., Philadelphia, Pennsylvania.

Haller, Douglas M. 1999. Architectural Archaeology: A Centennial View of the Museum Buildings. *Expedition* 41(1):31–47.

Harper's Weekly. 1897. Morgan's Appointment 'Out of Ordinary.' This Busy World. May 1, 1897.

Haynes, Gary. 2002. *The Early Settlement of North America: The Clovis Era*. Cambridge University Press, Cambridge.

Haynes, Henry W. 1883. The Argillite Implements Found in the Gravels of the Delaware

River, at Trenton, N.J., Compared with the Palaeolithic Implements of Europe. *Proceedings of the Boston Society of Natural History* 21:132–137.

———. 1893. Palaeolithic Man in North America. *Science* 21(522):66–67.

Heizer, Robert F. 1962. *Man's Discovery of his Past: Literary Landmarks in Archaeology*. Prentice-Hall, New Jersey.

Herweijer, Celene, Richard Seager, and Edward R. Cook. 2006. North American Droughts of the mid to late Nineteenth Century: A History, Simulation and Implication for Mediaeval Drought. *The Holocene* 16(2):159–171.

Hinsley, Curtis. 1976. Amateurs and Professionals in Washington Anthropology, 1879 to 1903. In *American Anthropology: The Early Years*, edited by J. Murra, pp. 36–68. West Publishing, St. Paul, Minnesota.

———. 1981. *Savages and Scientists: The Smithsonian Institution and the Development of American Anthropology*. Smithsonian Institution Press, Washington, D.C.

———. 1988. From Shell-Heaps to Stelae: Early Anthropology at the Peabody Museum. In *Objects and Others: Essays on Museums and Material Culture*, edited by George W. Stocking, pp. 49–74. History of Anthropology Volume 3. University of Wisconsin Press, Madison.

———. 1992. The Museum Origins of Harvard Anthropology, 1866–1915. *Science at Harvard University: Historical Perspectives*, edited by Clark A. Elliott and Margaret W. Rossiter, pp. 121–145. Lehigh University Press, Bethlehem, Pennsylvania.

———. 2003. Drab Doves Take Flight: The Dilemmas of Early Americanist Archaeology in Philadelphia, 1889–1900. In *Philadelphia and the Development of Americanist Archaeology*, edited by Don D. Fowler and David R. Wilcox, pp. 1–20. University of Alabama Press, Tuscaloosa.

Hitchcock, Edward. 1857. Illustrations of Surface Geology. *Smithsonian Contributions to Knowledge* 9(3):1–155.

Holmes, William Henry. 1890. A Quarry Workshop of the Flaked Stone Implement Makers in the District of Columbia. *American Anthropologist* 3:1–26.

———. 1892a. Modern Quarry Refuse and the Paleolithic Theory. *Science* 20(512):295–297.

———. 1892b. Aboriginal Quarries of Flakeable Stone and Their Bearing upon the Question of Palaeolithic Man. *Proceedings of the American Association for the Advancement of Science* 41:279–280.

———. 1892c. On the So-Called Palaeolithic Implements of the Upper Mississippi. *Proceedings of the American Association for the Advancement of Science* 41:280–281.

———. 1893a. Gravel Man and Palaeolithic Culture: A Preliminary Word. *Science* 21(520):29–30.

———. 1893b. A Question of Evidence. *Science* 21(527):135–136.

———. 1893c. Are There Traces of Man in the Trenton Gravels? *Journal of Geology* 1:15–37.

———. 1893d. Traces of Glacial Man in Ohio. *Journal of Geology* 1:147–163.

Horan, Sharon. 1992. Charles Conrad Abbott: Associations with the Peabody and the Museum of Archaeology and Paleontology. *Bulletin of the Archaeological Society of New Jersey* 47.29 36.

Howard, Edgar B. 1935. Evidence of Early Man in North America. *University Museum Journal* 24:2–3.

———. 1939. The Clovis Finds Are Not Two Million Years Old. *American Antiquity* 5(1):43–51.

Hudson, Kenneth. 1981. *A Social History of Archaeology: The British Experience*. MacMillan, London.

Huey, Paul R. 1991. The Dutch at Fort Orange. In *Historical Archaeology in Global Perspective*, edited by Lisa Falk, pp. 21–68. Smithsonian Institution Press, Washington, D.C.

Hughes, Howard L. 1929. Schools and Libraries. In *A History of Trenton, 1679–1929*, edited by Edwin Robert Walker, Hamilton Schuyler, and John J. Cleary. Trenton Historical Society. http://www.trentonhistory.org/His/Schools.html, Accessed December 7, 2015.

Hunter, Richard, and Damon Tvaryanas. 2009. The Abbott Farm National Historic Landmark Interpretive Plan, Cultural Resource Technical Document, Hamilton Township, Mercer County, Bordentown Township and the City of Bordentown, Burlington County, New Jersey. Report prepared by Hunter Research, Inc. Prepared for the County of Mercer.

Hurry, Silas D., and Robert W. Keeler. 1991. A Descriptive Analysis of the White Clay Tobacco Pipes from the St. John's Site in St. Mary's City, Maryland. In *The Archaeology of the Clay Tobacco Pipe, XII. Chesapeake Bay*, edited by Peter Davey and Dennis J. Pogue, pp. 37–72. Liverpool Monographs in Archaeology and Oriental Studies No. 14, BAR International Series 566.

Hutton, James. 1788. *Theory of the Earth*. Royal Society of Edinburgh, Scotland.

Huxley, Thomas. 1863. *Evidences as to Man's Place in Nature*. Williams and Norgate, London.

Jacobs, Jaap. 2004. *New Netherland, a Dutch Colony in 17th-Century America*. Brill Academic Publishers, Bedfordshire, U.K.

Jackson, John P., Jr., and Nadine M. Weidman. 2004. *Race, Racism, and Science: Social Impact and Interaction*. ABC-CLIO, Santa Barbara, California.

James, Frank A. L. J. 2005. An 'Open Clash between Science and the Church'?: Wilber-force, Huxley and Hooker on Darwin at the British Association, Oxford, 1860. In *Science and Beliefs: From Natural Philosophy to Natural Science 1700–1900*, edited by David M. Knight and Matthew D. Eddy, pp. 171–193. Ashgate, Burlington, Vermont.

Jelks, Edward B. 1993. The Founding Meeting of the Society for Historical Archaeol-ogy, 6 January 1967, *Historical Archaeology* 27(1):10–11.

Karklins, Karlis. 1983. Dutch Trade Beads in North America. In *Proceedings of the 1982 Glass Trade Bead Conference, Research Records No. 16*, edited by Charles F. Hayes III, pp. 111–126. Rochester Museum and Science Center, Rochester, New York.

Kehoe, Alice B. 1999. Introduction. In *Assembling the Past: Studies in the Profession-alization of Archaeology*, edited by Alice B. Kehoe and Mary Beth Emmerichs, pp. 1–18, University of New Mexico Press, Albuquerque.

Kelly, Robert. 1988. The Three Sides of a Biface. *American Antiquity* 53(4):717–734.

Kidd, Kenneth E. and Martha A. Kidd. 1970. A Classification System for Glass Beads for the Use of Field Archaeologists. *Canadian Historic Sites: Occasional Papers in Archaeology and History* 1:45–89, Parks Canada, Ottawa. Reprinted in Proceed-ings of the 1982 Glass Bead Conference, edited by Charles F. Hayes, Appendix, pp. 219–257, Research Records 16, Rochester Museum and Science Division, Roches-ter, New York, 1983.

Kinsey, W. Fred, III. 1975. Faucett and Byram Sites: Chronology and Settlement in the Delaware Valley. *Pennsylvania Archaeologist* 45(1–2):1–103.

Kirakosian, Katie. 2015. Mapping the Social Worlds of Shell Midden Archaeology in Massachusetts. *Bulletin of the History of Archaeology* 25(3):6, 1–11.

Kohler, Robert E. 2006. *All Creatures: Naturalists, Collectors, and Biodiversity 1850–1950*. Princeton University Press, Princeton, New Jersey.

Kopytoff, Igor. 2006. A Short History of Anthropology at Penn. *Expedition* 48(1):29–36.

Kosty, Pam. 1999. In the Beginning. *Expedition* 41(1):48.

Kraft, Herbert C. 1975. *The Archaeology of the Tocks Island Area*. Archaeological Re-search Center, Seton Hall University Museum, South Orange, New Jersey.

———. 1986. *The Lenape: Archaeology, History, and Ethnography*. New Jersey Histori-cal Society, Newark.

———. 1993. Dr. Charles Conrad Abbott, New Jersey's Pioneer Archaeologist. *Bul-letin of the Archaeological Society of New Jersey*. 48:1–12.

———. 2001. The *Lenape-Delaware Indian Heritage: 10,000 BC to AD 2,000*. Lenape Books, Stanhope, New Jersey.

Kroeber, Alfred L. 1915. Frederic Ward Putnam. *American Anthropologist, New Series*. 17(4):712–718.

Kuhn, Thomas. 1962. *The Structure of Scientific Revolutions.* University of Chicago Press, Chicago.

Kummel, Henry. 1898. The Age of the Artifact-Bering Sand at Trenton. *Proceedings of the American Association for the Advancement of Science* 46:348–350.

Lamdin-Whymark, Hugo. 2009. Sir John Evans: Experimental Knapping and the Origins of Lithic Research. *Lithics* 30:45–52.

Lattanzi, Gregory D. 2007. The Provenance of Pre-Contact Copper Artifacts: Social Complexity and Trade in the Delaware Valley. *Archaeology of Eastern North America* 35:125–137.

Lee, Francis Bazley. 1907. *Genealogical and Personal Memorial of Mercer County, New Jersey.* Lewis Publishing Company, New York.

Leitch, Alexander. 1978. *A Princeton Companion.* Princeton University Press, Princeton, New Jersey.

Leopold, Aldo. 1949. *A Sand Country Almanac.* Oxford University Press, Oxford.

Lepper, Bradley T., and David J. Meltzer. 1991. Late Pleistocene Human Occupation of the Eastern United States. In *Clovis Origins and Adaptations,* edited by Robson Bonnichsen and Karen L. Turnmire, pp. 175–184. Center for the Study of the First Americans, Oregon State University, Coravallis.

Levine, Philippa. 1986. *The Amateur and the Professional: Antiquarians, Historians and Archaeologists in Victorian England, 1838–1886.* Cambridge University Press, Cambridge.

Lewis, Henry Carvill. 1880a. The Trenton Gravel and its Relation to the Antiquity of Man. *Proceedings of the Academy of Natural Sciences of Philadelphia.* 32:296–309.

————. 1880b. The Antiquity of Man in Eastern America, Geologically Considered. *Science* 1(17):192–193.

Lightfoot, John. 1642. *A Few and New Observations Upon the Booke of Genesis.* T. Badger, London.

Long, William J. 1906. *Brier-Patch Philosophy by "Peter Rabbit".* Ginn and Company, Boston, Massachusetts.

Louis Berger and Associates. 1998. Historic Sites. Trenton Complex Archaeology Report 12. Federal Highway Administration and New Jersey Department of Transportation, Bureau of Environmental Analysis, Trenton, New Jersey. On file, New Jersey Historic Preservation Office (NJDEP), Trenton, New Jersey.

Lubbock, John. 1865. *Pre-Historic Times, As Illustrated by Ancient Remains, and the Manners and Customs of Modern Savages.* D. Appleton and Company, New York.

Luce, Stephen B. 1895. History of the Participation of the United States in the Columbian Historical Exposition at Madrid. In *Report of the United States Commission to the Columbian Historical Exposition at Madrid 1892–1893*, Volume 31, No. 100, Columbian Historical Exposition, pp. 7–17. The Executive Documents of the House of Representatives for the Third Session of the Fifty-third Congress 1894–1895, U.S. Government Printing Office, Washington, D.C.

Lutts, Ralph H. 1990. *The Nature Fakers: Wildlife, Science, and Sentiment*. Fulcrum, Golden, Colorado.

Lyell, Charles. 1830–1833. *Principles of Geology, Being an Attempt to Explain the Former Changes of the Earth's Surface, by Reference to Causes Now in Operation*, vols. 1–3. John Murray, London.

———. 1863. *The Geological Evidences of the Antiquity of Man*. Murray, London.

Lyell, Katharine M. 1881. *Life, Letters, and Journals of Sir Charles Lyell, Bart*. Murray, London.

Madiera, Percy C., Jr. 1964. *Men in Search of Man: The First Seventy-Five Years of the University Museum of the University of Pennsylvania*. University of Pennsylvania Press, Philadelphia.

Martin, Jane. 2006. The Vital Power of a Great Affection. *Princeton Alumni Weekly*, March 8, 2006. https://www.princeton.edu/~paw/columns/under_the_ivy/uti030806.html. Accessed June 20, 2016.

McAvoy, Joseph M., and Lynn D. McAvoy. 1997. *Archaeological Investigations of Site 44SX202, Cactus Hill, Sussex County, Virginia*. Virginia Department of Historic Resources, Research Report Series, No. 8. Sandston, Virginia.

McCann, Catherine. 1972. Some Caches and So-called Caches from Eastern Pennsylvania. *Pennsylvania Archaeologist* 42(1–2):15–26.

McCullough, David. 1992. *Brave Companions*. Prentice Hall, New York.

McGee, William J. 1889a. An Obsidian Implement from Pleistocene Deposits in Nevada. *American Anthropologist* 2(4):301–312.

———. 1889b. The Geologic Antecedents of Man in the Potomac Valley. *American Anthropologist* 2(3):227–234.

———. 1892. Letters to the Editor: Man and the Glacial Period. *Science* 20(513):317.

———. 1893. Man and the Glacial Period. *American Anthropologist* 6(1):85–95.

McKusick, Marshall B. 1970. *The Davenport Conspiracy*. University of Iowa Press, Iowa City.

———. 1988. *The Davenport Conspiracy Revisited*. Iowa State University Press, Ames.

McLearen, Douglas, and Michael Fokken. 1986. White Horse West Site (28-Me-119) Data Recovery. Trenton Complex Archaeology Report 4. The Cultural Resource Group, Louis Berger and Associates, Inc., East Orange, New Jersey. Prepared for the Federal Highway Administration and New Jersey Department of Transportation,

Bureau of Environmental Analysis, Trenton, New Jersey.

Meltzer, David J. 1983. Prehistory, Power and Politics in the Beau of American Ethnology, 1879–1906. In *The Socio-Politics of Archaeology*, edited by Joan M. Gero, David M. Lacy, and Michael L. Blakey, pp. 67–77. University of Massachusetts, Amherst.

———. 1988. Late Pleistocene Human Adaptations in Eastern North America. *Journal of World Prehistory* 2:1–53.

———. 1991. On 'Paradigms' and 'Paradigm Bias' in Controversies over human Antiquity in America. In *The First Americans: Search and Research*, edited by Thomas D. Dillehay and David J. Meltzer, pp. 13–49. CRC Press, Boca Raton, Florida.

———. 1993. *Search for the First Americans*. St. Remy Press, Montreal; and Smithsonian Books, Washington, DC.

———. 2002. What Do You Do When No One's Been There Before? Thoughts on the Exploration and Colonization of New Lands. In *The First Americans: The Pleistocene Colonization of the New World*, edited by Nina G. Jablonski, pp. 27–58. California Academy of Sciences, San Francisco.

———. 2003. In the Heat of Controversy: C. C. Abbott, the American Paleolithic, and the University Museum 1889–1893. In *Philadelphia and the Development of Americanist Archaeology*, edited by Don D. Fowler and David R. Wilcox, pp. 48–87. University of Alabama Press, Tuscaloosa.

———. 2004. Modeling the Initial Colonization of the Americas: Issues of Scale, Demography, and Landscape Learning. In *The Settlement of the American Continent: A Multidisciplinary Approach to Human Biogeography*, edited by C. Michael Barton, Geoffrey A. Clark, David R. Yesner, and Georges A. Pearson, pp. 123–137. University of Arizona Press, Tucson.

———. 2015. *The Great Paleolithic War: How Science Forged an Understanding of America's Ice Age Past*. University of Chicago Press, Chicago, Illinois.

Meltzer, David J., and Robert C. Dunnell. 1992. The Archaeology of William Henry Holmes. In *William Henry Holmes and the Origins of American Archaeology*, edited by David J. Meltzer and Robert C. Dunnell, pp. vii–1. Smithsonian Institution Press, Washington, D.C.

Menyuk, Rachel. 2012. Alanson B. Skinner: Collecting in the Wild Aurora. Smithsonian Collections Blog. Smithsonian Institution. Electronic document http://si-siris.blogspot.com/2012/04/alanson-b-skinner-collecting-in-wild.html Accessed July 21, 2016.

Mercer, Henry Chapman. 1885. *The Lenape Stone: Or the Indian and the Mammoth*. G. P. Putnam's Sons, New York.

———. 1893. Trenton and Somme Gravel Specimens Compared with Ancient Quarry

Refuse in America and Europe. *The American Naturalist* 27(323):962–978.

———. 1894. The Result of Excavations of the Ancient Argillite Quarries Recently Discovered near the Delaware River on Gaddis Run. *Proceedings of the American Association for the Advancement of Science* 42:304–307.

———. 1895. Chipped Stone Implements at the Columbian Historical Exhibition at Madrid, in January, 1893. In *Report of the United States Commission to the Columbian Historical Exposition at Madrid 1892–1893*, Volume 31, No. 100, Columbian Historical Exposition, pp. 367–397. The Executive Documents of the House of Representatives for the Third Session of the Fifty-third Congress 1894–1895, U.S. Government Printing Office, Washington, D.C.

———. 1898. A New Investigation of Man's Antiquity at Trenton. *Proceedings of the American Association for the Advancement of Science* 46:370–378.

Mighetto, Lisa. 1985. Science, Sentiment, and Anxiety: American Nature Writing at the Turn of the Century. *Pacific Historical Review* 54(1):33–50.

Miller, Henry M. 1991. Tobacco Pipes from Pope's Fort, St. Mary's City, Maryland: An English Civil War Site on the American Frontier. In *The Archaeology of the Clay Tobacco Pipe, XII, Chesapeake Bay*, edited by Peter Davey and Dennis J. Pogue, pp.73–88. Liverpool Monographs in Archaeology and Oriental Studies No. 14, BAR International Series 566.

Montgomery, David R. 2012. The Evolution of Creationism. *GSA Today* 22(11):4–9.

Moore, James R. 1979. *The Post-Darwinian Controversies*. Cambridge University Press, Cambridge.

Morlot, Adolphe. 1861. General Views on Archaeology. *Annual Report of the Smithsonian Institution for 1860*:284–343.

Morrell, Jack, and Arnold Thackray. 1981. *Gentlemen of Science: Early Years of the British Association for the Advancement of Science*. Clarendon Press, Oxford.

de Mortillet, Gabriel. 1879. Haches Quaternaires de New-Jersey. *Bulletins de la Société d'anthropologie de Paris*. 3(2):439–440.

Mulford, Isaac. 1853. The History and Location of Fort Nassau on the Delaware. *Proceedings of the New Jersey Historical Society* 6:187–207.

Murray, David. 1899. *History of Education in New Jersey*. United States Bureau of Education Circular of Information No. 1, Contributions to American Educational History, No. 23, edited by Herbert B. Adams. Government Printing Office, Washington, D.C.

New Jersey, District and Probate Courts, Mercer County. 1785–1924. *Will of Job Olden, April 11, 1874, pg. 491. Ancestry.com, New Jersey, Wills and Probate Records*, accessed December 16, 2015.

Newman, Andrew. 2010. The Walam Olum: An Indigenous Apocrypha and its Readers. *American Literary History* 22(1):26–56.

Nelson, William. 1886. Some Notes on Matinneconck, or Burlington Island. *The Pennsylvania Magazine of History and Biography* X:214–216.

Ozbun, Terry. 1991. Boulders to Bifaces: Initial Reduction of Obsidian at Newberry Crater, Oregon. *Journal of California and Great Basin Anthropology* 13(2):147–159.

Parezo, Nancy J., and Don D. Fowler. 2007. *Anthropology Goes to the Fair: The 1904 Louisiana Purchase Exposition*. University of Nebraska Press, Lincoln.

Parris, David C., and Lorraine E. Williams. 1986. Possible Sources of Mica from the Abbott Farm Site, Mercer County, New Jersey. *Bulletin of the Archaeological Society of New Jersey* 40:1–6.

Pennsylvania Historical and Museum Commission. 1969. Centennial Exhibition of 1876. *Historic Pennsylvania Leaflet* 30:1–4.

Perazio, Philip. 1986. Abbott's Lane Site (28-Me-1I) Data Recovery. Trenton Complex Archaeology Report 7. The Cultural Resource Group, Louis Berger and Associates, Inc., East Orange, New Jersey. Prepared for the Federal Highway Administration and New Jersey Department of Transportation, Bureau of Environmental Analysis, Trenton, New Jersey.

Pezzati, Alessandro, with Jane Hickman and Alexandra Fleischman. 2012. A Brief History of the Penn Museum. *Expedition* 54(3):4–19.

Pickering, Sam. 2007. An Unseen Stream. *The Concord Saunterer, New Series* 15:112–122.

Pitblado, Bonnie L. 2011. A Tale of Two Migrations: Reconciling Recent Biological and Archaeological Evidence for the Pleistocene Peopling of the Americas. *Journal of Archaeological Research* 19(4):327–375.

Pollak, Janet S. 1977. Case Report – Route I-195 Arena Drive to I-295 Interchange, Route I-295–U.S. 130 to Kuser Road, Route N.J. 29–Ferry Street to I-295 Interchange, Route N.J. 129–U.S. 1 to N. J. 29; Cities of Trenton and Bordentown, Townships of Hamilton and Bordentown, Counties of Mercer and Burlington, State of New Jersey. Prepared for the Federal Highway Administration and the New Jersey Department of Transportation, Trenton, New Jersey.

Powell, John Wesley. 1894. Report of the Director. *Eleventh Annual Report of the Bureau of Ethnology, 1889–1890*, pp. xxiii–xlvii. Government Printing Office, Washington, D.C.

Proudfit, Samuel Victor. 1889. Ancient Village Sites and Aboriginal Workshops in the District of Columbia. *American Anthropologist* 2(3):241–246.

Putnam, Frederic Ward. 1872. Report of the Director for the Year 1871. In *Fourth Annual Report of the Trustees Peabody Academy of Science, for the Year 1871*. pp.

7–14. Salem, Massachusetts.

———. 1873. Report of the Director for the Year 1872. In *Fifth Annual Report of the Trustees Peabody Academy of Science, for the Year 1872.* pp. 7–14. Salem, Massachusetts.

———. 1876. Report of the Curator. In *Ninth Annual Report of the Trustees of the Peabody Museum of American Archaeology and Ethnology.* pp. 7–15. Harvard University, Cambridge, Massachusetts.

———. 1877. Report of the Curator. In *Tenth Annual Report of the Trustees of the Peabody Museum of American Archaeology and Ethnology*, Vol 2, No. 1. pp. 7–12. Harvard University, Cambridge, Massachusetts.

———. 1881. Report of the Curator. In *Fourteenth Annual Report of the Trustees of the Peabody Museum of American Archaeology and Ethnology*, Vol 3, No. 1. pp. 7–28. Harvard University, Cambridge, Massachusetts.

———. 1882. Notes on the Copper Objects from North and South America, Contained in the Collections of the Peabody Museum. In *Fifteenth Annual Report of the Trustees of the Peabody Museum of American Archaeology and Ethnology*, Vol 3, No. 2. pp. 83–148. Harvard University, Cambridge, Massachusetts.

———. 1883. Concluding Remarks. *Proceedings of the Boston Society of Natural History* 21:147–149.

———. 1888. On a Collection of Paleolithic Implements from America and Europe. *Proceedings of the Boston Society of Natural History* 23:421–424.

———. 1889. Discussion. *American Anthropologist* 2(3):266–268.

———. 1890. On Collection of Paleolithic Implements. *Proceedings of the Boston Society of Natural History* 24:157–159.

———. 1891. Abstract from the Records. In *Twenty-Third Annual Report of the Trustees of the Peabody Museum of American Archaeology and Ethnology*, Vol. 4, No. 3. pp. 67–72. Harvard University, Cambridge, Massachusetts.

———. 1898. *Guide to the Peabody Museum of Harvard University with a Statement Relating to Instruction in Anthropology.* Salem Press, Salem, Massachusetts.

———. 1900. The Peabody Museum of American Archaeology and Ethnology. In *Annual Reports of the President and the Treasurer of Harvard College 1898–99.* pp. 271–279. Harvard University, Cambridge, Massachusetts.

———. 1911. Editorial Note. In Ernest Volk *The Archaeology of the Delaware Valley.* Papers of the Peabody Museum of American Archaeology and Ethnology, Vol. 5.

Randall, Asa R. 2015. How Jeffries Wyman Put Florida and Shell Mounds on the Map (1860–1875). *Bulletin of the History of Archaeology* 25(2):5, 1–12.

Rau, Charles. 1882. Observations on Cup-shaped and Other Lapidarian Sculptures in the Old World and in America. *Bureau of American Ethnology, Contributions to North American Ethnology*, Vol. 5. Washington, D.C.

Reed, H. Clay, and George J. Miller. 1944. *The Burlington Court Book: A Record of Quaker Jurisprudence in West New Jersey 1680–1709*. The American Historical Association, Washington, D.C.

Ritchie, William, and Robert Funk. 1973. *Aboriginal Settlement Patterns in the Northeast*. Memoir 20. New York State Museum and Science Service, State Education Department, Albany, New York.

Riverview Cemetery Corporation. 2010. History. Riverview Cemetery. http://www.riverview-cemetery.com/history.html Accessed July 26, 2016.

Roberts, Alison, and Nick Barton. 2008. Reading the Unwritten History: Evans and Ancient Stone Implements. In *Sir John Evans 1823–1908: Antiquity, Commerce and Natural Science in the Age of Darwin*, edited by Arthur MacGregor, pp. 95–115. Ashmolean Museum, University of Oxford.

Robins, Julia Stockton. 1896. A Willing Captive. *The Observer* 7(2):295–296.

Rollins, Phillip A. 1932. Junius Spencer Morgan, A.B. '88, A.M., '96. *Biblia* 3(1):1–6.

Romer, Alfred S. 1964. Cope versus Marsh. *Systematic Zoology* 13(4):201–207.

Rudwick, Martin J. S. 1970. The Strategy of Lyell's Principles of Geology. *Isis* 61(1):4–33.

———. 2005. Picturing Nature in the Age of Enlightenment. *Proceedings of the American Philosophical Society* 149:3.

———. 2008. *Worlds Before Adam: The Reconstruction of Geohistory in the Age of Reform*. University of Chicago Press, Chicago.

Rudwick, Martin J. S., and William D. Conybeare. 1967. A Critique of Uniformitarian Geology: A Letter from W. D. Conybeare to Charles Lyell, 1841. *Proceedings of the American Philosophical Society* 111(5):272–287.

Ruse, Michael. 1979. *The Darwinian Revolution*. University of Chicago Press, Chicago.

Schindler, III, William. 2008. Rethinking Middle Woodland Settlement and Subsistence Patterns in the Middle and Lower Delaware Valley. *North American Archaeologist* 29(1):1–12.

Schrabisch, Max. 1909. Indian Rockshelters in Northern New Jersey and Southern New York. In *The Indians of Greater New York and the Lower Hudson*, edited by Clark Wissler, pp. 141–165. Anthropological Papers of the American Museum of Natural History, Vol. 3. American Museum of Natural History, New York.

———. 1915. Indian Habitations in Sussex County New Jersey. *Geological Survey of New Jersey*, Bulletin 13. Dispatch Printing Co., Union Hill, New Jersey.

———. 1917. Archaeology of Warren and Hunterdon Counties. *Reports of the Department of Conservation and Development, State of New Jersey*, Bulletin 18.

MacCrellish and Quigley, Trenton, New Jersey.

———. 1930. *Archaeology of the Delaware River Valley between Hancock and Dingman's Ferry in Wayne and Pike Counties.* Vol. 1. Pennsylvania Historical Commission, Harrisburg.

Schutt, Amy C. 2007. *People of the River Valleys: The Odyssey of the Delaware Indians.* University of Pennsylvania Press, Philadelphia.

Schuyler, Robert L. 1977. *Historical Archaeology: A Guide to Substantive and Theoretical Contributions.* Baywood Publishing Company, Inc., Farmingdale, New York.

Shaeffer, Megan. 2016. Professional Identity and Professionalization in Archaeology: A Sociological View. Unpublished Ph.D. Dissertation, Department of Sociology, Kent State University.

Sigler, Bernadette M. 1990. The Egyptian Movement in American Decorative Arts 1865–1935. In *The Sphinx and the Lotus: The Egyptian Movement in American Decorative Arts 1865–1935,* pp. 11–31. Publication to accompany exhibit, Hudson River Museum (ed.), The Hudson River Museum, Yonkers, New York.

Skinner, Alanson B. 1917. Chronological Relations of Coastal Algonquian Culture. In *Proceedings of the Nineteenth International Congress of Americanists,* edited by Frederick W. Hodge, pp. 52–58. International Congress of Americanists, Washington, D.C.

Skinner, Alanson, and Max Schrabisch. 1913. A Preliminary Report of the Archaeological Survey of the State of New Jersey. Bulletin of the Geological Survey of New Jersey, No. 9. MacCrellish and Quigley, Trenton, New Jersey.

Slack, Robert H. 1878. Letter report to the Building Committee, Peabody Museum of American Archaeology and Ethnology, In *Eleventh Annual Report of the Trustees of the Peabody Museum of American Archaeology and Ethnology,* Vol. 2, No. 2. pp. 185–190.

Smallwood, Ashley M. 2012. Clovis Technology and Settlement in the American Southeast: Using Biface Analysis to Evaluate Dispersal Models. *American Antiquity* 77(4):689–713.

Smith, Bruce D. 1986. The Archaeology of the Southeastern United States: From Dalton to De Soto, 10,500 to 500 B.P. *Advances in World Archaeology* 5:1–92.

Smith, Samuel. 1765. *The History of the Colony of Nova-Caesaria, or New Jersey: Containing an Account of Its First Settlement, Progressive Improvements. The Original and Present Constitution, and Other Events, to the Year 1721. With Some Particulars Since; and a Short View of its Present State.* James Parker, Burlington, New Jersey.

Soderlund, Jean R. 2015. *Lenape Country: Delaware Valley Society before William Penn.* University of Pennsylvania Press, Philadelphia.

Spier, Leslie. 1918. The Trenton Argillite Culture. *Anthropological Papers of the American Museum of Natural History*, Vol. 22, Part 4. American Museum of Natural History, New York.

Stanford, Dennis J. 1991. Clovis Origins and Adaptations: An Introductory Perspective. In *Clovis Origins and Adaptations*, edited by Robson Bonnichsen and Karen L. Turnmire, pp. 1–14. Center for the Study of the First Americans, Oregon State University, Corvallis.

Stanzeski, Andrew J. 1974. The Three Beeches: Excavations in the House of an Archaeologist. *Bulletin of the Archaeological Society of New Jersey* 31:30–32.

Stebbins, Robert A. 1979. *Amateurs: On the Margin Between Work and Leisure.* Sage Publications, Beverly Hills, California.

Stewart, R. Michael. 1986a. Shady Brook Site (28-Me-20 and 28-Me-299) Data Recovery. Trenton Complex Archaeology Report 1. The Cultural Resource Group, Louis Berger and Associates, Inc., East Orange, New Jersey. Prepared for the Federal Highway Administration and New Jersey Department of Transportation, Bureau of Environmental Analysis, Trenton, New Jersey.

———. 1986b. Lister Site (28-Me-1A) Data Recovery. Trenton Complex Archaeology Report 6. The Cultural Resource Group, Louis Berger and Associates, Inc., East Orange, New Jersey. Prepared for the Federal Highway Administration and New Jersey Department of Transportation, Bureau of Environmental Analysis, Trenton, New Jersey.

———. 1987. Gropp's Lake Site (28-Me-100G) Data Recovery. Trenton Complex Archaeology Report 2. The Cultural Resource Group, Louis Berger and Associates, Inc., East Orange, New Jersey. Prepared for the Federal Highway Administration and New Jersey Department of Transportation, Bureau of Environmental Analysis, Trenton, New Jersey.

———. 1989. Trade and Exchange in Middle Atlantic Prehistory. *Archaeology of Eastern North America* 17:47–78.

———. 1990. The Middle Woodland to Late Woodland Transition in the Lower/Middle Delaware Valley. *North American Archaeologist* 11(3):231–254.

———. 1993. Comparison of Late Woodland Cultures: Delaware, Potomac, and Susquehanna River Valleys, Middle Atlantic Region. *Archaeology of Eastern North America* 21:163–178.

———. 1994a. Strategraphic Sequences and Archaeological Sites in the Delaware Valley: Implications for Paleoenvironmental Change in the Middle Atlantic Region. *Bulletin of the Archaeological Society of New Jersey* 49:99–105.

———. 1994b. Late Archaic through Late Woodland Exchange in the Middle Atlantic

Region. In *Prehistoric Exchange Systems in North America*, edited by T. Baugh and J. Ericson, pp. 73–98. Plenum Press, New York.

———. 1995. The Status of Woodland Prehistory in the Middle Atlantic Region. *Archaeology of Eastern North America* 23:177–206.

———. 1998. Ceramics and Delaware Valley Prehistory: Insights from the Abbott Farm. Trenton Complex Archaeology Report 14. The Cultural Resource Group, Louis Berger and Associates, Inc., East Orange, New Jersey. Prepared for the Federal Highway Administration and New Jersey Department of Transportation, Bureau of Environmental Analysis, Trenton, New Jersey.

———. 2007. Assessing Current Archaeological Research in the Delaware Valley. *Archaeology of Eastern North America* 35:161–174.

Stryker, William S. 1876. *Record of Officers and Men of New Jersey in the Civil War, 1861–1865*. John L. Murphy, Steam Book and Job Printer, Trenton, New Jersey.

Sydmondson, Anthony. 1970. *The Victorian Crisis of Faith*. SPCK, London.

Tankersley, Kenneth B. 2004. The Concept of Clovis and the Peopling of North America. In The Settlement of the American Continent: A Multidisciplinary Approach to Human Biogeography, edited by' C. Michael Barton, Geoffrey A. Clark, David R. Yesner, and Georges A. Pearson, pp. 49–63. University of Arizona Press, Tucson.

Taylor, Brian. 1995. Amateurs, Professionals and the Knowledge of Archaeology. *The British Journal of Sociology* 46(3):499–508.

Thoreau, Henry David. 1854. *Walden; or, Life in the Woods*. Ticknor and Fields, Boston, Massachusetts.

———. 1864. *The Maine Woods*. Ticknor and Fields, Boston, Massachusetts.

Tozzer, Alfred M. 1936. Biographical Memoir of Frederic Ward Putnam 1839–1915. *National Academy of Sciences Biographical Memoirs* 16(4):125–153.

Trigger, Bruce. 1986. *Native Shell Mounds of North America*. Garland, New York.

———. 1989. *A History of Archaeological Thought*. Cambridge University Press, Cambridge.

Trustees of the Peabody Academy of Science. 1869. Minutes of the Meeting of Trustees, April 13, 1867. In *First Annual Report of the Peabody Academy of Science*. Essex Institute Press, Salem, Massachusetts.

Trustees of the Peabody Museum of American Archaeology and Ethnology. 1868. *First Annual Report of the Trustees of the Peabody Museum of American Archaeology and Ethnology*. Harvard University, Cambridge, Massachusetts.

Ussher, James. 1650 [1658]. *Annals of the Old Testament, Deduced from the First Origins of the World*. E. Tyler, London.

Van Houten, Franklyn B. 1960. Composition of Upper Triassic Lockatong Argillite,

West-Central New Jersey. *Journal of Geology* 68:666–669.

———. 1964. Cyclic Lacustrine Sedimentation, Upper Triassic Lockatong Formation, Central New Jersey and Adjacent Pennsylvania. *Kansas Geological Survey Bulletin* 169:497–531.

———. 1965. Composition of Triassic Lockatong and Associated Formations of Newark Group, Central New Jersey and Adjacent Pennsylvania. *American Journal of Science* 263:825–863.

Van Ingen, Gilbert. 1908. The New Natural Science Laboratory at Princeton University. *The Museums Journal* 7(12):415–422.

Van Laer, Arnold J. F. (editor). 1924. *Documents Relating to New Netherlands, 1624–1626, in the Henry E. Huntington Library*. Henry E. Huntington Library and Art Gallery, San Marino, California.

Van Riper, A. Bowdoin. 1993. *Men among the Mammoths: Victorian Science and the Discovery of Human Prehistory*. University of Chicago Press, Chicago.

Veit, Richard. 2000. Following the Yellow Brick Road: Dutch Bricks in New Jersey, Facts and Folklore. *Bulletin of the Archaeological Society of New Jersey* 55:70–77.

———. 2002. Digging New Jersey's Past: Historical Archaeology in the Garden State, Rutgers University Press, New Brunswick, New Jersey.

Veit, Richard, and Charles A. Bello. 1999. "A Unique and Valuable Historical and Indian Collection": Charles Conrad Abbott Explores a 17th Century Dutch Trading Post in the Delaware Valley. *Journal of Middle Atlantic Archaeology* 15:95–123.

Veit, Richard, Gregory D. Lattanzi, and Charles A. Bello. 2004. More Precious than Gold: A Preliminary Study of the Varieties and Distribution of Pre-Contact Copper Artifacts in New Jersey. *Archaeology of Eastern North America* 32:73–88.

Volk, Ernest. 1911. The Archaeology of the Delaware Valley. *Papers of the Peabody Museum of American Archaeology and Ethnology*, Vol. 5. Cambridge, Massachusetts.

Von Sydow, Momme. 2005. Charles Darwin: A Christian Undermining Christianity? In *Science and Beliefs: From Natural Philosophy to Natural Science 1700–1900*, edited by David M. Knight and Matthew D. Eddy, pp. 141–156. Ashgate, Burlington, Vermont.

W. S. 1895. Review of "The Birds About Us." *The Auk* 12(1):67–69.

Wall, Robert D., and R. Michael Stewart. 1996. Sturgeon Pond Site (28-Me-114) Data Recovery. Trenton Complex Archaeology Report 10. The Cultural Resource Group, Louis Berger and Associates, Inc., East Orange, New Jersey. Prepared for the Federal Highway Administration and New Jersey Department of Transportation, Bureau of Environmental Analysis, Trenton, New Jersey.

Wall, Robert D., R. Michael Stewart, John Cavallo, Douglas McLearen, Robert Foss,

Philip Perazio, and John Dumont. 1996a. Prehistoric Archaeological Synthesis. Trenton Complex Archaeology Report 15. The Cultural Resource Group, Louis Berger and Associates, Inc., East Orange, New Jersey. Prepared for the Federal Highway Administration and New Jersey Department of Transportation, Bureau of Environmental Analysis, Trenton, New Jersey.

Wall, Robert D., R. Michael Stewart, John Cavallo, and Virginia Busby. 1996b. Area D Site (28-Me-1D) Data Recovery. Trenton Complex Archaeology Report 9. The Cultural Resource Group, Louis Berger and Associates, Inc., East Orange, New Jersey. Prepared for the Federal Highway Administration and New Jersey Department of Transportation, Bureau of Environmental Analysis, Trenton, New Jersey.

Wall, Robert D., R. Michael Stewart, and John Cavallo. 1996c. The Lithic Technology of the Trenton Complex. Trenton Complex Archaeology Report 13. The Cultural Resource Group, Louis Berger and Associates, Inc., East Orange, New Jersey. Prepared for the Federal Highway Administration and New Jersey Department of Transportation, Bureau of Environmental Analysis, Trenton, New Jersey.

Wallace, Alfred Russel. 1887. The Antiquity of Man in North America. *The Nineteenth Century* 22:667–679.

Warren, Leonard. 2005. *Constantine Samuel Rafinesque: A Voice in the American Wilderness*. University Press of Kentucky, Lexington.

Weslager, Clinton Alfred. 1961. *Dutch Explorers, Traders and Settlers in the Delaware Valley 1609–1664*. University of Pennsylvania Press, Philadelphia.

———. 1967. *The English on the Delaware 1610–1682*. Rutgers University Press, New Brunswick, New Jersey.

Williams, Lorraine E. and Ronald A. Thomas. 1982. The Early/Middle Woodland Period in New Jersey: c. 1,000 B.C.–A.D. 1,000. In New Jersey's Archaeological Resources from the Paleo-Indian Period to the Present: A Review of Research Problems and Survey Priorities, edited by Olga Chesler, pp. 103–138. Historic Preservation Office, Trenton, New Jersey.

Williams, Lorraine E., Anthony Puniello, and Lawrence E. Aten. 1976. Abbott Farm Historic District, National Register of Historic Places Nomination Form. On file, New Jersey Historic Preservation Office (NJDEP), Trenton, New Jersey.

Wilson, Thomas. 1889. The Paleolithic Period in the District of Columbia. *American Anthropologist* 2(3):235–240.

Winegrad, Dilys Pegler. 1993. *Through Time, Across Continents: A Hundred Years of Archaeology and Anthropology at the University Museum*. University of Pennsylvania Press, Philadelphia.

Winthrop, Robert C. 1878. Introductory Remarks. In Eleventh Annual Report of the

Trustees of the Peabody Museum of American Archaeology and Ethnology, pp. 174–184. Harvard University, Cambridge, Massachusetts.

Wissler, Clark. 1920. Charles C. Abbott. *American Anthropologist* 22(1):70–71.

Witthoft, John. 1948. A Bucks County Argillite Cache. *Pennsylvania Archaeologist* 18(1–2):13–14.

Wray, Charles F., Martha L. Sempowski, and Lorraine P. Saunders. 1990. *Two Early Contact Era Seneca Sites: Tram and Cameron.* C. F. Wray Series in Seneca Archaeology, Vol. 2, Rochester Museum and Science Center, Research Record 21, Rochester, New York.

Wright, George Frederick. 1881. On the Age of the Trenton Gravels. *Proceedings of the Boston Society of Natural History* 21:137–145.

———. 1882. Glacial Phenomena of North America and their Relation to the Question of Man's Antiquity in the Delaware Valley. *Bulletin Essex Institute* 14:71–73.

———. 1883. An Attempt to Estimate the Age of the Palaeolithic-Bearing Gravels in Trenton, N.J. *Proceedings of the Boston Society of Natural History* 21:137–146.

———. 1889. *The Ice Age in North America and its Bearing upon the Antiquity of Man.* D. Appleton, New York.

———. 1892a. *Man and the Glacial Period.* D. Appleton, New York.

———. 1892b. Communications: Man and the Glacial Period. *The Dial* 13:380.

———. 1893. Some Detailed Evidence of an Ice-Age Man in Eastern America. *Science* 21:65–66.

———. 1896. Fresh Geological Evidence of Glacial Man at Trenton, New Jersey. *American Geologist* 18:238.

———. 1919. Charles Conrad Abbott and Ernest Volk. *Science* 50(1298):451–453.

Wyman, Jeffries. 1868. Report of the Curator. In *First Annual Report of the Trustees of the Peabody Museum of American Archaeology and Ethnology*, pp. 5–18. Harvard University, Cambridge, Massachusetts.

———. 1870. Report of the Curator. In *Third Annual Report of the Trustees of the Peabody Museum of American Archaeology and Ethnology*, pp. 5–12. Harvard University, Cambridge, Massachusetts.

———. 1872. Report of the Curator. In *Fifth Annual Report of the Trustees of the Peabody Museum of American Archaeology and Ethnology*, pp. 5–30. Harvard University, Cambridge, Massachusetts.

———. 1875. *Fresh-Water Shell Mounds of the St. John's River, Florida.* Peabody Academy of Science, Salem, Massachusetts.

Youmans, William J. 1893. The Insolence of Office. *Popular Science Monthly* 42:841–842.